EXPLANATORIUM OF THE EARTH

SMITHSONIAN
EXPLANATORIUM OF THE EARTH

Senior Editor Ben Morgan
Senior Art Editor Smiljka Surla
Editors Joseph Barnes, Shaila Brown, Jolyon Goddard, Matteo Orsini Jones
Designers Tory Gordon-Harris, Anna Pond, Rhys Thomas
Illustrators Peter Bull, Sofian Moumene, Simon Mumford, Simon Tegg
Photographers Ruth Jenkinson, Gary Ombler
Creative Retouching Steve Crozier
Picture Researcher Laura Barwick
Managing Editor Rachel Fox
Managing Art Editor Owen Peyton Jones
Production Editor Rob Dunn
Production Controller Meskerem Berhane
Jackets Design Development Manager Sophia MTT
Senior Jackets Coordinator Priyanka Sharma Saddi
Jacket Designer Stephanie Cheng Hui Tan
Senior DTP Designer Harish Aggarwal
Publisher Andrew Macintyre
Art Director Karen Self
Publishing Director Jonathan Metcalf

Authors
Joseph Barnes, Abigail Beall,
Professor Joseph Holden, Wendy Horobin,
Dr. Peter Innes, Dr. Kate Ravilious,
Giles Sparrow, Isabel Thomas,
Dr. Rebecca Williams

Consultants
Professor Joseph Holden, Dr. Peter Innes,
Professor Stephen Marshak,
Cally Oldershaw, Dr. Rebecca Williams

First American Edition, 2024
Published in the United States by DK Publishing,
a division of Penguin Random House LLC
1745 Broadway, 20th Floor, New York, NY 10019

Copyright © 2024 Dorling Kindersley Limited
25 26 27 28 10 9 8 7 6 5 4 3
004–334051–May/2024

All rights reserved.
Without limiting the rights under the copyright reserved above, no part of this publication may be reproduced, stored in or introduced into a retrieval system, or transmitted, in any form, or by any means (electronic, mechanical, photocopying, recording, or otherwise), without the prior written permission of the copyright owner.

No part of this publication may be used or reproduced in any manner for the purpose of training artificial intelligence technologies or systems.

Published in Great Britain by Dorling Kindersley Limited

ISBN 978-0-7440-9205-9

DK books are available at special discounts when purchased in bulk for sales promotions, premiums, fund-raising, or educational use.
For details, contact: DK Publishing Special Markets, 1745 Broadway, 20th Floor, New York, NY 10019
SpecialSales@dk.com

Printed and bound in China

www.dk.com

Smithsonian

Established in 1846, the Smithsonian is the world's largest museum and research complex, dedicated to public education, national service, and scholarship in the arts, sciences, and history. It includes 21 museums and galleries and the National Zoological Park. The total number of artifacts, works of art, and specimens in the Smithsonian's collection is estimated at 155.5 million.

This trademark is owned by the Smithsonian Institution and is registered in the U.S. Patent and Trademark Office.

MIX
Paper | Supporting responsible forestry
FSC C018179

This book was made with Forest Stewardship Council™ certified paper—one small step in DK's commitment to a sustainable future. Learn more at www.dk.com/uk/information/sustainability

CONTENTS

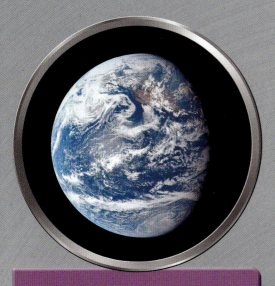
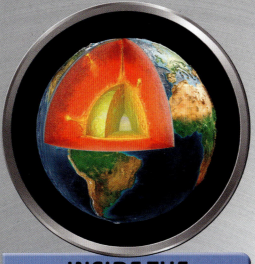
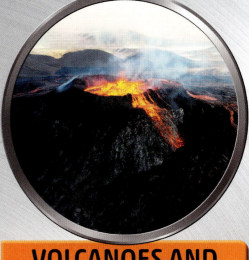

EARTH IN SPACE

- 10 How **Earth** formed
- 12 **Impact crater**
- 14 How the **solar system** works
- 16 **Day** and **night**
- 18 How **seasons** work
- 20 How **eclipses** work
- 22 How **tides** work

INSIDE THE PLANET

- 26 What's inside **Earth**?
- 28 How Earth's **magnetism** works
- 30 How the **aurora** works
- 32 How **tectonic plates** work
- 34 **Torn apart**
- 36 How **tectonic plates** move
- 38 How plates **collide**
- 40 How **continents** change

VOLCANOES AND EARTHQUAKES

- 44 **Volcanic world**
- 46 How **volcanoes** work
- 48 How **volcanoes** erupt
- 50 Types of **volcanoes**
- 52 How **lava** flows
- 54 **Liquid rock**
- 56 How **lava** cools
- 58 How **pyroclastic flows** work
- 60 How a **caldera** forms
- 62 How **hot spots** work
- 64 How **atolls** form
- 66 How **geysers** and **mud pots** work
- 68 **Limestone pools**
- 70 How **supervolcanoes** work
- 72 How **earthquakes** work
- 74 How **seismic waves** work
- 76 How **tsumanis** work

IMPORTANT

The experiments shown in this book are for demonstration purposes and to illustrate scientific principles. The experiments should not be attempted at home. The authors and publisher disclaim as far as the law allows any liability arising directly or indirectly from the use or misuse of the information contained in this book.

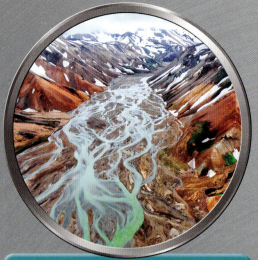

CHANGING LANDSCAPES

- 80 How **landscapes** form
- 82 How **mountains** rise
- 84 How **rift valleys** sink
- 86 How **weathering** works
- 88 How **erosion** works
- 90 How **landslides** work
- 92 How **sand dunes** work
- 94 How **glaciers** work
- 96 Glacial features
- 98 How **icebergs** work
- 100 How **rivers** work
- 102 How **rivers** bend
- 104 Braided river
- 106 How **waterfalls** work
- 108 Victoria Falls
- 110 How **floods** work
- 112 How **canyons** work
- 114 Antelope Canyon
- 116 How **groundwater** works
- 118 How **caves** work
- 120 How **deltas** and **estuaries** work
- 122 How **coastlines** change
- 124 How **waves** work

ROCKS AND MINERALS

- 128 How the **rock cycle** works
- 130 How **igneous rock** works
- 132 How **igneous intrusions** form
- 134 How **metamorphic rock** works
- 136 How **sedimentary rock** works
- 138 How **soil** works
- 140 How **minerals** work
- 142 How **crystals** work
- 144 Crystal habits
- 146 Why **minerals** glow
- 148 How **pigments** work
- 150 Types of **gemstones**
- 152 How **diamonds** work
- 154 How **native elements** work
- 156 Sulfur ponds
- 158 Biominerals

THE ATMOSPHERE

- 162 How the **atmosphere** works
- 164 What is **air** made of?
- 166 How **air pressure** works
- 168 How the **wind** blows
- 170 How **hot** and **cold climates** work
- 172 How **wet** and **dry climates** work
- 174 How **ocean currents** work
- 176 How **weather fronts** work
- 178 How **hurricanes** work
- 180 How **tornadoes** work
- 182 How **clouds** form
- 184 Types of **clouds**
- 186 Supercell
- 188 How **rain** works
- 190 How **rainbows** work
- 192 How **mist, fog,** and **dew** work
- 194 How **hailstones** form
- 196 How **snowflakes** form
- 198 How **frost** works
- 200 How **lightning** works
- 202 Power surge
- 204 How **dust storms** work
- 206 How **climate change** works

THE BIOSPHERE

- 210 How **life** began
- 212 How life changed the **atmosphere**
- 214 How **fossils** form
- 216 How **biomes** work
- 218 How **tundras** work
- 220 How **boreal forests** work
- 222 How **temperate forests** work
- 224 How **temperate grasslands** work
- 226 How **deserts** work
- 228 How **tropical rainforests** work
- 230 How **tropical grasslands** work
- 232 How **mountain life** works
- 234 How **arid scrublands** work
- 236 How **wetlands** work
- 238 How **ocean life** works
- 240 **Human impact**

REFERENCE

- 244 The **geological timescale**
- 246 Top ten longest **mountain ranges**
- 248 Top ten **longest rivers**
- 250 Top ten **largest lakes**
- 252 Top ten **longest cave systems**
- 254 Top ten **deepest canyons**
- 256 **Volcanoes** around the world
- 258 **Glaciers** around the world
- 260 **Igneous** rocks
- 261 **Metamorphic** rocks
- 262 **Sedimentary** rocks
- 264 **Minerals**
- 268 **Gemstones**
- 270 **Fossils**
- 272 **The continents**

- 274 Glossary
- 280 Index
- 288 Acknowledgments

Earth belongs to a family of eight planets orbiting the Sun, our **nearest star**. The Sun, planets, moons, and millions of smaller bodies like **comets** and **asteroids** make up our **solar system**. All the solar system's planets formed about 4.5 billion years ago in a series of **collisions**. These violent events shaped our world and its orbit, giving us our Moon, 24-hour days, 365-day years, seasons, and tides.

HOW EARTH FORMED

Planet Earth formed around 4.5 billion years ago from a swirling cloud of space debris that encircled the newborn Sun. Over millions of years, the tiny particles of matter in this cloud collided with each other and gradually clumped together, growing into whole planets.

▶ SPACE ROCKS

Meteorites are the oldest rocks known to science and contain the raw materials that formed our planet. The Imilac meteorite crashed into the Atacama Desert in Chile about 700 years ago. It consists of the metals iron and nickel—the same metals found in Earth's core—and is studded with yellow-green crystals of olivine—the main mineral found in Earth's mantle (the layer between the planet's crust and core). Scientists think the Imilac meteorite was once part of a planet or asteroid that was smashed by a collision in the solar system's early years.

BIRTH OF THE SOLAR SYSTEM

The solar system began to form when an interstellar gas and dust cloud (a nebula) began to shrink due to gravity. The Sun formed about 4.6 billion years ago and the planets developed from the cloud of debris that surrounded it.

1 SWIRLING CLOUD
A giant cloud of gas and dust collapses. The force of gravity pulls the debris into a dense, spinning disk. Some of the lighter gases are flung to the

2 THE SUN
The dense core of the disk becomes so hot, it triggers a nuclear reaction and a star—our Sun—is born. The debris forms a spinning disk around the Sun.

3 PLANETESIMALS
Particles of dust and rock within the spinning disk collide and clump together, forming massive objects called planetesimals. One of these will become Earth.

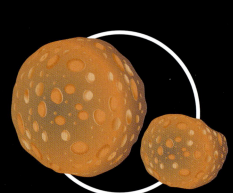

4 NEW PLANET
The planetesimals repeatedly crash into each other. These collisions heat and melt their interiors, and gradually, an irregularly shaped Earth forms.

HOW EARTH FORMED

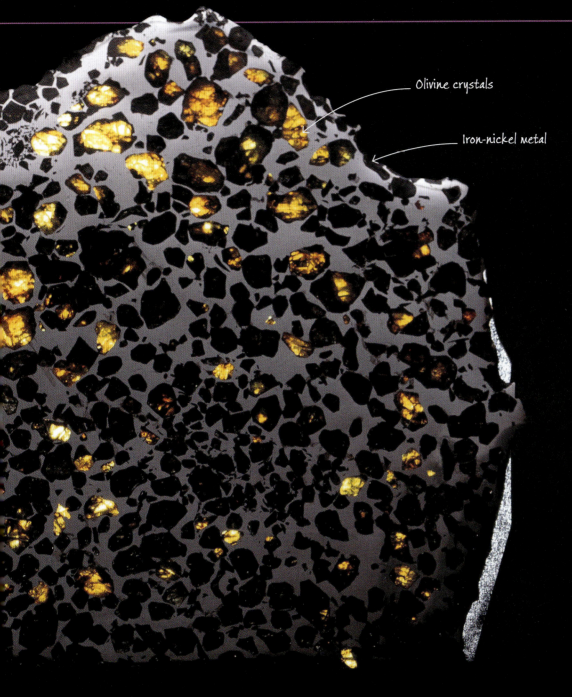

Olivine crystals

Iron-nickel metal

When small meteors collide with Earth's atmosphere, they burn up and create shooting stars.

The Moon was much closer to Earth than it is today.

5 EARLY EARTH
The inward pull of gravity reshapes Earth into a sphere. Heavier materials such as iron and nickel sink to form the core. Lighter materials such as rock minerals form the mantle.

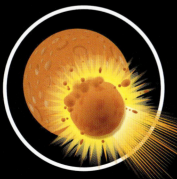

6 COLLISION COURSE
Late in Earth's formation, a collision with a small planet creates a cloud of debris around Earth. The collision also gives Earth's axis its tilt.

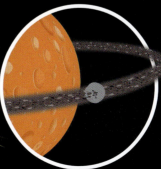

7 NEW MOON
The debris from the collision forms a ring around early Earth. The material—a mixture of rock and metal—clumps together to form the Moon.

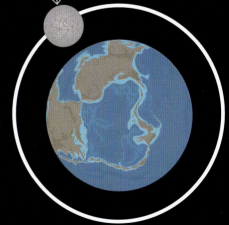

8 CHANGING EARTH
Outpouring of volcanic gases—composed mainly of carbon dioxide and water—creates early Earth's atmosphere. As Earth cools and moisture condenses, it rains to form the oceans.

IMPACT CRATER

Violent collisions with space rocks are less common today than in Earth's early years, but the threat still exists. Tenoumer Crater formed as recently as 20,000 years ago when a huge meteorite smashed into the Sahara desert, leaving a scar 1.2 miles (1.9 km) wide. Large impact craters are rare on our planet because erosion and weathering soon wear them away. The best preserved craters are found in deserts.

HOW THE SOLAR SYSTEM WORKS

The solar system is the area of space dominated by our local star, the Sun. Earth is the third of eight major planets that orbit (travel around) the Sun, trapped by the pull of its gravity. The solar system is also home to hundreds of moons, more than a million asteroids, and countless icy objects called comets.

▼ **SOLAR MODEL**
This simple model made from a ball and marbles shows the order of the planets in the solar system. The four inner planets are balls of rock and metal. The outer planets are gas giants—giant spinning globes of hydrogen and helium.

VENUS
Venus is about the same size as Earth but is smothered by a dense atmosphere of toxic gases and clouds of sulfuric acid. Carbon dioxide traps heat to make it the hottest planet in the solar system.

THE SUN
The Sun is a vast ball of hot gas containing 99.8 percent of the solar system's mass. The tremendous force of gravity from this great mass keeps the rest of the objects in the solar system trapped in orbit around it.

MERCURY
The smallest planet, Mercury has a huge metal core and a crater-covered surface.

EARTH
Earth is just the right distance from the Sun for water to exist as a liquid on the surface, making life possible. Earth is also the only planet with a crust broken into moving tectonic plates. Their motion creates volcanoes, mountains, and Earth's varied landscapes.

MARS
Mars is the outermost of the rocky planets and a little less than half the diameter of Earth. It is a bitterly cold, desert world but shows signs of being warmer and wetter in the distant past.

DISTANCE FROM SUN
Distances in space can be hard to grasp intuitively. If the Sun was the size of a basketball at one end of a basketball court, Earth would be a grain of sand at the other end. The Earth–Sun distance is known as one astronomical unit.

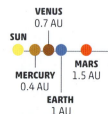

| SUN | MERCURY 0.4 AU | VENUS 0.7 AU | EARTH 1 AU | MARS 1.5 AU | JUPITER 5.2 AU | SATURN 9.5 AU |

HOW THE SOLAR SYSTEM WORKS

ORBITS
Objects in the solar system travel around the Sun along paths called orbits. Orbits are not perfectly circular. Instead they have shapes known as ellipses, which vary from highly elongated to nearly circular. The major planets all orbit the Sun in the same plane—the plane formed by the ring of debris that surrounded the newborn Sun 4.6 billion years ago. Smaller objects, including the dwarf planet Pluto, have more elliptical orbits that are tipped relative to the plane of the planets.

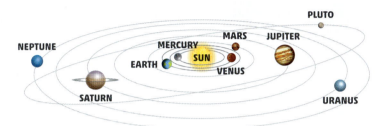

COMETS
Comets swoop in and out of the inner solar system on highly elliptical orbits. When a comet is near the Sun, its icy surface evaporates and forms a tail.

ASTEROID ITOKAWA

ASTEROIDS
These giant rocks vary from a few feet to hundreds of miles wide. They have irregular shapes and are mostly found in the asteroid belt, a zone between the orbits of Mars and Jupiter.

JUPITER
Jupiter is the largest planet and has more than 90 moons. It is a fast-spinning globe of hydrogen and helium, wrapped in colorful bands of windswept cloud. These include the Great Red Spot, a storm large enough to swallow Earth.

SATURN
Saturn is a gas giant with more than 140 moons and a spectacular system of rings. The rings consist of trillions of chunks of debris from the catastrophic destruction of an icy moon or comet millions of years ago.

SOLAR POWER
The Sun is powered by nuclear-fusion reactions in its core. These generate light energy, which sustains life on Earth. It takes thousands of years for light to travel from the Sun's core to its surface but only eight minutes to reach Earth.

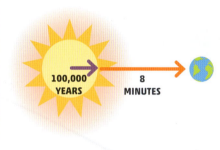

URANUS
Uranus is an ice giant with a hydrogen- and helium-rich atmosphere surrounding layers of slushy chemicals. Due to an interplanetary collision long ago, it spins like a rolling ball, with a horizontal axis of rotation.

NEPTUNE
Neptune is another ice giant and the outermost major planet. Despite receiving little energy from the Sun, it has surprisingly active, stormy weather and the highest wind speeds in the solar system—up to 1,200 mph (2,000 kph).

URANUS
19 AU

NEPTUNE
30 AU

EARTH IN SPACE

DAY AND NIGHT

Earth's daily rotation creates the natural cycle of light and shade we know as day and night. A whole day is 24 hours, but the number of daylight hours varies depending on where you live and the time of year. These variations happen because Earth spins round on a tilted axis.

▶ **SPINNING GLOBE**
Earth rotates eastward on an imaginary line called an axis. As the planet turns, different parts of the surface face the Sun and receive daylight, while other parts are in shadow, causing night. Because Earth's axis is tilted, the number of sunlight hours varies from place to place, ranging from as little as zero hours a day to 24 hours a day.

At the poles, the Sun sets and rises only once each year. There are six months of continuous daylight followed by six months of twilight or darkness.

Earth's axis is tilted 23.5° from upright in relation to the planet's orbit around the Sun. As a result, day and night are a different length in most places.

DAY AND NIGHT

Milan in Italy is halfway between the equator and the North Pole. Here, the number of daylight hours varies from about 9 hours in midwinter to nearly 16 hours in midsummer.

Points on Earth's surface move east as the planet rotates. As a result, the Sun rises in the east and sets in the west.

At the Equator, people get 12 hours of daylight and 12 hours of darkness every day of the year. Sunrise is always around 6 am and sunset is around 6 pm.

DAYS AND YEARS
A day lasts 24 hours from noon to noon, but it takes Earth only 23 hours, 56 minutes, and 4 seconds to rotate once. The times are different because Earth moves a little along its orbital path round the Sun over the course of a day. As a result, it has to rotate slightly more than one turn to face the Sun directly again. Over a year, these extra bits of rotation add up to more than a full turn. Earth actually rotates 366.24 times a year, even though there are only 365 days.

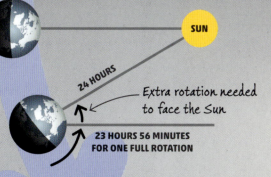

EARTH'S ROTATION
In the past, people watched the Sun and stars crossing the sky and naturally concluded that they travel around Earth. One of the first people to realize that Earth was rotating was the Indian mathematician Aryabhata in the 6th century. He also accurately calculated the length of one rotation as 23 hours, 56 minutes, and 4 seconds.

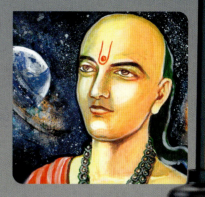

CHANGING DAYS
Powerful earthquakes can change the way Earth spins. In 2004, a huge earthquake in the Indian Ocean rocked the whole planet, shifting the North Pole by about 1 in (2.5 cm) and reducing the length of a day by 2.7 microseconds.

EPICENTER OF 2004 EARTHQUAKE

SPEEDY EQUATOR
Because Earth is spherical, different places on its surface move at different speeds as the planet rotates. The poles are stationary, but the Equator whizzes round at about 1,000 mph (1,600 kph). Rockets are often launched from near the Equator to give them an extra boost so they can reach orbit more easily.

LAUNCH OF ARIANE ROCKET IN FRENCH GUIANA, NEAR THE EQUATOR

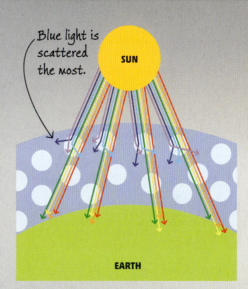

WHY IS THE SKY BLUE?
At night the sky is black, revealing the vastness of space, but during the day it turns bright blue. This happens because the brilliant light from the Sun is scattered by air molecules in Earth's atmosphere. White light is a mix of all the colors of the rainbow, but blue light is scattered more easily than other colors. The scattered blue light makes the whole sky look blue.

EARTH IN SPACE

▶ **AROUND THE SUN**
Earth orbits the Sun once a year. As it goes, each day it spins around an imaginary line called an axis, which runs from pole to pole. But the axis tilts at an angle of 23.5° and, as a result, the northern and southern hemispheres lean toward the Sun at different times of the year, causing the cycle of seasons.

NORTHERN SPRING
Around March 20, Earth's axis is at right angles to the Sun. Days and nights are about the same length everywhere in the world. It is spring in the northern hemisphere and fall in the southern hemisphere.

Earth's orbit around the Sun

NORTHERN SUMMER
The longest day of the year in the northern hemisphere is around June 21 (summer solstice). Around this time, the northern hemisphere tilts directly toward the Sun, causing long, warm days and short nights. But in the southern hemisphere, because the Earth tilts away from the Sun, this is the shortest day of the year (winter solstice).

SUN

HOW SEASONS WORK

Most of the world experiences seasons. As the months pass, the weather gradually changes from cold to warm or from dry to wet and then back again. These seasons are not caused by Earth getting closer to the Sun or further away. They are the result of our planet's tilt.

NORTHERN AUTUMN
Around September 23, instead of tilting toward the Sun, Earth's axis is at right angles to the Sun, and days and nights are about the same length everywhere. It is now fall in the northern hemisphere and spring in the southern hemisphere.

HOW SEASONS WORK 19

MIDNIGHT SUN
Places at the equator get roughly equal hours of day and night all year round, but near the poles, the seasonal variation between day and night is extreme. At midsummer in the Arctic, there is no night as the Sun stays above the horizon 24 hours a day. Meanwhile, in Antarctica, the Sun doesn't rise and it stays dark for weeks on end.

The equator is an imaginary line between the northern and southern hemispheres.

NORTHERN WINTER
The darkest day of the year in the northern hemisphere is around December 21 and is called the winter solstice. This is when the northern hemisphere tilts directly away from the Sun, causing the short days and cold weather of winter. The southern hemisphere tilts toward the Sun and so experiences summer.

By December, the South Pole tilts toward the Sun, bringing summer in the southern hemisphere.

FOUR SEASONS
In spring, as days start to get longer, leaves begin to appear and flowers start to bloom. The long days and the warmth of summer coincide with plants growing quickly. In fall, the days start to shorten and many leaves turn red or orange, before falling. In winter, when it is coldest and the days are shortest, most plants are bare. Then, it's spring once again.

SPRING

SUMMER

FALL

WINTER

TROPICAL SEASONS
Countries near the equator don't have the four seasons. However, most tropical countries have a dry and wet season. In tropical parts of the northern hemisphere, the wet season takes place at the same time as the northern summer, and the dry season happens in the northern winter. The opposite happens in the southern hemisphere.

DRY SEASON

WET SEASON

SEASONAL SURVIVORS
Baobab trees have adapted to severe dry seasons in the tropics. In the wet season, their massive trunks store thousands of liters of water for the dry season.

HOW ECLIPSES WORK

Every so often, the Sun, Earth, and the Moon line up directly in space. When the Moon passes between Earth and the Sun, it casts a shadow on Earth and we see a solar eclipse. When Earth casts a shadow on the Moon, we see a lunar eclipse.

▶ TOTAL SOLAR ECLIPSE
The most spectacular kind of eclipse is a total solar eclipse. For a few minutes, day turns almost to night and stars appear as the Moon crosses the Sun and blocks its light. You need to be in the center of the Moon's shadow to see a total solar eclipse. In other locations, people see a partial eclipse.

By a strange coincidence, the Sun is 400 times wider than the Moon and 400 times further away. As a result, the two appear the same size in our sky and fit almost perfectly during a total solar eclipse.

DIAMOND RING
All total solar eclipses begin as partial eclipses, as the Moon starts to make its way across the Sun. Just before the Sun is completely blocked, the last rays of sunlight pass through valleys on the Moon, creating a bright spot known as a diamond ring. This spectacular effect only lasts for a few seconds.

PARTIAL AND ANNULAR ECLIPSES
Partial solar eclipses happen when only some of the Sun's disk is blocked. If the Moon isn't perfectly aligned with Earth and the Sun, the Sun appears as a crescent. An annular eclipse happens when the Moon lines up perfectly but is slightly further from Earth than normal and doesn't completely cover the Sun.

PARTIAL

ANNULAR

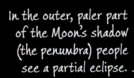

A total eclipse is only visible to people in the dark, central part of the Moon's shadow—the umbra.

In the outer, paler part of the Moon's shadow (the penumbra) people see a partial eclipse.

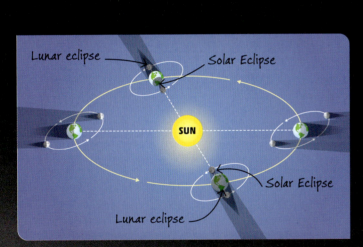

TILTED ORBIT
If the Moon orbited Earth in the same plane as Earth orbits the Sun, we'd have eclipses every month. However, the Moon's orbit is tilted a few degrees compared to Earth's, so it is usually too high or too low. Where it does cross the Sun-Earth lines, a total solar or lunar eclipse happens.

TOTALITY
During a total solar eclipse, the sky darkens and birds stop singing. The Sun's brilliant disk disappears entirely but its outer atmosphere—the corona—becomes visible as a glowing halo around the Moon. It's dangerous to look at the Sun directly, so never watch a total solar eclipse without eye protection.

LUNAR ECLIPSE
During a lunar eclipse the Moon passes through Earth's shadow but it doesn't disappear from view. Instead it turns a dark reddish color because red light can bend through Earth's atmosphere and reach it.

EARTH IN SPACE

▶ **HIGH AND LOW TIDE**
The sea level at any coastline changes daily. On the Island of Mont St Michel off the coast of France, the difference between high and low tide is about 33 ft (10 m) but can reach as much as 52 ft (16 m) during a spring tide. At low tide visitors can walk to the island, but at high tide it is cut off by the sea, which made it a natural fortress in the past.

HOW TIDES WORK

The Sun and Moon both pull on Earth through their gravity, playing a constant game of tug-of-war with our planet. Although the Moon is much smaller than the Sun, its gravitational pull on Earth is twice as strong because it is closer. The combined forces drag the ocean around, creating the tides.

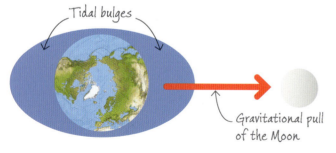

DOUBLE BULGE
There are two high and two low tides every day. This is because the Moon creates two bulges in the ocean. The tidal bulge nearest the Moon is caused by its gravitational pull. The opposite bulge is caused by inertia (the resistance to motion). Earth and the oceans are rotating, but inertia makes the water try to move in a straight line. As a result, it bulges outward where the Moon's gravity is weakest.

HOW TIDES WORK 23

SPRING TIDE
At full moon and new moon—when the Sun, Moon, and Earth line up—the Sun's and Moon's gravity combine to create the larger ocean bulges. This causes especially high and low tides, called spring tides (solar tide on the Sun's side and lunar tide on the Moon's side).

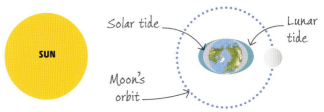

NEAP TIDE
When the Sun, Earth, and the Moon are at right angles to each other, the gravity of the Sun cancels out the gravity of the Moon, making the bulges smaller. This creates neap tides, when the difference between high tide and low tide is at its smallest.

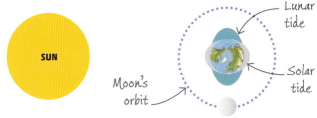

TIDAL BORE
In some parts of the world, the incoming tide is funneled by a wide bay toward a river mouth, temporarily reversing the flow of the river and causing a powerful wave called a tidal bore. These rare waves create a powerful roar as the opposing currents crash and churn together. They attract surfers and sightseers but are occasionally deadly.

If you could cut Earth in half like an onion, you'd see a series of inner layers that get hotter and hotter with depth. The surface layer is a skin of cold, brittle rock: the **crust**. Under this is a **mantle** of red-hot but solid rock and a partly molten **core** made of metal. Heat from the interior makes Earth's outer layers move, slowly but continually changing the shapes of **continents** and oceans.

INSIDE THE PLANET

26 INSIDE THE PLANET

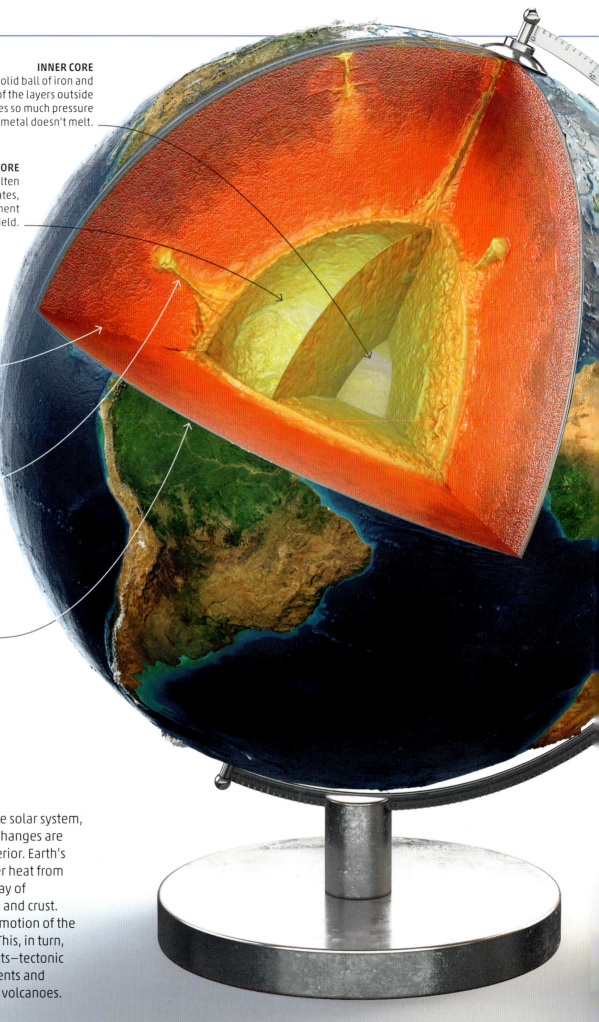

INNER CORE
The inner core is a solid ball of iron and nickel. The weight of the layers outside the inner core creates so much pressure that the superhot metal doesn't melt.

OUTER CORE
The outer core consists of molten iron and nickel. This liquid circulates, driven by heat, and the movement generates Earth's magnetic field.

MANTLE
The mantle is Earth's largest layer and makes up 82 percent of Earth's volume. It consists of dense rock, rich in the elements magnesium and iron. Although solid, the mantle is very hot, which makes it soft enough to flow very slowly.

Plumes of hot rock rise through the mantle, taking millions of years to reach the top.

CRUST
A thin layer of cooler, solid rock forms Earth's crust. The crust is thinnest under the oceans (oceanic crust), where it consists of a dense, volcanic rock called basalt. Continental crust is thicker and made of lots of different rock types.

▶ POWERED BY HEAT
Unlike the other rocky planets in the solar system, Earth is continually changing. The changes are driven by heat energy from the interior. Earth's inner heat has two sources: leftover heat from the planet's formation and the decay of radioactive elements in the mantle and crust. The heat drives the slow, churning motion of the mantle's hot, slightly pliable rock. This, in turn, breaks the crust into giant fragments—tectonic plates. Their motion shapes continents and oceans and creates mountains and volcanoes.

WHAT'S INSIDE EARTH?

Early in Earth's history, the planet was so hot that it was almost completely molten. Heavy, dense elements such as iron and nickel sank into the center to form a core. Lighter, molten rock, rich in the elements oxygen, silicon, and aluminum, rose to form a mantle and crust. And so the young planet separated into layers that still exist today.

Continental crust didn't start forming until Earth was over half a billion years old. The first crust was the solidified surface of the mantle and no longer exists. The crust we have today formed later, when magma rose beneath volcanoes and solidified to form rocks less dense than the mantle.

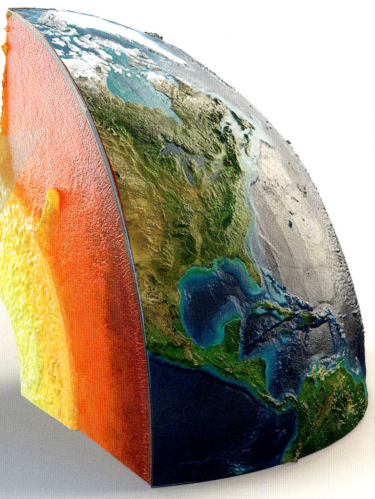

ROCKS FROM THE DEEP
Although we can't see the mantle directly, fragments of it are sometimes brought to the surface by volcanic eruptions. Mantle xenoliths are rocks from the upper mantle. They reveal that most of the upper mantle is a dense, grainy rock made of two minerals: olivine, which forms green crystals, and pyroxene, which is black.

RISING TEMPERATURE
The deeper you go into Earth, the hotter it gets. The temperature rises about 1°F per 70 ft (25°C per 1 km) until you reach the inner core, where it's about as hot as the surface of the Sun. Throughout the core and lower mantle, rock and metal are white-hot and emit dazzling light.

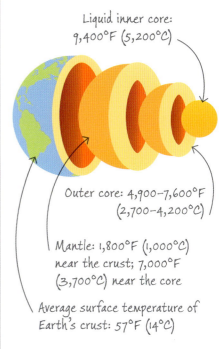

Liquid inner core: 9,400°F (5,200°C)

Outer core: 4,900–7,600°F (2,700–4,200°C)

Mantle: 1,800°F (1,000°C) near the crust; 7,000°F (3,700°C) near the core

Average surface temperature of Earth's crust: 57°F (14°C)

WATER WORLD
Earth is the only planet in the solar system with surface water in all three states: solid (ice), liquid, and gas (water vapor). There is also water deep inside the planet, where it exists as ions (charged particles) attached to minerals.

All Earth's surface water would make a sphere one ninth as wide as Earth.

HOW EARTH'S MAGNETISM WORKS

The swirling movement of molten metal in Earth's outer core creates a magnetic field around the planet through a process called the dynamo effect. This field is shaped like that of a bar magnet, but on a much larger scale. Earth's magnetic field shields us from dangerous cosmic radiation, and it makes compass needles point north. The field's direction is recorded in certain rocks as they form. Scientists can read this record to understand how the world has changed over time.

▼ **MAGNETIC FIELD**
The magnetic field around a magnet is the area where magnetic materials, such as iron, respond to the pull of a magnetic force. A magnetic field is normally invisible, but we can see the field around a magnet by sprinkling iron filings onto it. These tiny flecks of iron arrange themselves along lines of force, showing the direction in which the field pulls them.

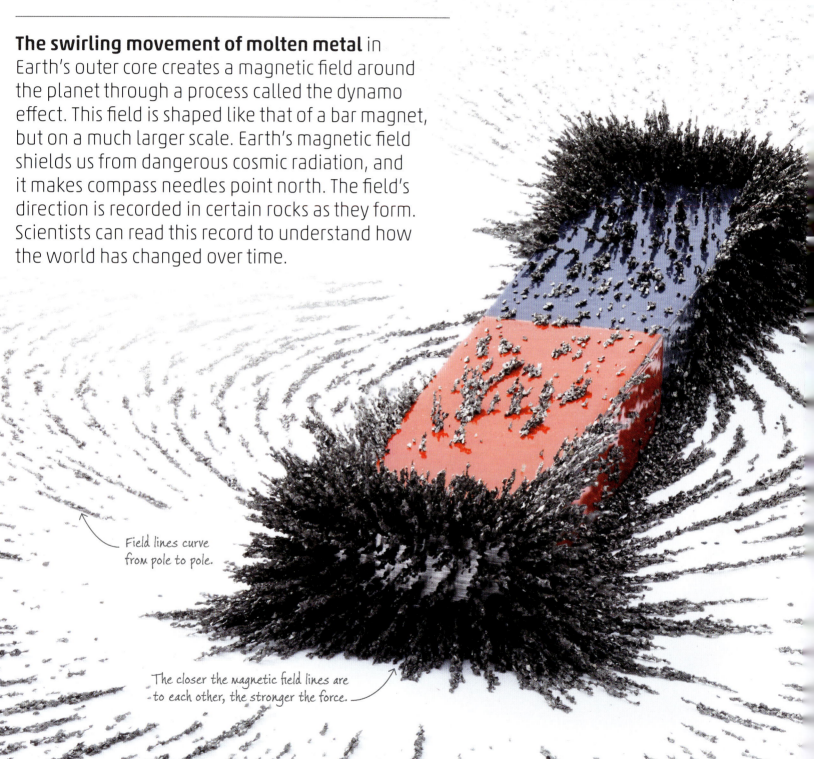

Field lines curve from pole to pole.

The closer the magnetic field lines are to each other, the stronger the force.

HOW EARTH'S MAGNETISM WORKS

EARTH'S FIELD
Earth's magnetic field is shaped as though the planet contains a gigantic bar magnet. However, Earth's field is more complex. It isn't perfectly symmetrical and it's currently tilted about 11° from the axis of rotation, which means the geographic poles are not in the same place as the magnetic poles.

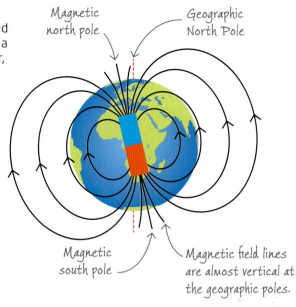

WANDERING POLES
The movement of Earth's molten core causes the magnetic poles to wander about randomly over time. The north and south magnetic poles even swap position every few hundred thousand years. Earth's magnetic north pole currently works like the south pole of a magnet, since it attracts the north pole of compasses (opposite poles attract).

MAGNETIC NORTH POLE OVER THE PAST 2,000 YEARS

PALEOMAGNETISM
When molten rock cools and hardens, minerals such as magnetite align with Earth's magnetic field. These patterns stay preserved in the rock crystals, and can tell scientists where on Earth the rock was formed. This branch of science is called paleomagnetism.

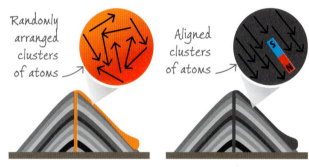

Molten rock
When rock is molten, the tiny magnetic fields around atoms are arranged randomly.

Solid rock
As rock solidifies and crystals from, clusters of atoms become aligned with Earth's magnetic field.

PLATE TECTONICS
Paleomagnetism helped scientists to confirm the theory of plate tectonics. They discovered that rocks around a diverging plate boundary had a symmetrical pattern, with bands of rock displaying alternating magnetic polarity. These formed over a long period of time, as the plates moved apart and Earth's magnetic field flipped repeatedly.

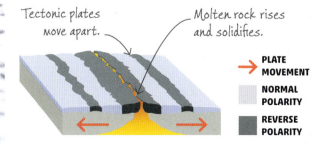

HOW THE AURORA WORKS

Visit Earth's polar regions in winter and you might be lucky enough to see the world's greatest natural light show. The aurora lights up the night sky with shimmering veils of color that pulse and wave from minute to minute. It is caused by the solar wind—a stream of charged particles from the Sun—colliding with gas atoms high in Earth's atmosphere.

AURORA COLORS
The colors in the aurora come from different elements in Earth's atmosphere. The most common color is green, which comes from oxygen atoms 60–200 miles (100–300 km) high. Oxygen higher than this emits red light, and nitrogen atoms give off blue and purple. Mixtures of colors occasionally produce other hues, including yellow and pink.

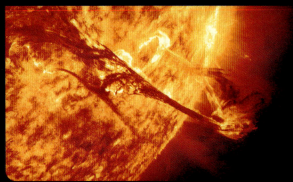

STORMS ON THE SUN
The strongest and most coloful auroras are seen after coronal mass ejections—occasional eruptions of matter from the Sun. These solar storms hurl vast quantities of energized particles toward Earth. As well as producing brilliant auroras, they sometimes damage satellites and GPS systems.

AURORAL ZONES
Auroras are seen most often in two rings about 3,000 miles (5,000 km) wide around the poles. The northern aurora is called the aurora borealis (northern lights). The southern aurora is called the aurora australis (southern lights). After a large solar storm, auroras can occasionally be seen further away too.

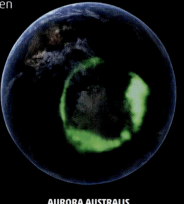

AURORA AUSTRALIS

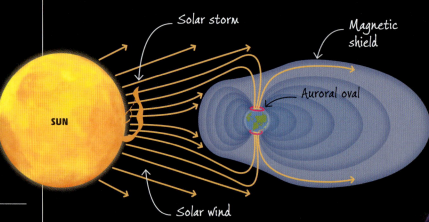

This charged metal ball represents the Sun.

Solar storm — Magnetic shield — Auroral oval — SUN — Solar wind

THE MAGNETOSPHERE
Earth's magnetic field acts as a kind of shield, protecting the planet's surface from the solar wind. However, some of the solar particles get through. They are funneled by the magnetic field toward the North and South Poles, where they collide with gas atoms in the atmosphere and create the auroras.

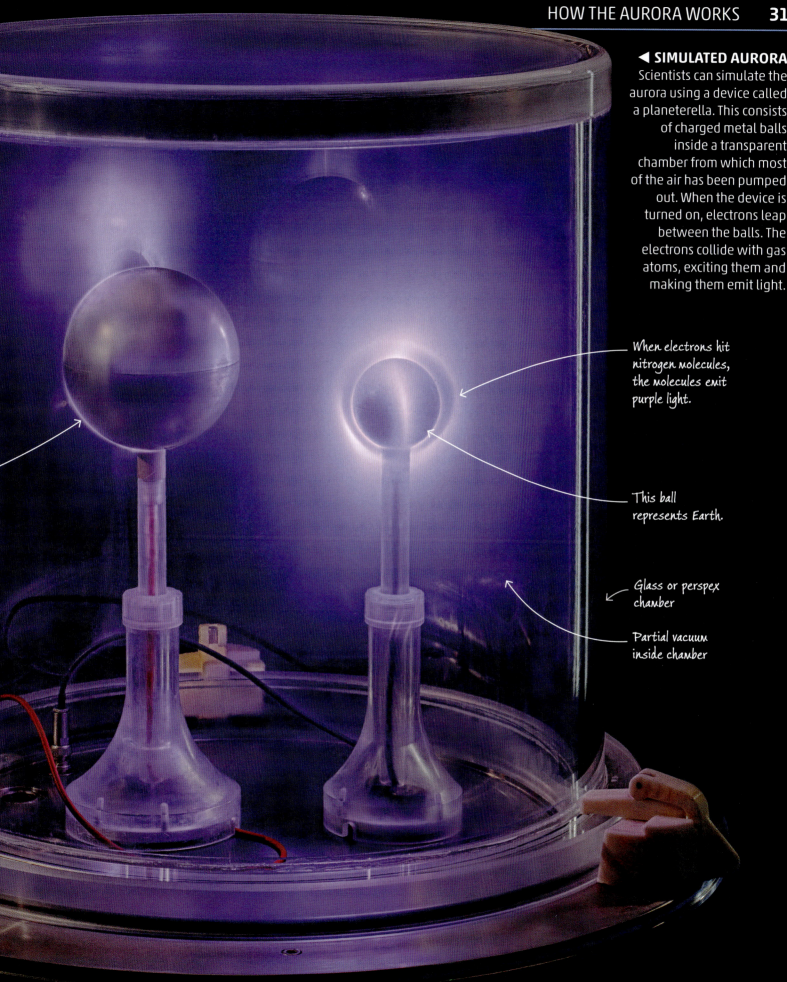

HOW THE AURORA WORKS 31

◄ SIMULATED AURORA
Scientists can simulate the aurora using a device called a planeterella. This consists of charged metal balls inside a transparent chamber from which most of the air has been pumped out. When the device is turned on, electrons leap between the balls. The electrons collide with gas atoms, exciting them and making them emit light.

When electrons hit nitrogen molecules, the molecules emit purple light.

This ball represents Earth.

Glass or perspex chamber

Partial vacuum inside chamber

INSIDE THE PLANET

HOW TECTONIC PLATES WORK

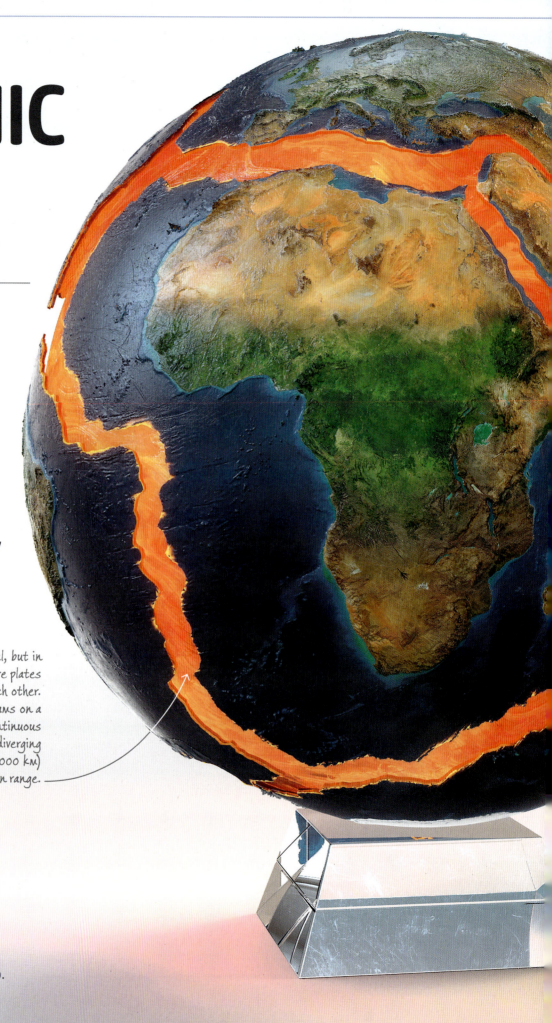

Earth's surface is broken up into 15 gigantic jigsaw pieces called tectonic plates. These move very slowly—just a few centimeters a year, which is about as fast your toenails grow. In some places they collide head-on, creating mountains and causing earthquakes and volcanic eruptions. In other places they move apart, with new crust forming between them.

The plates are separated in this model, but in reality they meet at boundaries where plates either converge, diverge, or slide past each other. Stretching around the planet like seams on a baseball is the mid-ocean ridge—a continuous range of underwater volcanoes along diverging plate boundaries. At 40,400 miles (65,000 km) long, it is the world's longest mountain range.

▶ AFRICAN PLATE

The African plate is one of the largest tectonic plates and includes part of the Atlantic seafloor as well as the continent of Africa. This plate is beginning to split into separate plates due to a rift running down the mountains of eastern Africa. Millions of years from now, a new ocean will form along this rift, dividing the continent in two.

HOW TECTONIC PLATES WORK

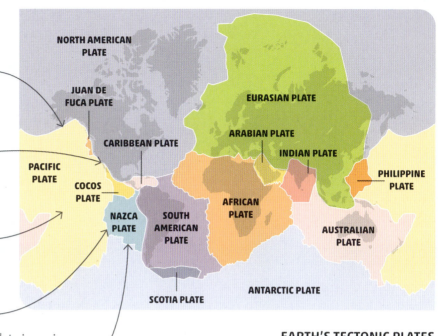

- Arabian plate
- The Pacific and North American plates are grinding past each other as they slide in opposite directions.
- At the Californian coast the tectonic plate is moving about 2 in (5 cm) a year, which is much faster than most plates.
- Nearly all of the Pacific Ocean is part of the Pacific plate, the largest of all the plates.
- The Pacific and Nazca plates are moving away from each other.
- The Nazca plate is moving toward and under the South American plate.
- Indian plate
- Antarctic plate

EARTH'S TECTONIC PLATES
There are seven major tectonic plates: the North American, South American, Pacific, African, Eurasian, Australian, and Antarctic plates. There are at least eight other minor plates. They fit together snugly at plate boundaries.

THE LITHOSPHERE
Tectonic plates are made of more than just Earth's crust. They also include the upper part of the mantle. Together the crust and upper mantle form a cool and very rigid layer called the lithosphere. Under the lithosphere, the mantle rock is hotter and almost at melting temperature. This rock is softer and flows very slowly, carrying tectonic plates along with it.

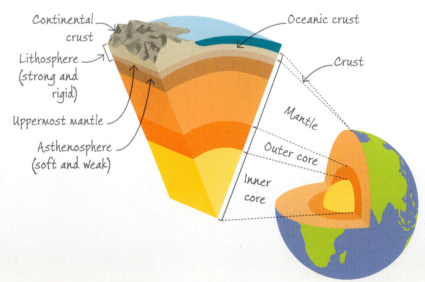

A TECTONIC DISCOVERY
US geologist Marie Tharp (1920–2006) was one of the scientists who discovered the mid-ocean ridge system, laying the foundations for the revolutionary theory of plate tectonics. Tharp and her colleague Bruce Heezen used depth measurements from ships to map the Atlantic seafloor. Their map revealed a huge mountain chain and rift valley running down the middle of the ocean.

TORN APART

In some parts of the world, tectonic plates are moving apart from each other, tearing open giant cracks and canyons in Earth's crust. The country of Iceland sits directly on the boundary between the North American and Eurasian tectonic plates, which are pulling apart. Such rifts are usually hidden below the sea, but in Iceland the tectonic scars are visible at the surface.

▶ CONVECTION IN A LAVA LAMP

Turn on a lava lamp to see convection in action. A bulb in the base heats up paraffin wax surrounded by liquid. The hot wax expands and so becomes less dense. This makes it buoyant, so it rises, expanding more as it goes. As it gets further away from the heat, it cools and becomes denser than the surrounding liquid, which makes it sink due to the pull of gravity. A similar process occurs in Earth's mantle.

Paraffin wax expands as it heats.

The wax rises as it expands.

The wax will start to cool as it moves away from the heat source.

A bulb in the base releases heat.

HOW TECTONIC PLATES MOVE

The tectonic plates that make up Earth's outermost layer are continually on the move, inching along at about the same speed that human toenails grow. This motion is driven by processes deep inside the planet. The details are not yet fully understood by science, but the most important drivers of tectonic plates are convection and the rise of hot, soft rock in Earth's mantle.

HOW TECTONIC PLATES MOVE

MANTLE CONVECTION

Although Earth's mantle is mostly solid rock, it is softened by heat from the core. Over millions of years, softened rock rises by convection like paraffin wax in a lava lamp. This transfer of heat energy from the core to the crust drives the motion of tectonic plates. However, convection inside Earth is more complex than in a lava lamp: the mantle might be divided into multiple layers, and the brittle crust does not flow like a liquid.

In some parts of the mantle, hot rock rises toward the surface in plumes like the hot wax in a lava lamp.

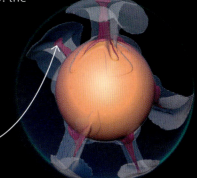

COMPUTER MODEL OF MANTLE CONVECTION

RIVAL THEORIES

Scientists have proposed two different models for mantle convection, but they aren't sure which is right.

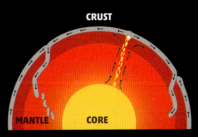

WHOLE MANTLE CONVECTION
According to this model, the whole mantle is stirred by convection. Plumes of hot rock rise from the core to the crust, where they cool, create new crust, and push tectonic plates apart. In other places, plates collide and can sink to the bottom of the mantle.

LAYER CAKE MODEL
In the layer cake model, the mantle is divided into different layers, each with its own convection cycle. The sinking tectonic plates stop at the boundary between the upper and lower mantle, and the plumes that push plates apart form at shallow depths.

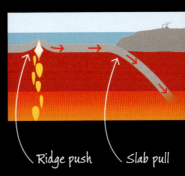

THE POWER OF GRAVITY

Gravity plays an important role in moving tectonic plates. At mid-ocean ridges, hot parts of the mantle rise and lift the ocean floor. As new crust forms at the ridge, it pushes the crust sideways and gravity pulls it down (ridge push). Gravity also pulls down the subducting (sinking) edges of tectonic plates, as the rock here is more dense and heavy than the surrounding mantle (slab pull).

HOW PLATES COLLIDE

The tectonic plates that make up Earth's crust meet at tectonic boundaries. At some boundaries, one plate slides under the other. At others, the plates move apart or they grind past each other horizontally. These three types of plate boundaries are called convergent, divergent, and transform.

▼ COLLISION ZONES
Tectonic boundaries can occur on land, under the sea, and where land meets sea. These meeting points are the most dynamic places on the planet. Here, mountain ranges rise as the crust buckles and folds. In the depths of the sea, giant trenches form where weaker oceanic crust is forced down (subducted) into the planet's interior.

CONVERGENT BOUNDARIES
Convergent boundaries are where two plates collide head-on. In a collision between continental and oceanic crust, the denser oceanic plate sinks below its lighter neighbor. This is called subduction. The subducting plate carries water into the mantle, which causes rock to melt and volcanoes to form. Meanwhile, the continental crust folds and buckles, creating mountains.

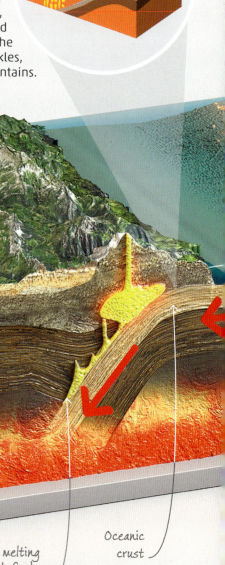

Some divergent boundaries occur within continents. Here, the crust tears apart to form a rift valley. This may flood, creating lakes.

Subduction causes melting in the mantle, which feeds a chain of volcanoes.

Continental crust

Oceanic crust

HOW PLATES COLLIDE 39

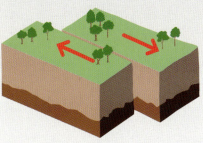

TRANSFORM BOUNDARIES
Transform plate boundaries are where neighboring plates move parallel, grinding past each other. Most transform faults are on the seafloor, but some are on land.

LAND DIVIDED
The San Andreas fault is a transform boundary that cuts across California. On average, the two plates move past each other by only 1 in (2.5 cm) a year. However, the movement occurs in fits and starts, generating powerful earthquakes.

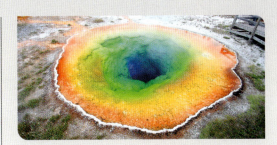

HOT SPRINGS
Geothermal features such as hot springs, geysers, and boiling mud pots are common at tectonic boundaries. These all form when groundwater is heated by magma that has risen into the crust.

DIVERGENT BOUNDARIES
Divergent plate boundaries are where neighboring plates move apart (diverge). As the plates shift, long cracks develop. Hot rock from the mantle rises, partially melts, and fills the cracks. This very slowly creates new crust.

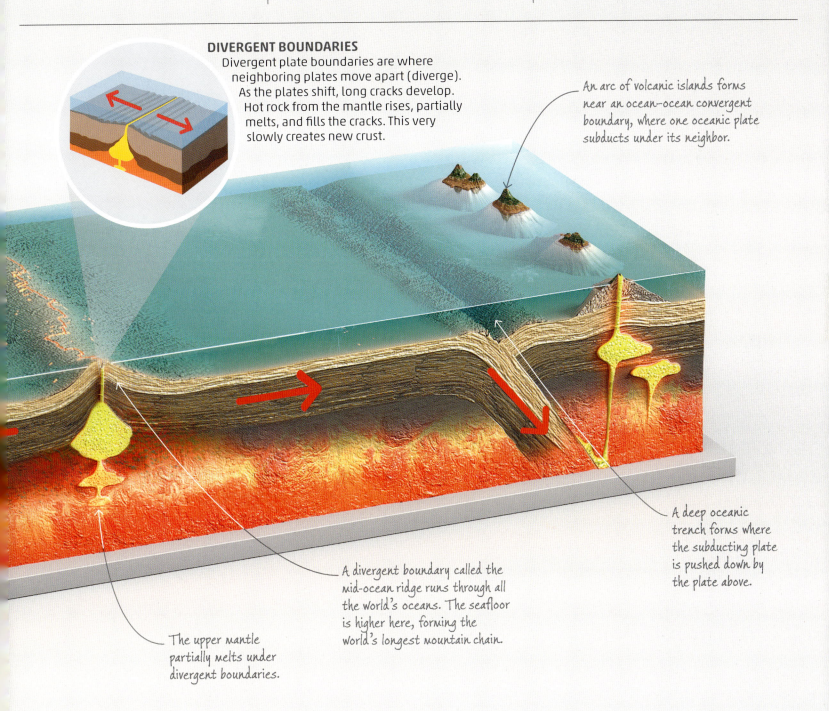

An arc of volcanic islands forms near an ocean–ocean convergent boundary, where one oceanic plate subducts under its neighbor.

A deep oceanic trench forms where the subducting plate is pushed down by the plate above.

A divergent boundary called the mid-ocean ridge runs through all the world's oceans. The seafloor is higher here, forming the world's longest mountain chain.

The upper mantle partially melts under divergent boundaries.

INSIDE THE PLANET

360 MILLION YEARS AGO
Laurentia and Baltica combined to form the supercontinent of Laurasia. This was separated from Gondwana by sea, but the two supercontinents were heading toward each other on a collision course.

420 MILLION YEARS AGO
The continents of Baltica (including parts of modern Europe) and Laurentia (North America and Greenland) moved together. The ocean between them slowly shrank until it was gone.

500 MILLION YEARS AGO
Half a billion years ago, Earth's northern hemisphere was mostly ocean. A supercontinent called Gondwana, along with several smaller continents, lay in the southern hemisphere.

300 MILLION YEARS AGO
Laurasia and Gondwana collided to form a single, vast supercontinent: Pangaea. The collision created a mountain range across its center, stretching from present-day Mexico to Poland. A huge ocean, Panthalassa, surrounded Pangaea.

180 MILLION YEARS AGO
A rift tore Pangea into two tectonic plates. The rift valley flooded, forming the beginnings of the North Atlantic Ocean between what are now North America and Africa.

120 MILLION YEARS AGO
More rifting caused the South Atlantic Ocean to form, opening like a zipper to separate South America from Africa. India and Antarctica broke away from Africa and drifted slowly away.

CONTINENTAL DRIFT
The theory that continents move was put forward by German scientist Alfred Wegener in 1912. He noticed that South America and Africa fit like jigsaw pieces and suggested they were once joined. He found matching rocks and fossils on each continent, but he couldn't explain what had pushed them apart, and his idea was ridiculed. It wasn't until after he died attempting to cross Greenland's ice sheet that this theory was finally accepted.

HOW CONTINENTS CHANGE

Moving at about the speed that toenails grow, Earth's continents have shifted over time, carried by the moving tectonic plates that make up the planet's crust. Continents have merged into supercontinents and broken apart. Oceans have opened and closed. The evidence for these incredible changes comes from many sources, including fossils, seafloor surveys, and magnetic patterns in rocks.

THE WALLACE LINE
The Wallace Line is an imaginary line separating Asia from Australia and New Guinea. It marks the boundary between the ancient continents that formed when the Pangaea supercontinent broke up. After this separation, animals on either side of the line evolved in different ways. Marsupials such as kangaroos evolved to the east of the line, while mammals without pouches evolved to the west.

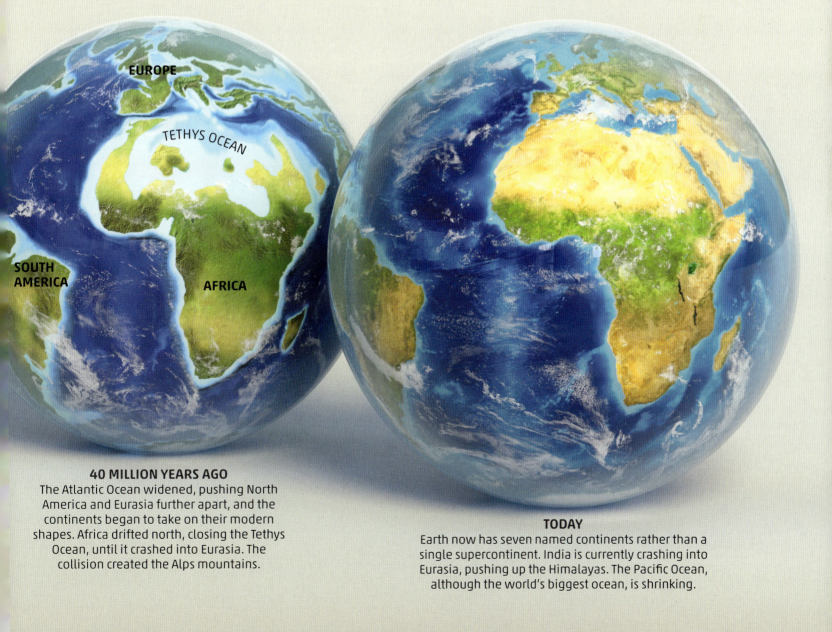

40 MILLION YEARS AGO
The Atlantic Ocean widened, pushing North America and Eurasia further apart, and the continents began to take on their modern shapes. Africa drifted north, closing the Tethys Ocean, until it crashed into Eurasia. The collision created the Alps mountains.

TODAY
Earth now has seven named continents rather than a single supercontinent. India is currently crashing into Eurasia, pushing up the Himalayas. The Pacific Ocean, although the world's biggest ocean, is shrinking.

The ground below your feet may feel rock solid, but the jigsaw of **tectonic plates** that make up Earth's **crust** is continually moving and cracking. Sudden jolts can shake the ground with great violence, causing **earthquakes**. Magma—liquid rock—oozes up through the crust from molten parts of the **mantle**, occasionally bursting out at the surface in **volcanic eruptions**.

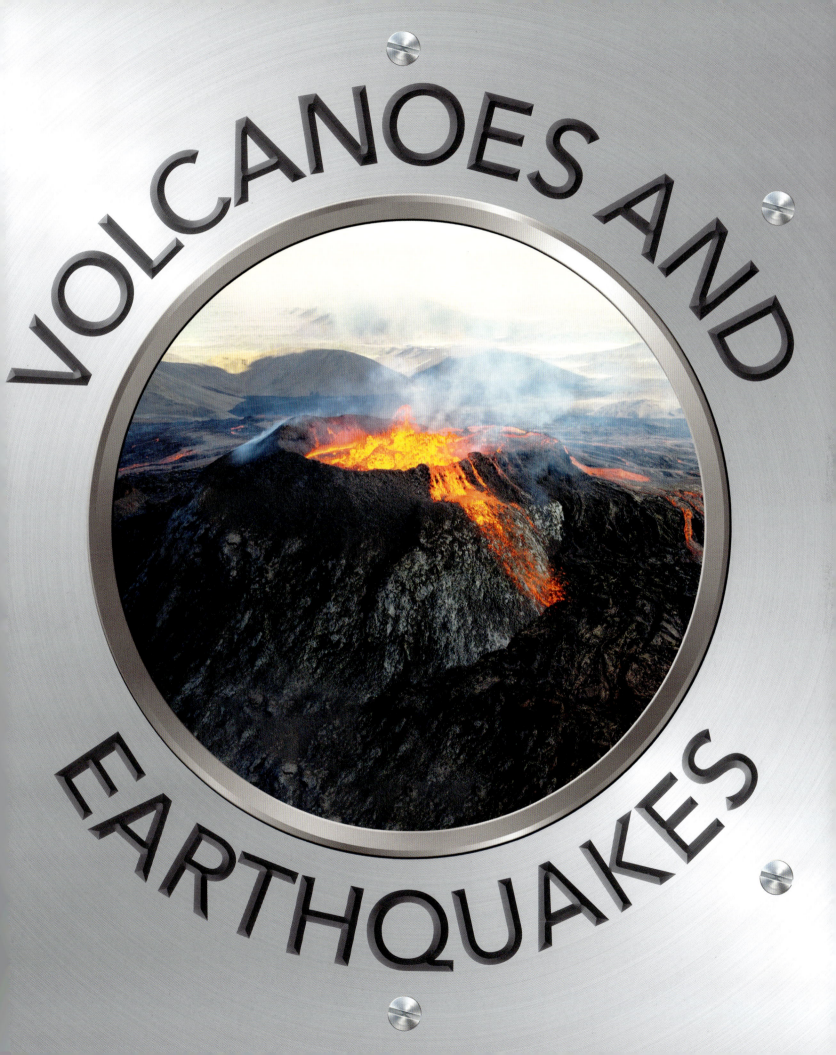
VOLCANOES AND EARTHQUAKES

VOLCANIC WORLD

Volcanoes and earthquakes are powerful reminders of the tectonic activity that takes place beneath our feet. We know where these deadly hazards are most likely to occur, but predicting when disaster will strike is very difficult.

The Aleutian Trench was formed by the Pacific plate sinking beneath the North American plate.

The Great Rift Valley is slowly splitting Africa apart.

MOUNT VESUVIUS
In 79 CE Mount Vesuvius erupted in Italy, burying the city of Pompeii under ash and rock. Most of the people died from the extreme heat of the scalding ash.

TŌHOKU TSUNAMI
In 2011, an earthquake in the Pacific Ocean triggered a tsunami that slammed into northeastern Japan, destroying thousands of homes and causing a nuclear disaster at the Fukushima power plant.

VOLCANIC WORLD

▼ DYNAMIC PLANET
Most volcanoes and earthquakes happen at the boundaries between tectonic plates. In these collision zones, magma forms where plates push into each other or tear apart, and the molten rock oozes into the crust to feed eruptions. Earthquakes happen when plates or parts of plates move past each other in sudden jolts, sending shockwaves through the ground.

● Volcanoes active in the last 10,000 years
● Earthquakes above magnitude 6 in the last 100 years

RING OF FIRE
The Pacific Ring of Fire is home to three-quarters of Earth's volcanoes and is where 90 percent of earthquakes happen. It is made up of several different plate boundaries and stretches from New Zealand to Russia and around the western coastlines of North and South America.

ACTIVE VOLCANOES
Active volcanoes (volcanoes still connected to a magma chamber) occur in clusters. The US has the most, with 165, whereas the continent of Australia has no volcanoes that have erupted in the last 1,000 years. About 500 volcanoes have erupted in the last century.

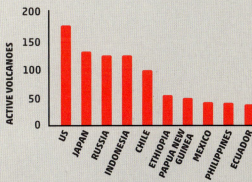

THE 2-MILLION-YEAR ERUPTION
About 252 million years ago, 90 percent of the world's species mysteriously died out. Some scientists think volcanoes were to blame: at around the same time, a massive volcano in Siberia produced floods of lava that kept flowing for 2 million years.

📍 VALDIVIA EARTHQUAKE
In 1960, the most powerful earthquake ever recorded struck near Valdivia, Chile, measuring a whopping 9.5 in magnitude. The quake triggered tsunamis, destroyed buildings, and left over 2 million people homeless.

VOLCANOES AND EARTHQUAKES

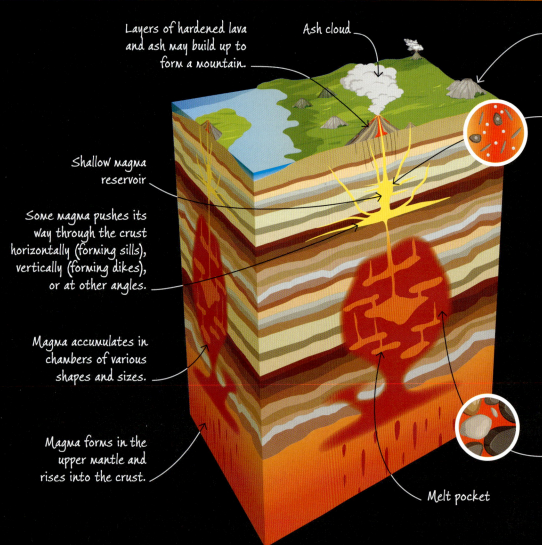

Layers of hardened lava and ash may build up to form a mountain.

Ash cloud

An extinct volcano has no magma supply and will never erupt again.

Magma is mostly molten but also contains solid rock crystals and bubbles of gas. Variations in the ratio of these affect whether a volcano erupts explosively or more calmly.

Shallow magma reservoir

Some magma pushes its way through the crust horizontally (forming sills), vertically (forming dikes), or at other angles.

Magma accumulates in chambers of various shapes and sizes.

Magma forms in the upper mantle and rises into the crust.

Melt pocket

DEEP ROOTS
The roots of volcanoes can reach more than 62 miles (100 km) deep, extending all the way to the mantle. From there, a series of magma chambers and pathways bring molten rock to the surface in a journey that can take millennia. Inside magma chambers, rock crystals and gas bubbles form as the temperature and pressure vary. If the pressure gets too high, the magma is forced out in a volcanic eruption.

Some magma chambers contain a substance called crystal mush, which is not fully molten and is mostly made of solid crystals.

When magma spills onto Earth's surface, we call it lava.

HOW VOLCANOES WORK

Volcanoes form when magma (molten rock) spills onto Earth's surface. Magma forms miles undergound in Earth's upper mantle. The mantle is normally solid, but small patches of melting happen at plate boundaries or other hot areas. The red-hot liquid then rises through the crust, seeping through cracks, melting through rock, and pooling in chambers. It can spend thousands of years in a magma chamber before finally erupting from a volcano.

HOW VOLCANOES WORK

Most lava erupts through the main conduit (vent) of a volcano.

▲ TUNGURAHUA
Tungurahua is one of Ecuador's most active volcanoes. Some of its eruptions produce rivers of lava, while others belch out ash clouds, rock fragments, and lava bombs. Layers of hardened lava and tephra (rock fragments) have piled up over thousands of years into a conical mountain, typical of this kind of volcano (a stratovolcano).

VOLCANO SCIENCE
Volcanologists (volcano scientists) forecast eruptions by looking for signs that magma is on the move. Sometimes the ground rises ominously, lifted by a bulging magma chamber. Earthquakes may be detected as magma bursts through cracks underground. Rising magma may also release telltale gases such as carbon dioxide and sulfur dioxide, which can be measured.

CHANGING MAGMA
As magma is held in a magma chamber, its composition slowly changes as one element after another forms crystals and then sinks out of the liquid rock.

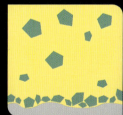

① COOLING
Rock crystals form as magma cools. They are denser than liquid rock, so they sink and settle at the bottom.

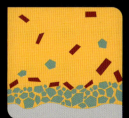

② New crystals
Crystallization uses up certain elements. After they run out, new kinds of crystal form.

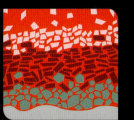

③ Magma changes
As the cycle continues, the chemical makeup of the magma changes. This affects how frequent and how dangerous any eruptions are.

▶ EXPLOSIVE ERUPTIONS

On May 18, 1980, Mount St Helens in Washington State exploded in a Plinian eruption—the most explosive kind of eruption. An earthquake triggered a landslide that allowed pressurized magma and gas to explode northward. The blast destroyed the summit and north face of the mountain, creating a crater 1 mile (1.6 km) wide and hurling 540 million tons of scalding ash into the sky.

1973 **1982**

HOW VOLCANOES ERUPT

Volcanic eruptions are among the most powerful natural events on Earth. They can blanket vast areas in ash, destroying towns and causing many deaths. But they also create new land and fertilize soil, which is good for farming. Every volcanic eruption is different. The type of eruption depends on the composition of the magma, how hot it is, how much gas it contains, and how sticky it is.

Crater

HOW VOLCANOES ERUPT 49

EFFUSIVE ERUPTIONS
Not all eruptions are explosive. When Russia's Tolbachik volcano burst into life in 2012, it produced rivers of runny lava that flowed for 12 miles (20 km). Eruptions of runny lava are called effusive eruptions and can continue for months. When the lava cools, it hardens to form a kind of rock called basalt.

ERUPTION STYLES
Volcanologists classify eruptions into several different types based on their size and how explosive they are.

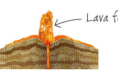 

Lava fountain

Hawaiian eruptions are the most effusive and are characterized by lava fountains and flows of runny, basaltic magma.

Strombolian eruptions are small explosions caused by gas bubbles in magma channels. They can throw lava bombs hundreds of meters high.

Pyroclastic flow

Vulcanian eruptions are short, explosive bursts that happen when sticky lava blocking a vent is suddenly blown out.

Pelean eruptions are explosive and deadly. They are powered by trapped gas and can cause pyroclastic flows of ash.

Volcanic ash is a mixture of hot gases and tiny specks of rock and glass. The ash cloud can drift on the wind for miles before settling as a dusty layer on the ground.

Ash plume

Plinian eruptions are the biggest and deadliest. So much gas is trapped in the sticky magma that it turns to foam in an instant when pressure is released. The foam explodes outward at terrific speed and immediately solidifies, breaking up into an ash cloud that can rise in a plume many miles high.

PRESSURE RELEASE
Explosive eruptions are powered by bubbles. Gas bubbles form in magma as it sits in a magma chamber. In runny magma, bubbles rise to the surface and pop, but in sticky magma they build up. A sudden release of pressure makes the bubbles expand, turning magma to foam. The result is an explosion—a bit like shaking a fizzy drink and opening it.

MAGMA AND WATER
When magma meets water, heat turns the liquid water into vapor, which can be explosive. In 1963, a massive eruption on the Atlantic seafloor created the island of Surtsey off the coast of Iceland. Such eruptions are now called Surtseyian after the island.

TYPES OF VOLCANOES

Every volcano is different. Some volcanoes tower over the landscape as mountains, while others are just holes in the ground or hidden entirely underwater. The most active volcanoes spew out lava continually, but other volcanoes can stay dormant for centuries before exploding without warning. There are six main types of volcanoes: lava domes, fissure volcanoes, cinder cones, calderas, shield volcanoes, and stratovolcanoes.

LAVA DOMES
When viscous (sticky) lava erupts, it can't flow away. Instead it oozes out slowly and builds up into a steep-sided dome. Sometimes the inside of the dome stays molten and forces its way out as a spike. Or the dome may completely collapse, resulting in an avalanche of volcanic debris.

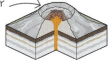

LAVA DOME AT NOVARUPTA VOLCANO, ALASKA

FISSURE ON KILAUEA VOLCANO, HAWAII

FISSURE VOLCANOES
A fissure volcano is a long crack in the ground through which runny lava erupts, often as a curtain. These eruptions feed some of the largest lava flows on Earth.

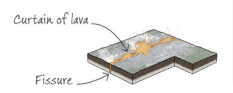

CINDER CONES
These small, conical volcanoes are heaps of loose volcanic fragments that pile up when a fountain of lava erupts from a volcanic vent. They have a central crater and steep slopes that are easily eroded. They can grow on the side of stratovolcanoes and sometimes occur in clusters.

MEKE CRATER, TURKEY

TYPES OF VOLCANOES

CALDERAS

If a violent volcanic eruption empties part of a magma chamber just below the volcano, the ground may collapse to form a crater called a caldera. Calderas can be miles wide and often flood with water to form lakes.

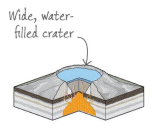
Wide, water-filled crater

QUILOTOA LAKE, ECUADOR

SHIELD VOLCANOES

Shield volcanoes build up from runny lava that spreads out over a large area. They are very wide with gentle slopes but can grow enormous. They include the largest volcanoes on Earth.

Gentle slope

SUMMIT OF MAUNA LOA, HAWAII

STRATOVOLCANOES

These large volcanoes have a distinctive conical shape that makes them easy to recognize as volcanoes. They grow layer by layer from eruptions of thick, sticky lava that doesn't flow far. Between the lava flows are layers of ash and pumice from explosive eruptions.

Alternating layers of lava and ash

MOUNT FUJI, JAPAN

HOW LAVA FLOWS

Lava is molten rock that flows onto Earth's surface from a volcano. Not all lava is the red-hot liquid we are familiar with. Depending on its temperature and composition, lava can be as runny as syrup, thick and gloopy like oatmeal, or so stiff that it resembles a sliding heap of rubble. Even thick lava can flow a surprisingly long way, while its molten interior stays insulated by a solid outer crust.

TYPES OF LAVA FLOWS
Lava takes a surprising variety of different forms, depending on its chemical makeup, its temperature, and how much water, gas, and rock crystals it contains. The names *aa* and *pahoehoe* come from Hawaii, where lava flows are common.

AA
Aa (pronounced ah ah) is a thick, rubbly basalt lava that bulldozes anything in its way. The outer edges of the stream harden as they cool, building up to form walls and raising the flow high above ground. The jagged surface of *aa* makes it hard to walk on once it's cooled.

▼ PAHOEHOE
Pahoehoe (pronounced pa-ho-ee-ho-ee) lava is fluid, with a consistency like pancake batter. The front of the flow moves in lobe shapes called toes. It forms beautiful shapes as the surface cools, hardens, and then stretches and folds while the runny interior keeps flowing.

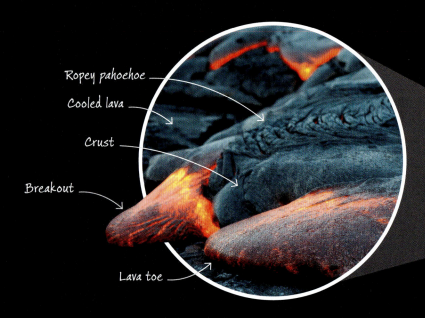

- Ropey pahoehoe
- Cooled lava
- Crust
- Breakout
- Lava toe

STICKY OR RUNNY?
If lava is very thick and sticky, we describe it as viscous. The viscosity of lava depends on how hot it is and how much silica (silicon dioxide) it contains—the higher the silica content, the thicker the lava. Very viscous lava can't flow easily, and it can cause explosive eruptions. Runny lava is less likely to cause explosions, but it can flow a long way.

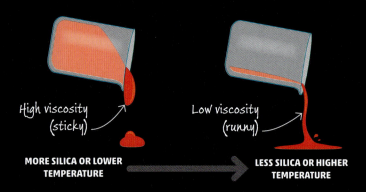

High viscosity (sticky) — Low viscosity (runny)

MORE SILICA OR LOWER TEMPERATURE → LESS SILICA OR HIGHER TEMPERATURE

HOW LAVA FLOWS

PILLOW LAVA
When lava erupts underwater, it cools quickly and forms pillow shapes. While pillow lava might look unusual, it is actually the most common type of lava, as most lava flows happen in the sea.

BLOCKY LAVA
Blocky lavas are very viscous, thick, and slow-moving compared to other lavas. Sharp-edged blocks form on the surface as the lava cools. These can grow very large and sometimes tumble off the front of the flow.

CARBONATITE LAVA
Carbonatite is a rare, black kind of lava that can only be seen at one volcano in Tanzania in Africa. It contains less silica than other lavas, so it is much runnier. It also erupts at lower temperatures, which is why it doesn't glow.

LAVA TUBES
Lava tubes form in *pahoehoe* as the solidified crust insulates the lava underneath. This allows the lava to flow long distances in underground rivers, which form tube-shaped caves after the lava stops flowing and drains out.

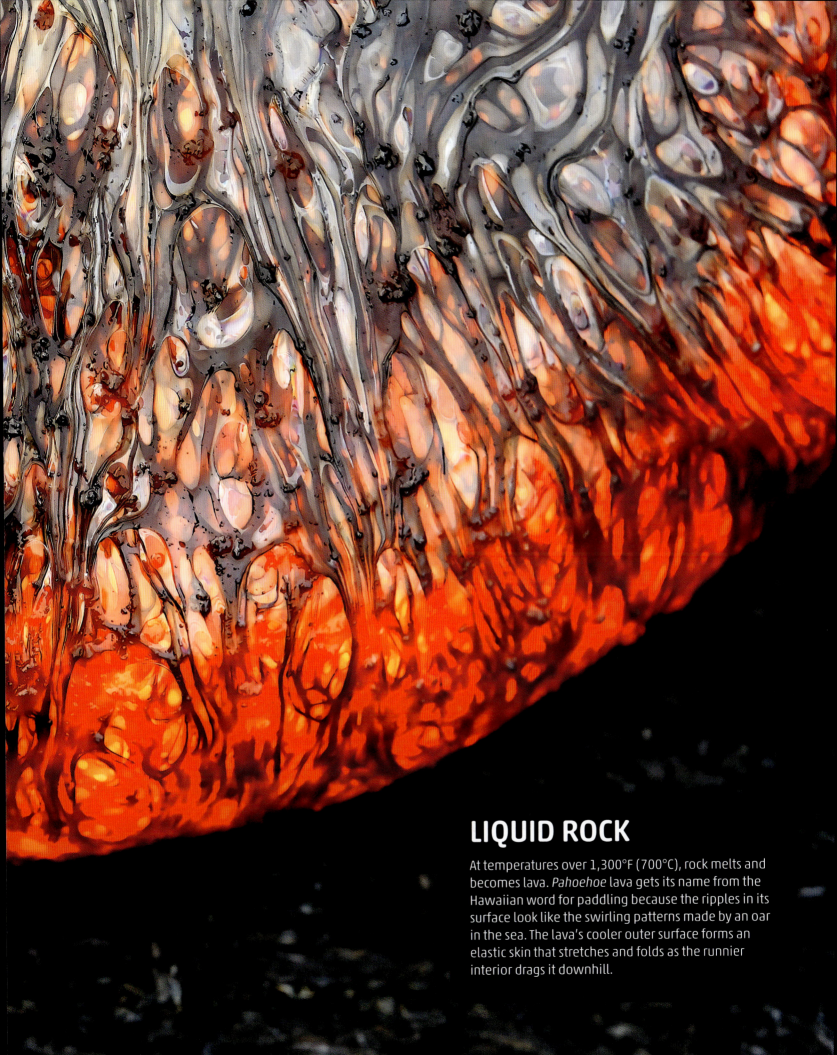

LIQUID ROCK

At temperatures over 1,300°F (700°C), rock melts and becomes lava. *Pahoehoe* lava gets its name from the Hawaiian word for paddling because the ripples in its surface look like the swirling patterns made by an oar in the sea. The lava's cooler outer surface forms an elastic skin that stretches and folds as the runnier interior drags it downhill.

HOW LAVA COOLS

Different types of volcanic eruptions result in many different kinds of lavas, which cool and solidify into a variety of wonderful rock structures called pyroclasts. By studying pyroclasts, volcanologists can work out what kind of eruption a volcano is likely to have in the future.

SCORIA
Scoria is a vesicular volcanic rock—a rock full of vesicles (bubbles) formed by gas inside lava. It has larger and fewer air pockets than pumice, but is denser and doesn't float. The lava that forms scoria is usually less viscous than lava that forms pumice, allowing trapped air to escape more easily.

PELE'S HAIR
When lava drips off a cliff or gets shot high in the air, droplets can stretch into long, thin threads. These are called Pele's hair, after the Hawaiian goddess of fire, volcanoes, and creation.

STRANDS OF PELE'S HAIR

Pumice is less dense than water

FLOATING ROCKS
Explosive volcanic eruptions eject ash and pumice into the air. The sticky magma inside an explosive volcano traps gas, making it foamy and full of tiny gas bubbles (vesicles). It cools to form pumice, a rock that is so light it can float on water. Rafts of pumice can appear floating on the ocean after underwater eruptions.

VOLCANIC GLASS
Obsidian, also known as volcanic glass, is a smooth, dark rock that forms when lava cools too quickly for crystals to form. Just like ordinary glass, it's rich in silicon dioxide (silica). Obsidian breaks into razor-sharp fragments and has been used since the Stone Age to make arrowheads and knives.

Sharp, glasslike edges

Reticulite has so many bubbles that you can often see straight through it.

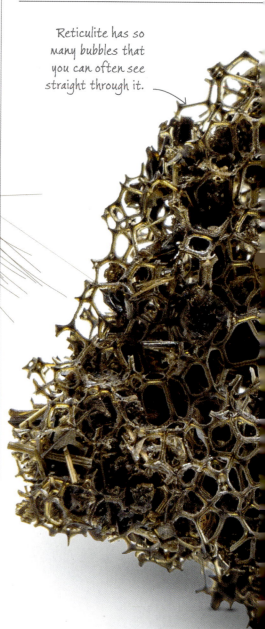

HOW LAVA COOLS 57

Thin, broken ends may have detached from a strand of Pele's hair.

PELE'S TEARS
Small blobs of liquid lava form teardrop shapes as they fall to the ground. These are called Pele's tears, and they can form at the end of Pele's hair strands.

CROPS COVERED IN VOLCANIC ASH

VOLCANIC ASH
Ash clouds from volcanoes consist of billions of tiny fragments of volcanic glass. During an explosive eruption, gases in magma expand and shatter the magma into minute flecks that harden in air to become ash. Near Mount Etna in Italy, drivers must replace the tires on their cars as often as twice a year because volcanic ash on the ground shreds and wears away the rubber.

LAVA BOMBS
These volcanic hazards are often thrown into the air during eruptions. Bread-crust bombs cool and solidify on the outside first, cracking later like bread-crust as gas escapes. Cow-pie bombs are still soft as they land and so form flatter, uneven disks.

BREAD-CRUST LAVA BOMB

COW-PIE LAVA BOMB

RETICULITE
This volcanic rock forms in tall lava fountains. It is full of air bubbles and so lightweight that the wind blows it across the ground like tumbleweed.

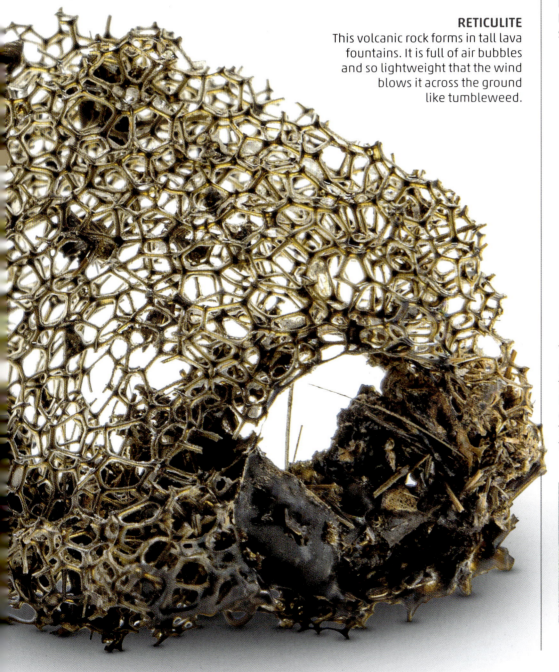

LAVA TREES
These stumps are made of solidified lava. Flowing lava can engulf living trees, then cool and form a solid crust around them. This leaves a cast of the tree where the real tree—long since burned away—used to be.

LAVA TREES, HAWAII

HOW PYROCLASTIC FLOWS WORK

The deadliest thing a volcano can produce is a pyroclastic flow, which is a dense, ground-hugging avalanche of superhot gas, ash, and rocks that races downhill. Pyroclastic flows demolish and burn everything in their path and can bury the landscape under tons of volcanic debris.

Temperatures can reach 390–1300°F (200–700°C) inside a pyroclastic flow.

▶ MOUNT PINATUBO
The eruption of Mount Pinatubo in the Philippines on June 15, 1991, was the second-largest eruption in the 20th century. It sent pyroclastic flows sweeping down the slopes of the volcano, filling valleys with volcanic deposits. This photo was captured by a photographer who was racing away in the back of a truck.

Dense, scalding ash cloud

The rising ash cloud is called a phoenix cloud.

Flows downhill at great speed

Large boulders are carried at the bottom.

INSIDE A PYROCLASTIC FLOW
Pyroclastic flows have a violent and turbulent interior and carry debris ranging from scalding dust and ash to large boulders. The fast-flowing clouds of rock fragments strip vegetation from the volcano's slope, erode the ground, and set fire to anything in their path.

The pyroclastic flows from Pinatubo filled valleys with volcanic debris up to 660 ft (200 m) thick.

HOW PYROCLASTIC FLOWS WORK

HOW PYROCLASTIC FLOWS FORM
Pyroclastic flows form in several different ways. Some are mostly ash and gas, while others are full of rubble. All hurtle downhill at terrific speed—some as fast as 435 mph (700 kph).

Sideways blast
The volcano erupts sideways rather than vertically.

Dome collapse
An eruption shatters an unstable lava dome, creating an avalanche of hot rock.

Ash cloud collapse
A large ash cloud partially collapses as heavy material falls back.

Boiling over
Heavy ash rises a short distance before falling and rolling downhill.

MOUNT VESUVIUS
In 79 CE, the city of Pompeii in Italy was engulfed by pyroclastic flows from Mount Vesuvius. Around 1,500 years later, archaeologists discovered the buried town and found body-shaped cavities. They created casts of the victims, revealing they had died from the scalding heat and from breathing in ash.

KRAKATAU
The 1883 eruption of Krakatau in Indonesia was one of the deadliest in history, killing over 36,000 people. Pyroclastic flows ploughed into the sea, generating tsunamis. In 1927, Anak Krakatau began to emerge from the caldera that was formed by Krakatau, and continues to erupt today.

ANAK KRAKATAU, INDONESIA

HOW A CALDERA FORMS

Massive eruptions can make a volcano collapse inward and form a giant crater—a caldera. Calderas often fill with water to create lakes or lagoons and are among the most tranquil landscapes on Earth. But these beautiful places are evidence of incredibly violent events that took place in the past.

RISE AND FALL
The city of Pozzuoli in southern Italy sits inside a caldera. Roman ruins that are above sea level today have holes made by marine mussels, which shows that the land has sunk below sea level since Roman times only to rise again. This is evidence of an active magma chamber making the ground rise and fall over time.

▼ **CRATER LAKE**
Crater Lake in Oregon is a caldera that formed 7,700 years ago as a result of an explosive eruption. Later eruptions created Wizard Island, a small conical volcano in the lake. At 1,949 ft (594 m) deep, Crater Lake is the US's deepest lake and the ninth deepest lake in the world. No rivers flow into or out of it—the crystal clear water comes solely from rain and melted snow.

Caldera wall

Crater Lake is 6 miles (10 km) across at its widest point.

HOW A CALDERA FORMS

SANTORINI
The island of Santorini in Greece is a submerged caldera. Around 3,600 years ago, one of the largest volcanic eruptions in recorded history destroyed the prehistoric city of Akrotiri and triggered tsunamis that devastated nearby islands. The eruption obliterated the center of the volcano, leaving a ring of islands.

SLOW COLLAPSE
Not all calderas form suddenly. In 2014–2015, volcanologists observed the gradual formation of a caldera at Bardarbunga in Iceland. The crater developed over six months as lava slowly drained from the magma chamber to the surface, forming what is now a flat plain.

FORMATION OF CRATER LAKE
A caldera forms when a large eruption empties or partially empties a magma chamber and the volcano collapses into the empty space. Crater Lake formed when a stratovolcano called Mount Mazama self-destructed.

1 PRESSURE BUILDS
Before the eruption, Mount Mazama's peak was 12,000 ft (3,650 m) high, with a vast magma chamber below.

2 ERUPTION
An explosive eruption partly emptied the magma chamber, making its roof unstable.

3 COLLAPSE
The peak collapsed, creating a crater. More than 8,000 ft (2,400 m) of Mount Mazama's height was destroyed.

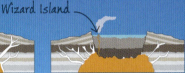

4 FLOOD
The crater flooded to form a lake. Later eruptions produced lava domes and small cones. One of these became Wizard Island.

How HOT SPOTS Work

Some of the largest volcanoes on Earth occur in sites that geologists call hot spots. These sites in Earth's crust lie over mantle plumes—columns of hot rock that rise from deep in the mantle or even the core, bringing heat to the planet's surface. Hot-spot volcanoes produce huge volumes of runny, basaltic lava that can build up on the seafloor to form islands. In places like Hawaii, chains of volcanoes have formed as the ocean floor has slowly moved across the hot spot.

HOW HOT SPOTS WORK

▼ KĪLAUEA, HAWAII
Kīlauea on Hawaii is one of the most active volcanoes in the world. At its summit is a crater called Halemaumau that sometimes fills with molten rock to form a lava lake. Lava lakes are rare—only another six exist on Earth. Eruptions from fissures in the sides of Kīlauea can drain this deep lake, producing rivers of lava that flow all the way to the sea.

THE HAWAIIAN ISLANDS
The Hawaiian Islands formed as the Pacific tectonic plate slowly moved over a hot spot. The hot spot melts the lithosphere above, creating magma that erupts to produce one new island after another. Only the newer islands still have active volcanoes. Further away, the older volcanoes have become dormant or extinct, and many have eroded and sunk below the ocean surface.

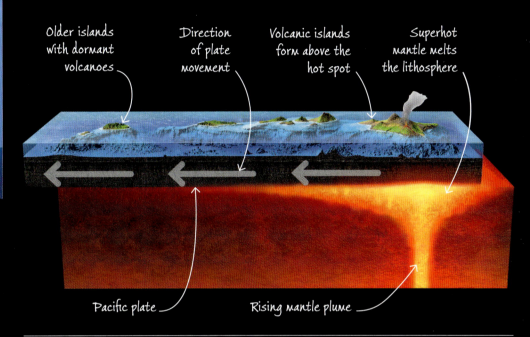

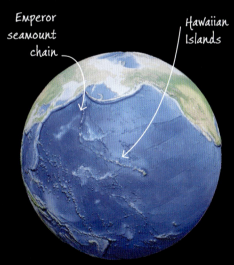

HAWAIIAN-EMPEROR SEAMOUNT CHAIN
The Hawaiian Islands are part of a longer chain of islands and underwater mountains (seamounts) extending for 3,900 miles (6,200 km): the Hawaiian-Emperor seamount chain. This vast structure formed over 85 million years as the Pacific plate moved across a hot spot. The shape of the chain tells us about the plate's movement, with a bend marking a change in direction.

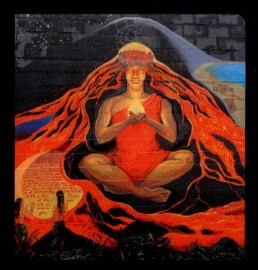

GODDESS OF VOLCANOES
According to Hawaiian mythology, the Halemaumau crater on Kīlauea is home to Pele, goddess of volcanoes and fire. Pele had a fiery personality and fought with her sister, the goddess of the sea. Pele was driven from island to island, each time digging a fire pit for herself and creating new eruptions. These ancient stories explained how the Hawaiian volcanoes formed, long before scientific theories developed.

HOW ATOLLS FORM

If you take a flight over a tropical ocean, you might spot ring-shaped islands or ring-shaped reefs with blue lagoons in the middle. These are atolls and are built by small sea creatures called corals. Corals grow in large colonies inside hard skeletons made of calcium carbonate. Over thousands of years, the skeletons of dead corals build up to form coral reefs, which are home to an amazing diversity of life.

▼ BORA BORA
The Bora Bora atoll formed around an extinct volcano in the South Pacific. The island is encircled by a lagoon, which is surrounded by a barrier reef. The barrier reef protects the lagoon from the ocean waves, making the calm waters a haven for stingrays, barracudas, sharks, and other fish.

Extinct volcanoes no longer have magma in their magma chamber and so will not erupt.

Lagoons are shallow, bodies of water protected from the sea by land or reefs.

SINKING ISLANDS
Almost 200 years ago the British naturalist Charles Darwin produced a map of all the atolls he found during a round-the-world sea trip, and proposed the theory that atolls form around sunken islands.

① ISLAND FORMATION
A hot-spot volcano forms an island, and a fringing reef then grows around the island. Once the magma chamber cools and solidifies, the volcano is extinct.

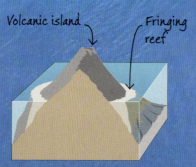

Volcanic island — *Fringing reef*

② EROSION AND SINKING
The island sinks due to erosion, sinking of the seafloor, or both. The reef grows upward, staying just below sea level. A lagoon forms between the land and the reef.

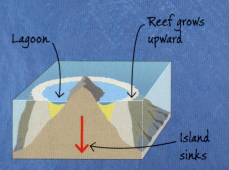

Lagoon — *Reef grows upward* — *Island sinks*

HOW ATOLLS FORM 65

CORAL COLONIES
Coral colonies come in all sorts of colors, shapes, and sizes. Some look like the branches of a tree, and some look like leaves or flowers. Fan-shaped corals reach into the water, trying to trap food, while vase-shaped corals are a hiding place for fish.

As the coral on the lagoon side dies, it breaks down to form sand.

Waves break on the outer edge of the reef.

❸ ATOLL GROWS
Eventually the island disappears, leaving just a circular reef—an atoll. The outside of the atoll grows upward and outward, and the inside gets broken up, depositing sand on the bottom of the lagoon.

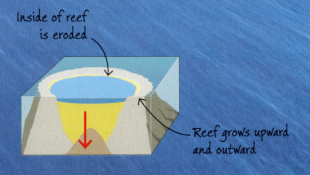

Inside of reef is eroded

Reef grows upward and outward

AN ATOLL NATION
The Maldives is a country in the Indian Ocean made up of around 1,200 small coral islands arranged in rings to form 26 huge atolls. The Maldives is the lowest-lying country in the world, with the highest point being only 8 ft (2.4 m) above sea level.

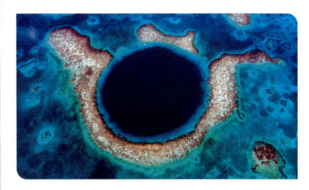

GREAT BLUE HOLE
Not all atolls develop from sinking islands. The Great Blue Hole in the Caribbean Sea was once a cave on dry land, when sea levels were lower than today. The cave's roof collapsed, forming a sinkhole, and the sea level later rose and filled it, creating an atoll.

NUKUORO ATOLL
Nukuoro in the Pacific is another atoll that formed due to changing sea levels. Long ago, a fall in sea level turned the shallow limestone seafloor here into land. The limestone eroded to form a bowl shape, which became an atoll when the water rose again.

HOW GEYSERS AND MUD POTS WORK

The ground beneath your feet contains more than just rock. It also contains groundwater, which trickles though a maze of hidden channels and soaks into layers of softer rock like water into a sponge. When volcanoes heat this groundwater, amazing geothermal features can form. Hot water and steam gush through cracks and other spaces to the surface, where the hot, mineral-rich water forms hot springs, geysers, mud pots, and unusual rock formations.

▶ **STROKKUR GEYSER, ICELAND**
Geysers are volcanic springs that shoot out boiling water and steam. The name comes from the Icelandic word *geysir*, meaning "to gush." Strokkur, a fountain geyser, is Iceland's most regularly erupting geyser. Every 6–10 minutes, a fountain of scalding water shoots 65 ft (20 m) high, though it has been known to reach twice this height.

HOW GEYSERS WORK
Geysers form when heat from volcanic activity boils groundwater but the steam gets trapped, builds up, and periodically erupts. At Strokkur, the trapped pocket of steam expands and pushes up the pool before bursting out. The sudden release of pressure creates an explosive fountain of hot water and steam. The pressure then starts to build again.

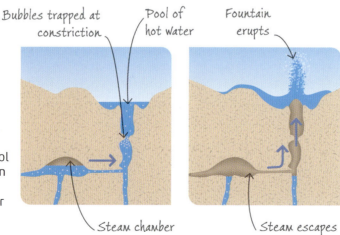

1 STEAM BUILDS UP
Bubbles of steam rise to a chamber that traps them. A constriction in the outlet traps more bubbles, causing pressure below to build up.

2 ERUPTION
Trapped steam escapes, releasing pressure. The sudden fall in pressure allows the scalding water to boil, creating an explosive fountain.

LIFE IN HOT SPRINGS
Not all hot springs are boiling—some are cool enough to bathe in. Even the hottest springs have life. Microorganisms called extremophiles can withstand the heat and can obtain energy from minerals dissolved in the water. Some scientists think the earliest forms of life on Earth may have lived this way.

CONE GEYSERS
Whereas fountain geysers erupt from pools, cone geysers erupt from chimneylike mounds of sinter, a rocky mineral deposited by the water. The Fly Ranch geyser in Nevada owes its vibrant colors to thermophilic (heat-loving) algae.

MUD POTS
Mud pots are pools of boiling mud. They form where a hot spring has relatively little water, and the underlying rock is eaten away by acidic gases and by extremophiles. This results in a gooey, gray mud through which steam and hot water erupt. Some mud pots are cool enough to sit in. The mud is thought to be good for the skin.

LIMESTONE POOLS

The water that bubbles out of hot springs is rich in minerals dissolved underground. As the water trickles away and evaporates, the minerals crystallize on the ground as a hard crust. In the mountains of Turkey, this process has created a natural wonder—a terrace of white limestone pools brimming with turquoise water. Called Pamukkale ("cotton castle" in Turkish), it has attracted tourists for more than 2,000 years.

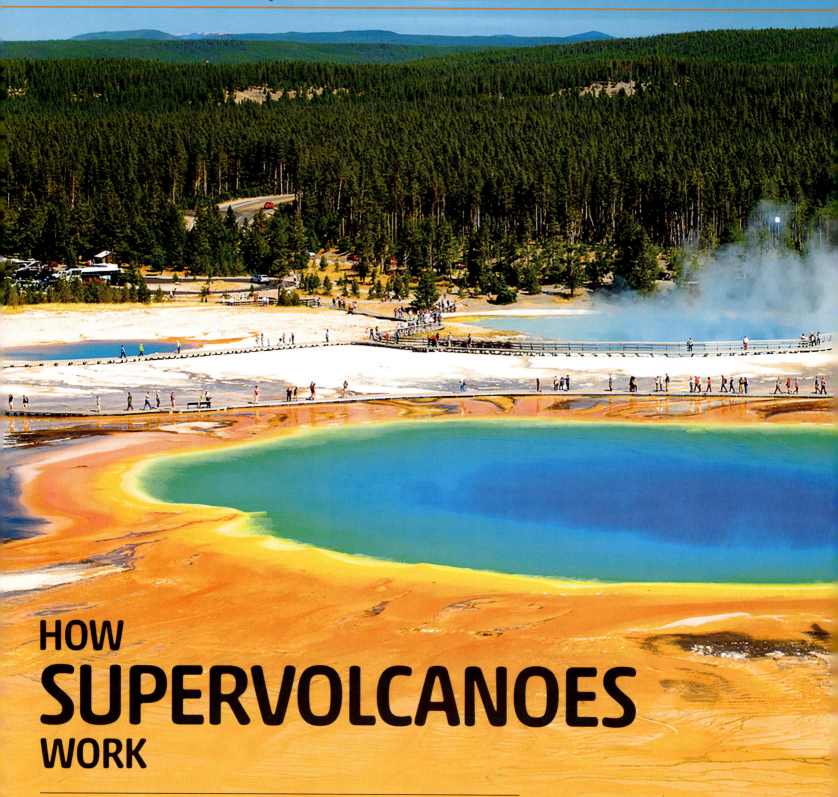

HOW SUPERVOLCANOES WORK

The most powerful volcanoes can produce catastrophic supereruptions. A supereruption can bury a whole country under a blanket of ash and release enough volcanic gas to change the climate. At the eruption site, pyroclastic flows destroy everything in their path, and the ground collapses into a gigantic crater (a caldera). Thankfully, supereruptions are rare—the last one was 27,000 years ago.

▲ **YELLOWSTONE**
The Yellowstone volcano has had three supereruptions in the last 2 million years. Each lasted for decades and covered North America in ash. Today, the caldera is a popular beauty spot, thanks to its spectacular hot springs (above) and geysers, kept active by the giant magma chamber still lurking deep below.

HOW SUPERVOLCANOES WORK 71

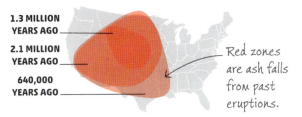

PAST ERUPTIONS
Traces of ash from past eruptions at Yellowstone show how devastating a supereruption can be. Most of Yellowstone's eruptions are now small lava flows, so the next eruption is unlikely to be a supereruption.

These rock layers, formed in lava floods, stretch thousands of miles across India.

LAVA FLOODS
Some of the mass extinctions in Earth's past may have been caused by supereruptions. About 65 million years ago, just before the dinosaurs died out, massive floods of lava spewed from volcanoes in India for thousands of years. The lava covered much of western India in igneous rock, forming geological structures now known as the Deccan Traps.

VOLCANIC WINTERS
In 1815, the eruption of Mount Tambora in Indonesia led to the "Year Without Summer." Gases released by the volcano interacted with water vapor in the atmosphere and blocked out the Sun. This caused global failed harvests and famines. Many horses had to be killed due to lack of food, prompting the invention of the bicycle.

Grand Prismatic Spring is a hot spring heated by the Yellowstone volcano.

UNDER YELLOWSTONE
Yellowstone's volcano sits over a mantle plume—a column of hot magma rising from deep in Earth's mantle. Heat from the plume has melted parts of the crust, creating two giant magma chambers. These are not caverns full of liquid rock, but hot zones containing scattered pockets of liquid magma. When enough pockets join, an eruption can occur.

HOW EARTHQUAKES WORK

Earthquakes happen when huge areas of rock grind and slip past each other at fractures called faults. Thousands of tiny earthquakes happen every day, but the most violent ones happen at the biggest faults, which are near the boundaries between tectonic plates. When these strike in highly populated areas, they can be devastating.

▶ **ALASKA, 2018**
When movement along faults is sudden, energy is released as powerful seismic waves. These cause the ground to shake, buckle, and rupture, which can demolish roads and buildings in seconds.

LOCK AND SNAP
Just as a squeezed spring stores energy, the rock in Earth's crust stores energy when compressed or stretched. If this stored energy is released by a sudden movement, it causes an earthquake. The hypocenter of an earthquake is where the movement happens. The epicenter is the point on the surface directly above.

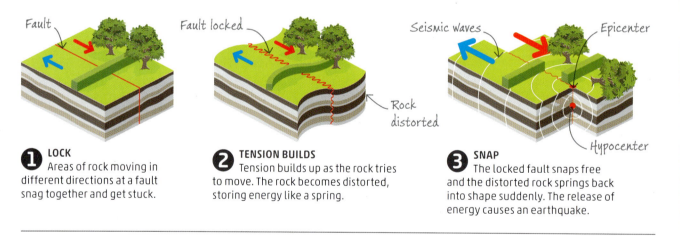

❶ LOCK
Areas of rock moving in different directions at a fault snag together and get stuck.

❷ TENSION BUILDS
Tension builds up as the rock tries to move. The rock becomes distorted, storing energy like a spring.

❸ SNAP
The locked fault snaps free and the distorted rock springs back into shape suddenly. The release of energy causes an earthquake.

EARTHQUAKE SCALES
Earthquakes are measured in two ways. The magnitude scale (below) is based on the energy released, which is measured with vibration-detecting instruments called seismometers. The intensity scale is based on how much damage is done.

| ❷ VERY MINOR | ❸ MINOR | ❹ LIGHT | ❺ MODERATE | ❻ STRONG | ❼ MAJOR | ❽ DEVASTATING |

- Strong enough to feel, but not strong enough to cause much damage
- Chance of damage near the epicenter
- Strong vibrations that may cause a lot of damage near the epicenter
- Major earthquake that is likely to cause extensive damage over a large area
- Huge earthquake that is likely to completely destroy buildings around its epicenter

MAGNITUDE SCALE

HOW EARTHQUAKES WORK

LIQUEFACTION
If the ground is wet and made of soil or loose material, a process called liquefaction can occur during an earthquake. The shaking moves the loose ground so much that it flows like a liquid and engulfs objects. Cars and buildings sink into the ground, while buried pipes and cables float to the surface.

EARTHQUAKE PROTECTION
Earthquakes are hard to predict, but scientists can detect warning signs, including foreshocks and changes in ground height. Most deaths are caused by the collapse of buildings, so an effective form of protection is to design buildings that can withstand being shaken, with shock-absorbing foundations and reinforced steel frames.

SAN FRANCISCO EARTHQUAKE
The deadliest earthquake in US history took place in San Francisco in 1906. It was caused by the San Andreas fault between the Pacific and North American tectonic plates. The Pacific plate lurched 33 ft (10 m) north, causing an earthquake with a magnitude of 7.9. The shaking and subsequent fires destroyed 80 percent of the city. It was one of the first earthquakes to be recorded on film.

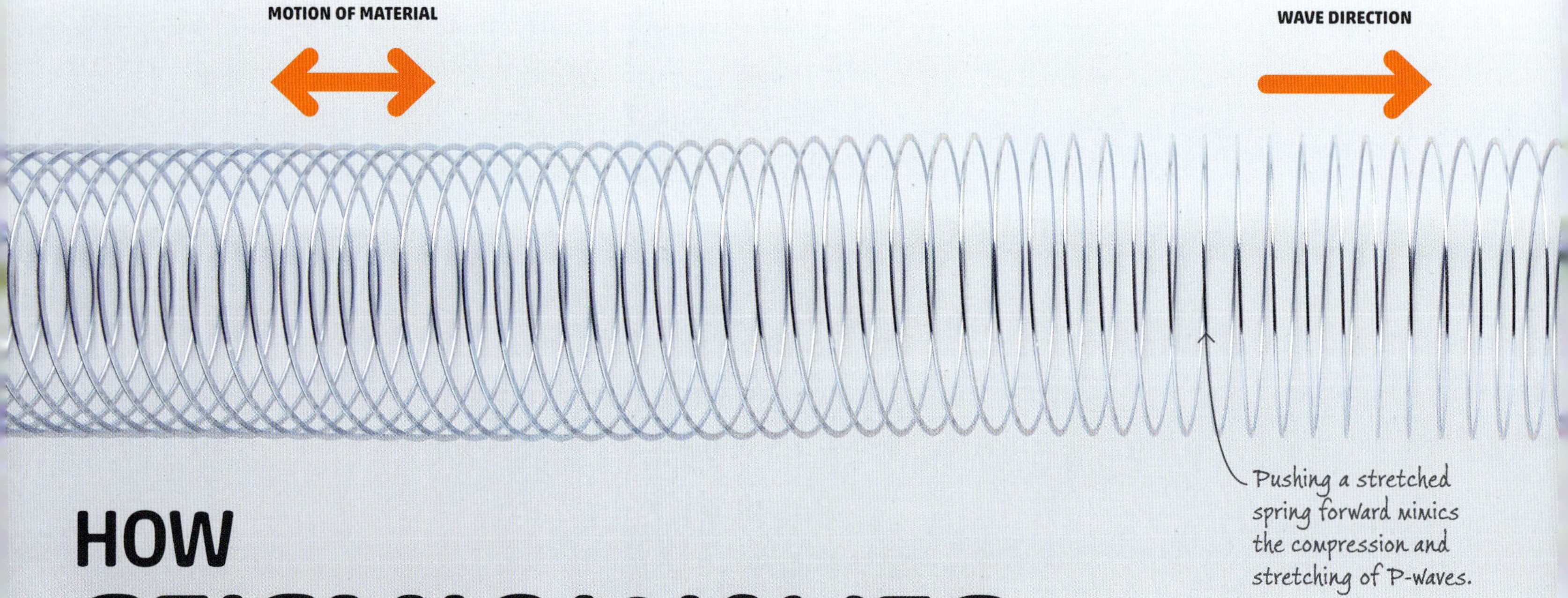

MOTION OF MATERIAL ⟷

WAVE DIRECTION →

Pushing a stretched spring forward mimics the compression and stretching of P-waves.

HOW SEISMIC WAVES WORK

Earthquakes unleash vast amounts of energy, triggering powerful vibrations that spread through the ground at thousands of miles an hour. These vibrations are called seismic waves. There are several different types, with some traveling only through rock on Earth's surface and others passing right through our planet's core. By studying these waves, scientists can figure out not only why earthquakes happen but also how Earth's inner layers work.

▲▼ P- AND S-WAVES

Surface waves travel in the rock layers just below Earth's surface, and body waves travel through the inside of Earth. Body waves are either primary (P-) waves or secondary (S-) waves. P-waves travel by compressing and expanding the rock they pass through, and S-waves travel in a side-to-side motion. P-waves and S-waves travel on a curved path through Earth because of changes in density in the mantle and the core.

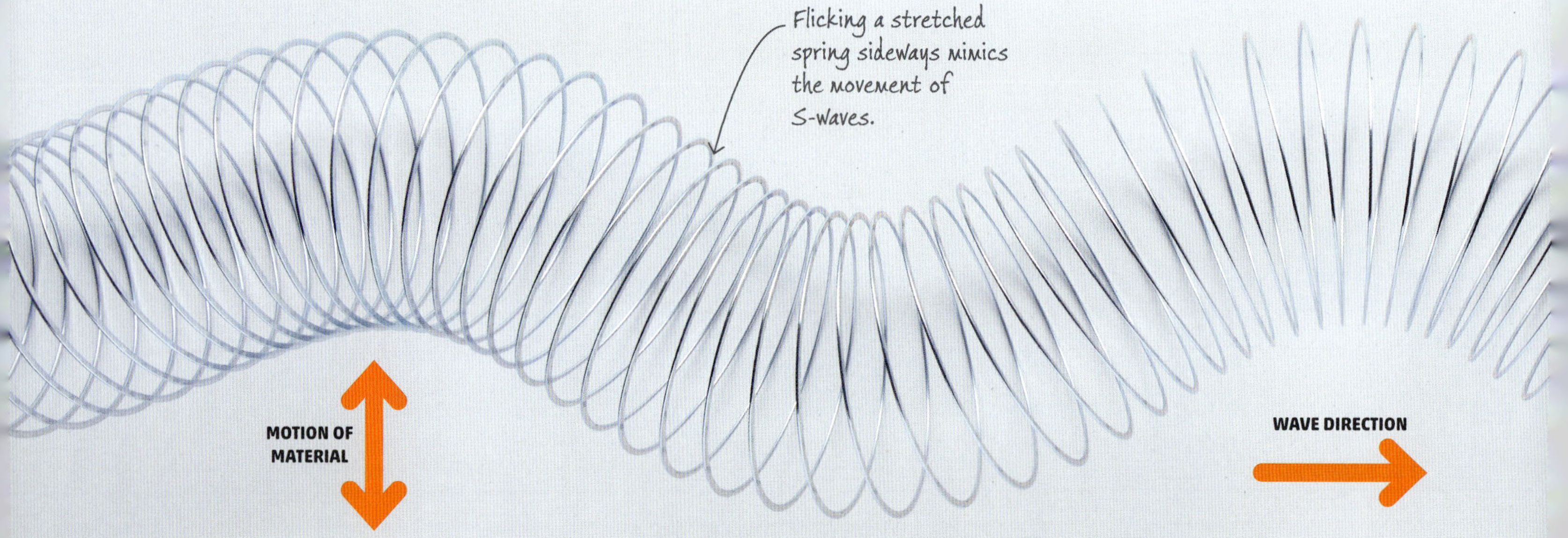

Flicking a stretched spring sideways mimics the movement of S-waves.

MOTION OF MATERIAL ↕

WAVE DIRECTION →

HOW SEISMIC WAVES WORK

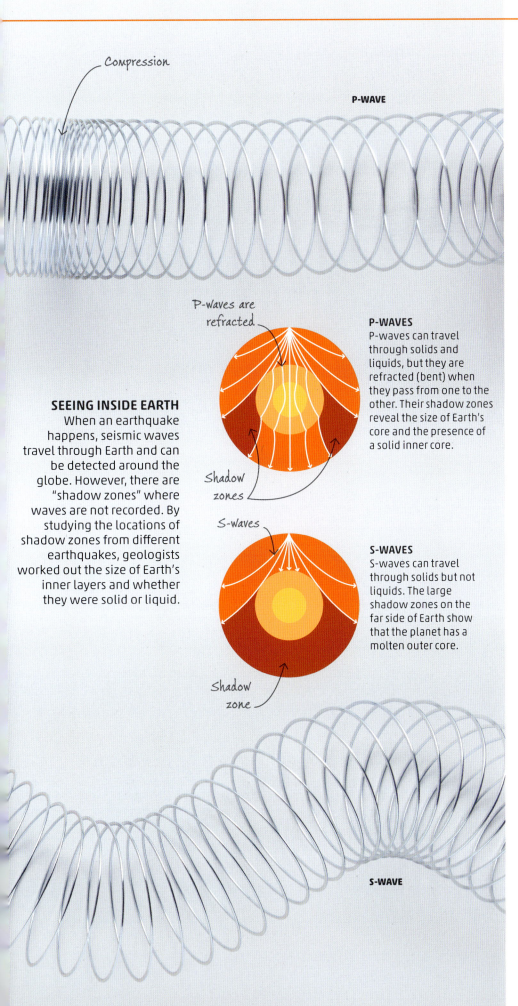

P-WAVE

Compression

P-WAVES
P-waves can travel through solids and liquids, but they are refracted (bent) when they pass from one to the other. Their shadow zones reveal the size of Earth's core and the presence of a solid inner core.

P-waves are refracted

Shadow zones

S-WAVES
S-waves can travel through solids but not liquids. The large shadow zones on the far side of Earth show that the planet has a molten outer core.

S-waves

Shadow zone

SEEING INSIDE EARTH
When an earthquake happens, seismic waves travel through Earth and can be detected around the globe. However, there are "shadow zones" where waves are not recorded. By studying the locations of shadow zones from different earthquakes, geologists worked out the size of Earth's inner layers and whether they were solid or liquid.

S-WAVE

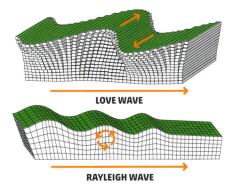

SURFACE WAVES
There are two types of surface waves. Love waves move the ground from side to side, a bit like S-waves trapped at the surface. These cause the most damage to roads and buildings. Rayleigh waves move the surface in a circular motion, a bit like ocean waves.

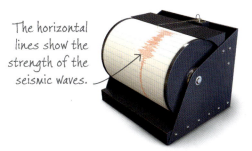

The horizontal lines show the strength of the seismic waves.

SEISMOMETERS
Scientists use instruments called seismometers to measure seismic waves and study earthquakes. The seismometer is securely attached to the ground so that it shakes when an earthquake happens. The motion was traditionally recorded by a pen drawing on a drum of paper, but modern seismometers record their data digitally.

Epicenter — Seismometer

FINDING THE EPICENTER
To work out exactly where the epicenter of an earthquake is, seismologists need three seismometers in different places. Each one can calculate the distance to the epicenter by measuring when P- and S-waves arrive (P-waves are faster). When the distance from all three seismometers is known, drawing intersecting circles on a map pinpoints the epicenter.

HOW TSUNAMIS WORK

When an earthquake, volcanic eruption, or landslide happens at sea, it can cause a powerful wave called a tsunami. Tsunamis are usually no taller than ordinary waves but they are thousands of times longer and can race across the open ocean at speeds of 500 mph (800 kph). Larger tsunamis build to a great height as they reach the coast, causing catastrophic floods as they rush inland.

TSUNAMI FORMATION
Most tsunamis are created by earthquakes that cause sudden movements of the seafloor. This displaces a colossal volume of ocean water, producing tsunami waves that radiate outward.

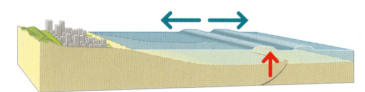

❶ SEAFLOOR DISPLACEMENT
The seafloor lurches upward, creating a wave that spreads in all directions. The wave is low but hundreds of miles long and moves at terrific speed.

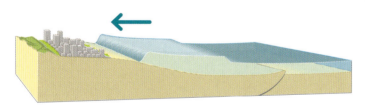

❷ WAVES BUILD
When a wave reaches the shore, its front slows down but the rear keeps moving. As a result, water accumulates and the wave grows taller. Water may retreat from the coast before the tsunami hits, as the trough (low point) of the wave may arrive first.

❸ COASTAL FLOODING
Now higher than the land, the tsunami washes inland faster than a person can run. The surge of water can carry boats, cars, trees, and debris from demolished buildings.

HOW TSUNAMIS WORK

▼ TŌHOKU TSUNAMI
In 2011, Japan was shaken by the largest earthquake in its history, caused by a sudden slip between the Eurasian and Pacific tectonic plates deep under the Pacific Ocean. The whole of Japan's main island lurched eastward by 8 ft (2.4 m) and the seafloor sprang upward by 23 ft (7 m), triggering a tsunami that struck Japan ten minutes later. The wave reached 133 ft (40.5 m) at its highest point and surged inland for up to 6 miles (10 km). The image below – a still from a bystander's video – shows the wave breaching tsunami defenses at Miyako.

TSUNAMI WARNINGS
Tsunamis can't be predicted, but tsunami buoys and sensors on the seafloor can detect them and give an early warning. After an earthquake, a tsunami alert is sent to coastal communities that could be affected. The sea draining away quickly from a beach is a sign that a deadly wave is coming and that people need to move to higher ground.

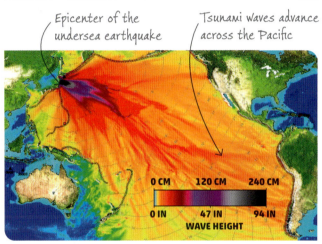

ACROSS THE OCEAN
Tsunami waves travel outward from their source. They carry a huge quantity of energy and can travel across an entire ocean. The 2011 tsunami that struck Japan also traveled 5,600 miles (9,000 km) across the Pacific Ocean to hit California with 9 ft (2.7 m) waves just a few hours later.

BOXING DAY TSUNAMI
The deadliest tsunami on record took place on December 26, 2004, after a massive earthquake in the Indian Ocean. The tsunami killed around 230,000 people and caused widespread destruction along the coasts of the Indian Ocean.

BANDA ACEH BEFORE TSUNAMI

BANDA ACEH AFTER TSUNAMI

Earth's surface is in a continual state of change. Over millions of years, **tectonic forces** raise **mountains** and reshape **continents**. At the same time, the forces of **weathering** and **erosion** wear away the land, turning solid rock into sand and mud. This endless cycle of creation and destruction has created all the world's **landscapes**, from alpine valleys to desert canyons and coastlines.

CHANGING LANDSCAPES

HOW LANDSCAPES FORM

Earth's surface is dynamic, which means that it's continually changing. Some changes are so slow that we barely notice them, but something that looks trivial—like rain falling on a hillside—can wear down a whole mountain range given enough time. Other processes, such as volcanic eruptions and landslides, can cause sudden, dramatic changes to landscapes. Every landscape has its own story to tell.

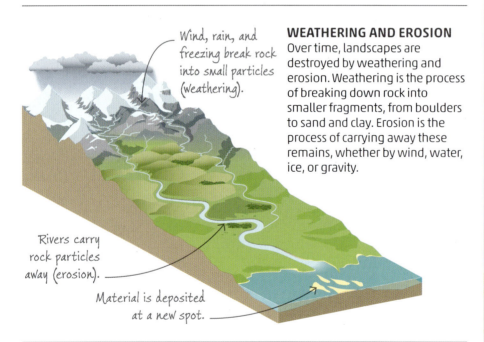

WEATHERING AND EROSION
Over time, landscapes are destroyed by weathering and erosion. Weathering is the process of breaking down rock into smaller fragments, from boulders to sand and clay. Erosion is the process of carrying away these remains, whether by wind, water, ice, or gravity.

Wind, rain, and freezing break rock into small particles (weathering).

Rivers carry rock particles away (erosion).

Material is deposited at a new spot.

KEY TO THE PAST
Mary and Charles Lyell were a geologist couple who visited the Swiss Alps for their honeymoon in 1832. They formed a theory that Earth's landscapes are shaped by gradual processes that have acted for vast spans of time and continue today. As Charles Lyell famously said, "the present is the key to the past."

MARY HORNER LYELL

SIR CHARLES LYELL

▼ ALPINE VALLEY
The Alps mountain range rose bit by bit as tectonic plates carrying Africa and Europe collided, folding and buckling layers of rock that once lay on the sea floor. During the Ice Age, vast glaciers carved deep valleys, like Lauterbrunnen in Switzerland.

Alpine glaciers form where centuries of snow build up on mountain peaks.

Lauterbrunnen valley was filled with a glacier during the Ice Age. Glaciers flow slowly and carve out U-shaped valleys with steep sides and wide, flat bottoms.

Snow and ice break down rock by seeping into crevices and expanding with each cycle of freezing and thawing.

Waterfalls cut through the cliffs creating dramatic gorges.

❶ SCREE
Broken rock fragments caused by weathering collect on steep slopes, forming heaps of loose debris called scree.

❷ RAPIDS
Rapids are areas of fast-flowing water in shallow rivers or streams with a rocky bottom. They form where the ground is steep and rocky.

❸ CAVES
Caves form where groundwater flows through soft rock such as limestone. Limestone reacts with natural acidity in rain and slowly dissolves.

❹ FLOODPLAINS
Rivers carry away sediment and deposit it in the valleys, where it forms lush floodplains.

❺ MEANDERS
Meanders are bends in rivers. They form when sediment is eroded on the outside of bends and deposited on the inner edges.

82 CHANGING LANDSCAPES

1 BEFORE COMPRESSION
Beds of colored sand representing sedimentary rock strata are carefully laid down in flat layers. Deeper layers represent older layers of rock.

Dyed sand represents layers of sedimentary rock.

2 FOLDING BEGINS
When the moving plate begins to push the sand, the layers bend and fold. The surface level rises as sand piles up, just as land rises when mountains begin to form.

Layers begin to fold

3 FAULTS DEVELOP
Fractures develop when the layers are pushed too much to fold any further. These fractures are known as thrust faults.

Thrust fault

As folding continues, older rock is pushed over younger layers, forming a structure called a nappe.

4 MOUNTAINS RISE
The crust continues to thicken, raising the sand to form mountains. In the real world, the thickening pushes downward too, giving mountains very deep roots.

Ridges and valleys form on the surface

▼ MODELING MOUNTAINS
To understand mountain formation, scientists use sandbox models. Layers of sand representing layers of rock in Earth's crust are slowly compressed by a machine. The sand layers fold and then break along faults, as happens in Earth's crust. The folded layers pile up, making the crust thicker and raising the land.

Far from the zone of folding, the tectonic plate remains thin and undeformed.

HOW MOUNTAINS RISE

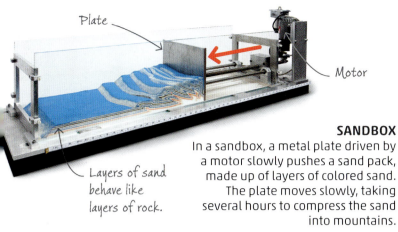

SANDBOX
In a sandbox, a metal plate driven by a motor slowly pushes a sand pack, made up of layers of colored sand. The plate moves slowly, taking several hours to compress the sand into mountains.

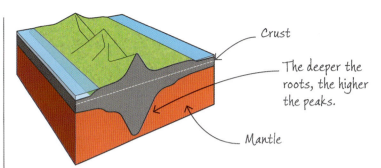

DEEP ROOTS
Mountains don't just have high peaks—they have deep roots too. A mountain range "floats" on the soft but denser mantle rock below, its roots submerged. As the peaks are worn away by erosion, the whole mountain range bobs up like an iceberg in water, keeping the peaks high.

FOLDED ROCK
Erosion can make the internal folds of mountains visible. The mountains of Crete in Greece formed when Africa and Europe collided, crumpling layers of sedimentary rock that were once on the seafloor.

FOLDED LIMESTONE, CRETE

Mountain ranges form at the boundaries between tectonic plates. The world's tallest mountains—the Himalayas—are still rising today by about 0.4 in (1 cm) a year as the plate carrying India collides with the Eurasian plate. These processes play out over millions of years, but scientists can simulate them in a few hours by using models made of sand.

A fold that bends upward like an arch is called an anticline.

Foothills

A thrust fault is a sloping fracture that moves older rocks over younger rocks.

A fold that bends downward in a u-shape or v-shape is called a syncline.

84 CHANGING LANDSCAPES

HOW RIFT VALLEYS SINK

HOW RIFT VALLEYS FORM
The process of stretching and breaking up a continent is called rifting. A rift valley takes millions of years to form and eventually evolves into a new ocean.

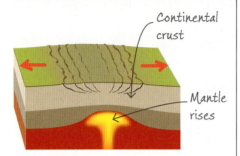

1. PLATES DIVERGE
When tectonic plates move away from each other, they stretch and thin the crust. The mantle rises and partly melts, forming magma.

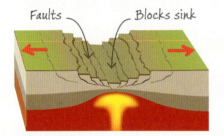

2. VALLEY FORMS
The crust breaks along faults, and large blocks sink. This forms an elongated valley called a continental rift.

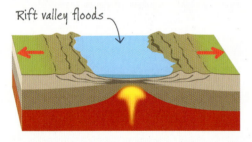

3. OCEAN FORMS
As the rifting continues, the land sinks below sea level and floods, forming a linear ocean like the present-day Red Sea.

In some parts of the world, neighboring tectonic plates are pulling apart. When this happens, the crust between them thins and breaks up. Magma wells up from the mantle, oozing through cracks and creating new crust. This process can happen on the sea floor or on land. In the sea, it creates new ocean basins. On land, it tears apart whole continents, forming mountains and rift valleys.

▶ THE GREAT RIFT VALLEY
Africa's Great Rift Valley stretches for more than 1,864 miles (3,000 km) from Jordan to Mozambique, and is slowly tearing the continent apart. The crust here has stretched and broken into separate blocks, separated by deep cracks called faults. Some sections have sunk, forming steep-sided valleys called grabens, flanked by highlands. Magma rising from the mantle feeds the Rift Valley's many volcanoes, including Mount Kilimanjaro—Africa's highest peak.

MODELING RIFTS
Geologists use sandbox models to study how rift valleys form. Layers of colored sand on a moving base are slowly pulled apart. A process that can take millions of years can be modeled in a few hours.

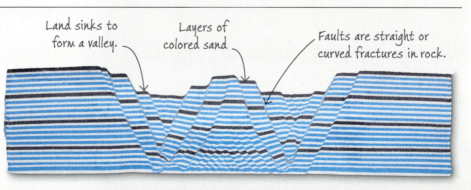

HOW WEATHERING WORKS

Some rocks are harder than others, but every kind of rock is eventually broken down by a process called weathering. Pattering rain, gusts of wind, and even your feet stomping along a mountain path all cause weathering. This process wears down rocks into tiny particles such as sand grains, while another process—erosion—carries these away. Working together over millions of years, weathering and erosion can wear away whole mountain ranges.

▼ **WEATHERED GRANITE**
This granite outcrop on a hill in Dartmoor, UK, is slowly wearing away due to weathering. Granite is a very hard rock made of the minerals feldspar, biotite, and quartz. Although tough, it eventually breaks down. Feldspar and biotite react chemically with the natural acidity in rain and turn into clay, which is softer, causing the rock to crumble. Quartz is much tougher but its crystals fall out as sand grains when the other minerals in granite are weathered away.

FERTILE SOIL
Soil is made from weathered particles of rock mixed with plant and animal remains. Soils made from a mix of rock types contain lots of different minerals. These soils are often the most fertile, making them perfect for growing crops.

HOW WEATHERING WORKS 87

PHYSICAL WEATHERING
When rocks are broken down by physical processes, it's called physical weathering. This rock in Antarctica has been split up by a process called freeze-thaw. Water trickles into cracks in a rock and expands when it freezes, causing the cracks to widen until the rock splits.

BIOLOGICAL WEATHERING
Weathering happens in three different ways. When living things break up rock, it's called biological weathering. For example, pieces of rock may be broken off when a plant's roots grow into a crack in a rock and widen it until the rock splits.

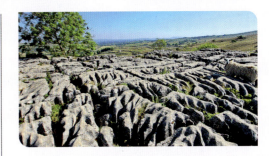

CHEMICAL WEATHERING
Chemical weathering occurs when rocks are broken down by chemical reactions. Rain picks up carbon dioxide from the air, making it slightly acidic. It trickles into cracks, where a chemical reaction occurs, changing and weakening some of the minerals.

Cracks in the rock allow rain to penetrate, causing chemical weathering.

SHRINKING MOUNTAINS
The inland mountain ranges of the western US, such as the White Mountains, were once as high as the Himalayas, with peaks rivaling Mount Everest. After millions of years of weathering, the tallest peak in this region—White Mountain in California—is now 14,252 ft (4,344 m)—less than half of Everest's height.

BREAKING UP
Solid rock falls apart and breaks down into its mineral grains when weathered. Fragments of broken rock are carried away by rivers and dumped far away, even in the sea.

HOW EROSION WORKS

Earth's landscapes are constantly changing due to erosion—the wearing away of rock and the removal of rock particles by wind, water, and gravity. Working together with weathering (the breakdown of rock into smaller particles), erosion can create spectacular landforms, from cliffs and canyons to rock arches and pinnacles.

SAND
Look closely at sand and you'll see it's made of tiny crystals. Most types of sand consist of grains of quartz—a hard, crystalline mineral found in igneous rocks like granite. When rocks break down, the quartz crystals fall out and are carried away by wind or water.

Quartz crystal

▶ ROCK PINNACLE
Pinnacles of rock, like this one in the Sahara desert, are shaped by erosion. This pinnacle has been worn away by windblown sand. Its tapering shape shows that the force of erosion is most powerful near the base, where a vortex of swirling wind has also made a depression in the sand. Eventually the pinnacle will become unstable and collapse.

❶ WALL
The side of a plateau (a raised area of land) is weathered and eroded by water and wind, leaving a narrow wall of rock.

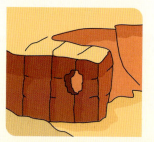

❷ WINDOW
The wall becomes thinner as weathering and erosion continue. Windows appear in the softer, weaker areas of the rock wall.

❸ PINNACLE
Eventually, a column of rock, known as a pinnacle, is all that remains of the wall. In time, the pinnacle will be eroded away too.

HOW EROSION WORKS 89

EROSION BY WIND
The sand-filled winds of the Sahara erode exposed soft rock into intricate patterns, such as this latticework of sandstone in Tassili n'Ajjer, Algeria.

EROSION BY RIVERS
Over millions of years, the Colorado River cut into the rocky ground to form this sharp turn, known as Horseshoe Bend, in Arizona.

EROSION BY WAVES
The pounding of ocean waves can erode cliffs, creating rock formations such as this sea arch, known as Durdle Door, in the UK.

EROSION BY ICE
Ice erodes land too. Glaciers, such as Elephant Foot in Greenland, drag rocks and grit downhill, reshaping valleys and creating new landforms.

The sides of this pinnacle are slowly eaten away by windblown sand.

The depression is due to wind swirling around the base. The same thing happens when a hollow forms in the snow around a fence post.

HOW LANDSLIDES WORK

When large amounts of earth, rock, and soil move down a steep slope under the force of gravity we call it a landslide. Every year, this type of erosion causes thousands of deaths and billions of dollars' worth of damage. Most landslides are triggered by rainfall, which soaks into the soil making it heavier, weaker, and more slippery. Shaking from earthquakes, volcanic rumbles, and human activities such as road cutting can also start rocks and soil tumbling.

Bare slope once covered in soil and forest

Houses engulfed by soil and uprooted trees

▶ **AFTER AN EARTHQUAKE**
In 2018, a powerful earthquake shook the island of Hokkaido in Japan, triggering landslides that killed 36 people. To make matters worse, heavy rains before the earthquake had loosened the soil covering the hills, making it more likely to slide downhill.

TYPES OF LANDSLIDES
Landslides can be fast or slow. They may be noticeable only after many years as rock and soil gradually move downhill. Others are much more dramatic as earth and rocks break away from a slope, forming a chaotic mixture of debris.

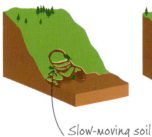 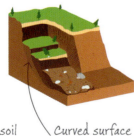 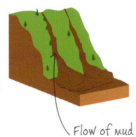 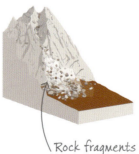

Slow-moving soil — *Curved surface* — *Flow of mud* — *Rock fragments*

CREEP
This is the slowest type of landslide. Dislodged soil gradually slides downhill and may show as a wavy surface on a hillside.

SLUMP
In this type of landslide, part of a mountainside or cliff detaches from the bedrock and slides downward, often along a curved surface.

MUDFLOW
Mudflows occur when heavy rain or melting snow turns soil into runny mud that surges down a slope in channels.

ROCKFALL
Rocks broken up by weathering may tumble down cliffs and mountainsides. A pile of fallen rocks is known as scree.

HOW LANDSLIDES WORK 91

LAHARS
Volcanic eruptions can cause deadly mudflows, called lahars, which race downhill and can bury settlements. Lahars happen when an eruption melts snow or ice at the top of a volcano or when torrential rain mixes with the loose volcanic debris.

LAHAR SEDIMENT AT MOUNT ST HELENS

RECEDING CLIFFS
Ocean waves pound away at cliffs with great power, weakening them and causing landslides. Over time, coastal cliffs recede, threatening communities that were once a safe distance from the sea.

COASTAL EROSION IN CALIFORNIA

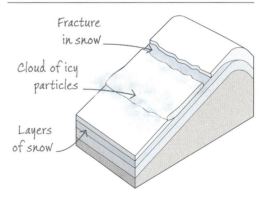

AVALANCHES
Avalanches are "landslides" of snow. They occur when a recent layer of snow on a steep slope separates and slides away from the older layers underneath, gathering speed as it falls and creating a cloud of icy particles.

CHANGING LANDSCAPES

TYPES OF SAND DUNES
The shape and size of sand dunes depend on how fast and strong the wind is, which direction it comes from, and how much sand it carries. There are five different types of sand dunes.

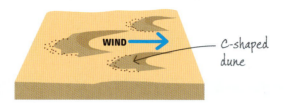

Barchan dunes
These C-shaped dunes are the most common type of dune. They form in places where the wind usually blows from one direction.

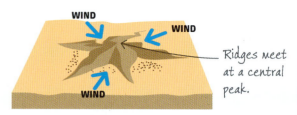

Star dunes
Many of the tallest dunes are star dunes. They have three or more ridges and form where the wind blows from different directions.

HOW SAND DUNES WORK

Sand dunes are ever-changing mountains of sand, created and shaped by the wind. They are common on windswept beaches, but the largest occur in deserts, where vast expanses of sand dunes—sand seas—can stretch for hundreds of miles.

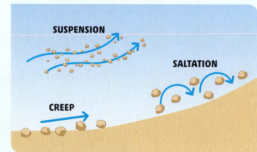

HOW PARTICLES MOVE
Wind moves sand grains in three different ways. Large sand particles roll along the ground (creep). Medium particles move in hops and skips (saltation), and the finest particles become airborne (suspension). The faster the wind, the larger the particles it can lift and carry.

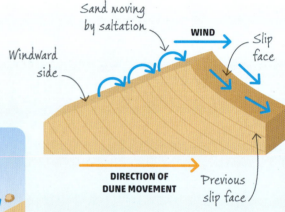

MOVING DUNES
A dune begins to form when an obstacle slows the wind, causing it to lose energy and dump its cargo of sand. The growing dune intercepts the wind, trapping yet more sand and so getting bigger. On the windward side, sand grains are blown up the shallow slope. They pile up at the top until the crest becomes unstable and collapses down the steep side. Each time this happens, the dune moves a little. Over a year, a barchan sand dune can migrate up to 330 ft (100 m).

Sand is blown onto the windward face of a sand dune.

HOW SAND DUNES WORK 93

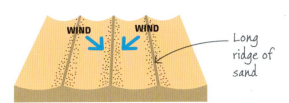

Linear dunes
These very long dunes sometimes stretch to 125 miles (200 km). They form where the wind varies between two directions.

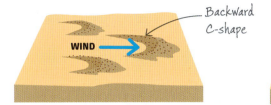

Parabolic dunes
Parabolic dunes form where the wind blows mainly from one direction. Their ends are held down by plants growing on the dune.

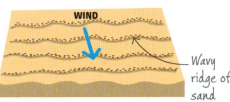

Transverse dunes
These are rows of very long, wavy dunes made when the wind blows from one direction and carries a lot of sand.

LIFE IN SAND DUNES
Sand dunes are difficult places to live, but some species have adapted to life here. The sandfish is a lizard that "swims" into the sand to avoid the Sun's heat. It tucks its limbs close to its smooth, streamlined body and slithers under the surface.

SINGING SAND DUNES
Sometimes a sand dune can make a low rumbling noise, like the hum of an aircraft. These sand-dune songs are caused by sand avalanches, which may be triggered by people, and can last for minutes and be heard miles away.

MARTIAN DUNES
Sand dunes form on other planets too. This false-colored image shows crescent dunes (blue) near the north pole of Mars. The dunes are made of volcanic sand, and their peaks poke through a layer of carbon dioxide frost (pale areas).

▼ RUSTY RED DUNES
The wonderful red Soussusvlei sand dunes in Namibia, Africa, formed over many millions of years. They contain some of the tallest dunes in the world—similar in height to the Eiffel Tower in France. Their rusty color comes from iron oxide in the sand, with the oldest dunes having the most intense red hue.

The slip face of a sand dune is the side that's sheltered from the wind.

HOW GLACIERS WORK

Glaciers are giant, flowing bodies of ice, like very slow-flowing rivers. They form in cold places where snow builds up faster than it melts, such as mountains and polar regions. Most glaciers move less than 3 ft (1 m) a day, but over time they drastically change the shape of landscapes, grinding down rock and gouging deep valleys between mountains.

GLACIER CAVES
Meltwater seeps down through crevasses and erodes ice until it reaches the base of the glacier, forming tunnels and caves. The Breidamerkurjökull caves in Iceland have a crystal blue color because the glacial ice filters out all colors of light except blue.

CREVASSES
Different sections of a glacier move at different rates, resulting in the formation of giant cracks called crevasses. These deep openings, with near-vertical sides, are a hazard to skiers and mountaineers.

▼ ALETSCH GLACIER
Stretching for over 12.5 miles (20 km), and with a maximum depth of 2,950 ft (900 m), the Aletsch Glacier in Switzerland is the largest glacier in the European Alps. This valley glacier has been gouging out a U-shaped valley for thousands of years but, like many glaciers, it is now shrinking due to climate change.

HOW GLACIERS WORK

VALLEY GLACIER
Valley glaciers are giant rivers of ice that get trapped between mountains as they flow downhill.

- Accumulation zone—where snowfall is greater than ice loss
- Cirque—a bowl-shaped valley made by glacial erosion
- Arête—a narrow ridge of rock that separates two glaciers
- Tidewater glacier—where icebergs break off into the sea
- Ablation zone—where ice melts or breaks off at a higher rate than it accumulates
- Glacial toe or terminus—where the glacier ends
- Meltwater stream
- End moraine—soil and rock that has been picked up by the glacier and dumped at its end
- When two glaciers meet, soil and rock debris from their edges combine to form a central streak—a medial moraine.

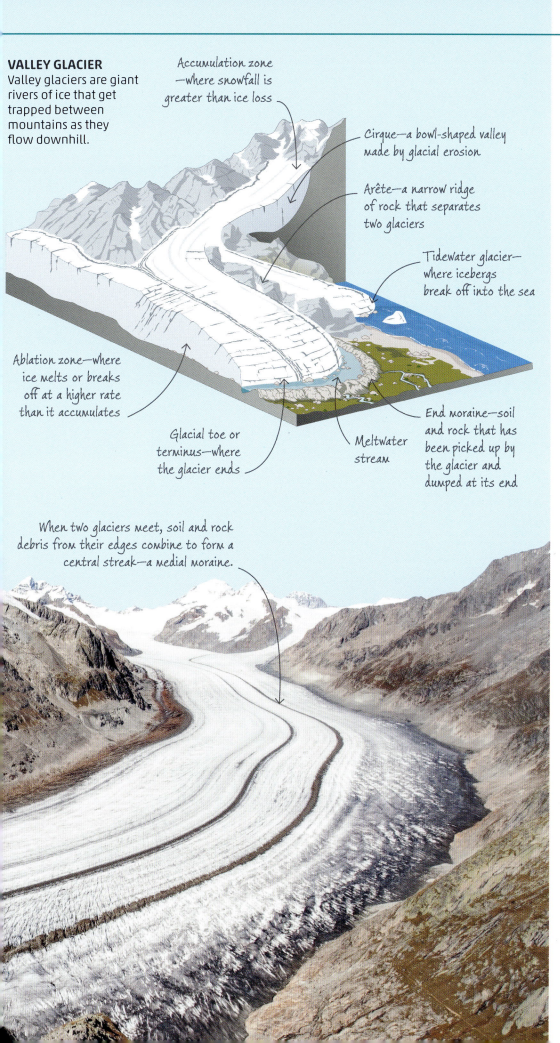

FORMATION OF GLACIAL ICE
Glaciers form when snow builds up in the same place. Over time, the snow is squashed by the weight of new snow, squeezing out air. This turns it into a denser, granular substance called firn, which resembles wet sugar, and finally into solid ice. It can take thousands of years for ice to reach the bottom of a glacier, and scientists estimate that ice at the bottom of the Antarctic ice sheet could be 1 million years old.

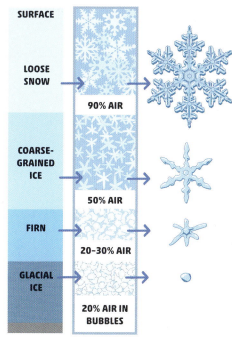

SURFACE
LOOSE SNOW — 90% AIR
COARSE-GRAINED ICE — 50% AIR
FIRN — 20–30% AIR
GLACIAL ICE — 20% AIR IN BUBBLES

GLACIAL VALLEYS
When glaciers melt, they leave behind U-shaped valleys with steep sides and a curved floor. These are different from the V-shaped valleys carved out by rivers, because erosion by the glacier happens across the whole valley, widening it and making the sides steeper. There are many glacial valleys in places that used to be covered in glaciers during the Ice Age—such as Yosemite National Park and the fjords of Norway.

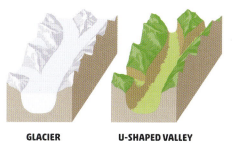

GLACIER | U-SHAPED VALLEY

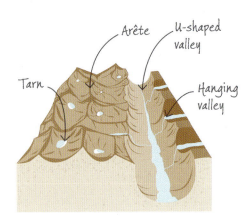

CARVED-OUT LANDSCAPE
In places once covered in glaciers, telltale signs remain showing that the rivers of ice carved mountains and valleys into different shapes.

HANGING VALLEY
A hanging valley is a high side valley created by a tributary glacier that once fed into a larger glacier. The valley is higher because the smaller glacier contained less ice and didn't erode as deeply as the main glacier. Hanging valleys often end in waterfalls.

◀ STIRLING FALLS, NEW ZEALAND

ARÊTE
An arête is a sharp, rocky ridge that was carved between neighboring glacial valleys. The name comes from the French word for a fish's backbone, which the ridge resembles.

◀ BEN NEVIS, SCOTLAND

▲ GRANITE CREEK TARN, ALASKA

TARN
Small lakes that form high in the mountains, in the bowl-shaped valley (cirque) once filled by the head of a glacier, are called tarns. The word comes from the old Norse *tjörn*, which means pond.

U-SHAPED VALLEY
As glaciers flow, they pick up rocks, which then grind away at V-shaped river valleys. This process results in U-shaped valleys, with steep sides and a rounded bottom.

YOSEMITE NATIONAL PARK ▶

GLACIAL FEATURES

Glaciers shape and mold our landscapes by carving out valleys, reshaping mountains, and shifting rocks and soil across huge distances. Glaciers once covered more than one-third of Earth's surface, and the features they left behind give us valuable information about past climates.

ERRATIC
Erratics are rocks carried by glaciers and dumped in a location where the local rock is different. They range from the size of a pebble to larger than a house. By studying erratics, geologists can work out where ancient glaciers once flowed.

YORKSHIRE, UK ▶

GLACIAL FEATURES 97

MORAINE
This is the name given to rocks and soil that are moved and then dumped by a glacier. The sediment that heaps up at the furthest reach of a glacier is called a terminal moraine and is a bit like the high-tide line on a beach.

◀ KASKAPAKTE GLACIER, SWEDEN

Terminal moraine

KETTLE LAKE
When big blocks of ice from retreating glaciers become stranded in the rocks and stones transported by the glaciers, they melt and create hollows in the ground. These hollows may later fill with water to form deep ponds called kettle lakes.

ALASKA ▶

ESKER
Eskers are winding ridges of sand and gravel deposited by meltwater rivers that once flowed through tunnels under glaciers. The longest eskers stretch for hundreds of miles, and the tallest are 98 ft (30 m) high.

▼ MANITOBA, CANADA

DRUMLIN
As glaciers slide across the landscape, they create new lumps and bumps, known as drumlins, from the debris they carry. The mounds are tapered on one side, pointing in the direction that the glacier once flowed in.

◀ CLEW BAY, IRELAND

GLACIAL DEPOSITS
Glaciers transport rocks and soil as they flow. When glaciers melt, this debris is left behind, forming distinctive landscape features such as drumlins, eskers, erratics, and moraines.

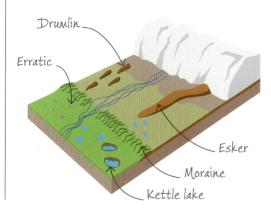

Drumlin, Erratic, Esker, Moraine, Kettle lake

HOW ICEBERGS WORK

Icebergs are like giant ice cubes floating in the ocean. They are made of freshwater ice that has broken off the end of a glacier or an ice shelf. Formed in the coldest parts of the world, icebergs are found in the Arctic and North Atlantic oceans and in the oceans around Antarctica. Icebergs may drift thousands of miles on ocean currents and take several years to melt.

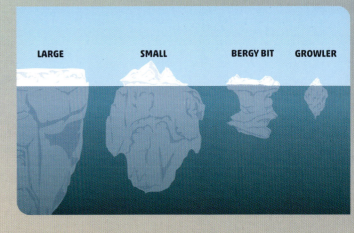

ICEBERGS, BERGY BITS, AND GROWLERS
Icebergs are classified by their size. The smallest ones, growlers, are about the size of a car. Bergy bits, next up in size, are roughly as big as a small house. The other four categories are simply called small, medium, large, and very large. The biggest icebergs of all can be larger than some countries.

UNDERWATER VIEW
Seen from under water, the iceberg has a mottled appearance because melting ice leaves pockmarks in its surface. Rock fragments and dirt picked up by the glacier's base on land sink to the seafloor as the iceberg melts, providing nutrients for marine life.

Tiny air bubbles inside ice reflect white light, giving icebergs their white appearance.

HOW ICEBERGS WORK 99

GIANT ICEBERGS
Rifts (cracks) in ice shelves around Antarctica create the most gigantic icebergs, which are flat in shape (tabular). In 2017, this rift in the Larsen C Ice Shelf allowed a vast iceberg, known as A-68, to break away. It was 110 miles (175 km) long and 30 miles (50 km) wide.

WHERE DO ICEBERGS COME FROM?
When icebergs form—a process called calving—they create a loud cracking or booming noise as the ice hits the sea. They can also cause large waves. Most icebergs in the northern hemisphere come from Greenland, with the West Greenland glaciers calving 10,000 or more icebergs every year. Most icebergs in the southern hemisphere come from Antarctica.

ICE SCULPTURES
Icebergs don't melt evenly all over. The ceaseless action of wind, rain, waves, and ocean currents can erode icebergs unevenly, sometimes carving them into fantastic shapes, such as this arched iceberg in the North Atlantic Ocean.

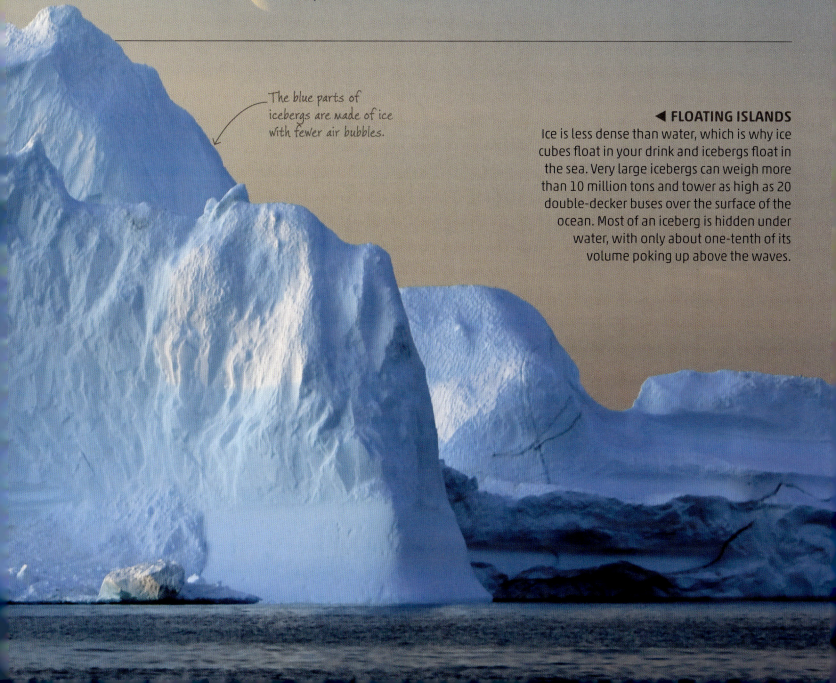

The blue parts of icebergs are made of ice with fewer air bubbles.

◀ **FLOATING ISLANDS**
Ice is less dense than water, which is why ice cubes float in your drink and icebergs float in the sea. Very large icebergs can weigh more than 10 million tons and tower as high as 20 double-decker buses over the surface of the ocean. Most of an iceberg is hidden under water, with only about one-tenth of its volume poking up above the waves.

CHANGING LANDSCAPES

HOW RIVERS WORK

Rain and melting snow flow off the land and drain away in rivers. As well as transporting water, rivers sweep away all sorts of sediment—rocks, pebbles, gravel, sand, silt, and clay. Over great spans of time, this slow but relentless process transforms landscapes. It carves out V-shaped valleys in the upper and middle parts of rivers, and it creates flat plains where sediment is dumped in the lowlands further downstream.

▼ **DRAINAGE BASIN**
A river doesn't have a single source. It is fed by many streams and by groundwater from a large area called a drainage basin. Rivers flow downhill all the way, often starting in mountains. The upper parts are steep, with fast-flowing water and rocky rapids. The middle parts pass through wider valleys formed by erosion over tens of thousands of years. Finally, the river, now flatter and calmer, snakes in wide curves across broad plains.

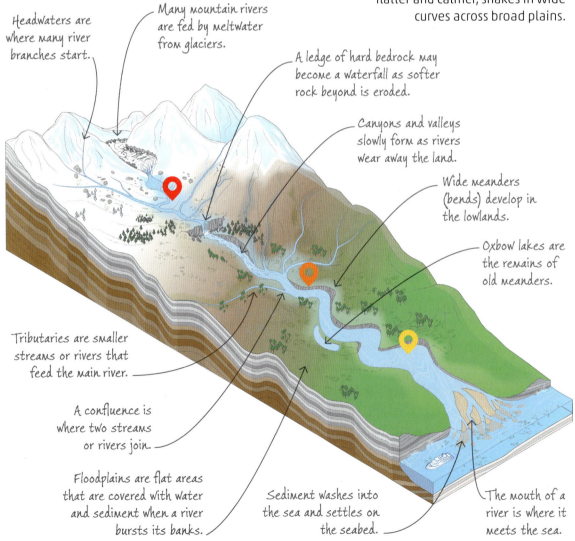

Headwaters are where many river branches start.

Many mountain rivers are fed by meltwater from glaciers.

A ledge of hard bedrock may become a waterfall as softer rock beyond is eroded.

Canyons and valleys slowly form as rivers wear away the land.

Wide meanders (bends) develop in the lowlands.

Oxbow lakes are the remains of old meanders.

Tributaries are smaller streams or rivers that feed the main river.

A confluence is where two streams or rivers join.

Floodplains are flat areas that are covered with water and sediment when a river bursts its banks.

Sediment washes into the sea and settles on the seabed.

The mouth of a river is where it meets the sea.

📍 HIGHLANDS
In mountains, fast-flowing streams called rapids cut vertically into the landscape, carving out V-shaped valleys. The uneven, steep ground makes the water turbulent. The steep hillsides cause rockfalls that send boulders tumbling into the stream. As the water flows around these obstacles, it forms powerful currents.

📍 TRANSITION ZONE
Swollen by water from many tributaries, rivers grow larger as they leave mountain valleys. Broader valleys form in the middle sections of a river under the force of the water flowing over thousands of years, and millions of rocks and pebbles are dumped on the riverbed as the water becomes less turbulent.

📍 LOWLANDS
The lower part of a river meanders in wide loops over flatter land. These bends continually change as sediment is eroded in some places but dumped in others. Occasional floods spread sediment over large floodplains. As the river slowly cuts down into the land, former floodplains are stranded as flat areas of land (terraces).

HOW RIVERS BEND

All natural rivers snake across the land with a wavy, bendy pattern. The bends in rivers are not fixed. They continually change as rivers erode the ground, shifting vast amounts of soil, sand, and pebbles from place to place. Over long periods, rivers change course, but dramatic changes can also happen suddenly during floods.

RIVER TABLE
Scientists study how rivers change over time by modeling them in a river table. Water is pumped to the upper end of the table and allowed to flow through a bed of artificial sediment. The flowing water washes sediment downstream and carves a channel that continually changes shape.

▼ MODELING RIVERS
It can take many years for large rivers to change course, but the same process takes minutes when a river is modeled in a lab. The water picks up sediment where it flows quickly and deposits it where it slows down. Bends grow larger over time because water flows fastest round the outside of a bend, eroding the ground there more powerfully.

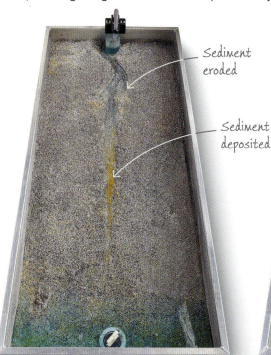

❶ CHANNEL FORMS
Flowing water creates a channel as it removes sediment. The most lightweight particles (yellow) are picked up first and deposited downstream in slower water.

❷ BENDS FORM
Bends can form wherever small obstacles divert the water to one side. Water flows faster around the outsides of bends, so the bends get progressively larger over time.

❸ BENDS WIDEN
A succession of bends develops, giving the river a wavy shape. Sediment builds up on the insides of bends, where water is slower, forming shallow banks called point bars. The river flows around these obstacles, making the bends even wider.

HOW RIVERS BEND

INSIDE A BEND
The river is not only faster but deeper in the outside of a bend. The water spirals around as it rushes downstream, cutting out a steeply eroded river bank. On the opposite, slower side of the river, sediment settles out to form a shallow bank of sand and pebbles—a point bar.

Gentle river bank where sediment is deposited on point bar
Steep eroding river bank
Flow spirals around

Shortcut forming

④ SHORTCUTS FORM
A bend may get so large that the river finds a shortcut. This can lead to the formation of an oxbow lake—a stretch of water cut off from the river.

OXBOW LAKES
River bends get larger and larger over time. Eventually only a narrow neck of land is left between neighboring loops. If the river breaks through this, the new channel has faster flow and cuts out a new riverbed, leaving sediment at the side. This cuts off the old loop, creating an oxbow lake.

BENDS WIDEN | **LOOP FORMS** | **OXBOW LAKE**

POOLS AND RIFFLES
Even a single pebble can give birth to a river bend. The tiny disturbance to water flow around a pebble causes changes that are magnified over time, creating features such as pools, riffles (submerged pebble banks), and bends.

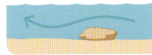

❶ OBSTRUCTION
When water meets a pebble on the riverbed, the flow is squeezed over the top.

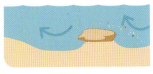

❷ HOLLOWS FORM
As water swirls around the pebble, it speeds up and collects sand grains from the riverbed. Hollows form where sand is removed.

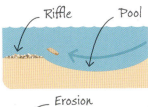

Riffle *Pool*

❸ POOL AND RIFFLE FORM
The pebble is swept away and the hollows merge and grow to form a pool. Downstream is a riffle, where pebbles and sand are dumped.

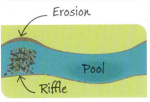

Erosion *Pool* *Riffle*

❹ BEND FORMS
The riffle is an obstacle, so water tries to flow around it, causing the river bank to erode and a bend to form.

BRAIDED RIVER

Most rivers form a single channel. However, if the water volume is large, the slope is steep, or the water is choked with fine sediment, a river may break up into a network of interweaving channels—a braided river. Like this one in Iceland, braided rivers have dozens of muddy islands where sediment collects. The islands are unstable. They expand, shrink, and vanish as the channels continually change course.

HOW WATERFALLS WORK

A waterfall shows the power of erosion in action. The plunging water and its cargo of pebbles continually pound the riverbed under the falls, gouging away bedrock and eating into the cliff. Waterfalls may look permanent, but they slowly inch their way upstream. Over thousands of years, all waterfalls eventually wear themselves away.

A sudden drop in a riverbed is called a knickpoint.

A hard rock overhang forms at the top of the waterfall.

Weaker rock is worn down by the force of water.

SEGMENTED WATERFALL
There are many different kinds of waterfalls. Iguaçu Falls in South America is a segmented waterfall, which means it consists of many channels separated by islands of rock.

BLOCK WATERFALL
Block waterfalls form on wide rivers. The water descends in a wide, uninterrupted curtain. Horseshoe Falls—one of the three waterfalls that form Niagara Falls on the US-Canada border—is a block waterfall.

CASCADE WATERFALLS
At a cascade waterfall, the river tumbles over a series of rocky steps. Detian Falls on the Vietnam-China border is a cascade waterfall.

FAN WATERFALLS
Fan waterfalls spread out horizontally on the rock as the water spills down. Union Falls in Montana is a fan waterfall.

HOW WATERFALLS WORK 107

◀ **PLUNGE WATERFALL**
Helmcken Falls in British Columbia, Canada, is a plunge waterfall. The water plunges over an overhanging ledge and falls vertically through the air, without touching the bedrock, until it hits the pool below.

HOW WATERFALLS FORM
Waterfalls are most common on steep ground, where rivers flow with greater force. Many begin to form where a band of hard rock meets a band of soft rock.

Hard rock
Soft rock

❶ BEDROCK CHANGE
A waterfall can begin to form if the river flows across a boundary between hard, erosion-resistant rock and a softer type of rock.

❷ DROP FORMS
The softer rock erodes faster than the hard rock, creating a drop. The falling water gains force, speeding up the process of erosion.

Overhang

❸ PLUNGE POOL
Plunging water and pebbles swirl around the base of the cliff, carving out a wide plunge pool. The cliff beneath the resistant rock recedes, creating an overhang.

❹ MOVING UPSTREAM
Eventually, the overhang collapses as it has nothing supporting it from underneath. The cliff continues to recede, and the process repeats, causing the waterfall to move upstream.

VICTORIA FALLS

In the language of Africa's Lozi people, Victoria Falls is the "smoke that thunders." Visitors can feel the thunderous noise in their feet before setting eyes on the waterfall—the largest in the world, twice as tall and wide as Niagara. It formed where a crack in the basalt bedrock created a weak area. Erosion turned the crack into a gorge that now swallows the Zambezi River—along with the occasional unfortunate crocodile or hippo.

HOW FLOODS WORK

Floods happen when large amounts of water submerge land that is normally dry. Some floods happen in minutes and take people by surprise, but others build up gradually over months. Floods can cause devastating damage, but some bring benefits. River floods, for example, spread sediment over land and fertilize soil.

▶ RIVER FLOODS
Melting snow or heavy rain can make rivers overflow. In 2019, a particularly wet winter and spring in the Midwest led to catastrophic floods of the Mississippi River. Urban areas were submerged, causing loss of lives and billions of dollars' worth of damage. These satellite images show flooding near the city of Memphis, which is on the right.

FLOOD DEFENSES
While some floods are inevitable, there are ways to reduce the damage they cause or even prevent them altogether.

NATURAL DEFENSES
Many wetlands are great at absorbing excess water, and then releasing it slowly during dry seasons. Trees also absorb a lot of water through their roots, and densely vegetated ground slows the flow of water. Restoring and promoting natural habitats, for example by reintroducing beavers to an area, can therefore protect us against flooding.

ARTIFICIAL DEFENSES
Most artificial flood defenses are physical barriers that hold back water, either inside a river or along its banks. The Thames Barrier in London, UK, protects the city from dangerously high tides by blocking the incoming water with rotating gates between concrete piers.

FEBRUARY 2014 (BEFORE FLOOD)

FEBRUARY 2019 (DURING FLOOD)

HOW FLOODS WORK 111

PLUVIAL FLOODS
When heavy rain hits hard ground in urban areas, drainage systems may be overwhelmed, causing pluvial (surface water) floods. Trapped by buildings and paved areas, the water pools in low spots, turning streets into temporary rivers.

COASTAL FLOODS
When high tides coincide with storms, large waves may flood coastal areas. Hurricanes can also raise the sea level, causing even bigger floods, and submarine earthquakes can cause tsunamis that sweep inland for miles.

GROUNDWATER FLOODS
Soil and porous rock layers underground absorb rainwater like a sponge. This groundwater normally drains away slowly toward rivers and the coast, but prolonged rain can raise it faster than it drains, until it appears above ground and causes flooding.

HOW CANYONS WORK

Canyons are deep, steep-sided valleys with rocky walls. They form over millions of years, as rivers slowly erode the rock and sink deeper into the ground. Most large canyons occur in hot, dry regions, where weathering and erosion mainly affect areas near the river. In wetter climates, rivers tend to create wider V-shaped valleys instead, as the weathering is more widespread.

▼ **GRAND CANYON**
The Grand Canyon in Arizona is so vast that if all of the water in all rivers on Earth was put into it, the canyon would only be half full. There are nearly 40 distinctive bands of rock that have been revealed on the sides of the canyon, with the oldest at the bottom dating back almost two billion years.

- The surrounding landscape is flat and dry.
- Bands of different rock types wear down at different rates, creating steps.
- Fallen rocks build up in piles of rubble (scree) at the base of the cliffs.
- The Colorado River slowly wears down rock on the bed of the river.

HOW CANYONS WORK

Exposed rock weakens and crumbles over time, widening the canyon at the top.

Hard rock   Soft rock

STAIR-STEP CANYON

HOW THE GRAND CANYON FORMED
The Grand Canyon is a stair-step canyon. Some parts began to form 70 million years ago, but most parts formed over the last 6 million years as the Colorado River carved down into the rock. The steps are formed because the Colorado plateau has alternating layers of soft and hard rock, which erode at different rates.

COLORED CANYON, EGYPT

SLOT CANYONS
Narrow canyons with vertical walls, such as the Colored Canyon in Egypt, form when water quickly cuts down through a single rock layer. The water erodes the rock through abrasion—it picks up debris and then acts like sandpaper against the canyon walls, particularly during flash floods.

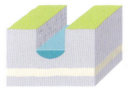 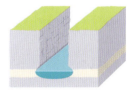

VERTICAL EROSION
Water carves quickly downward, through a single rock layer.

FLOOR FORMATION
If water hits a softer rock layer, the canyon will suddenly widen.

COMPUTER-GENERATED DEPTH MAP OF MONTEREY CANYON

CANYONS IN THE SEA
Submarine canyons are found on the seabed near continents. Rivers may have cut the upper parts of these canyons long ago, when sea levels were much lower. When sea levels later rose, underwater landslides and ocean currents deepened and lengthened the canyons.

ANTELOPE CANYON

The flowing shapes in the walls of this canyon in Arizona are a clue to how it formed. Antelope Canyon is a slot canyon that was carved from the desert sandstone by floods. For thousands of years, repeated flash floods laden with sand and grit have whipped through the canyon in a raging torrent, scouring the walls. Even today, floods fed by rainfall miles away can fill the canyon without warning.

116 CHANGING LANDSCAPES

HOW GROUNDWATER WORKS

More than 99 percent of Earth's unfrozen fresh water is hidden underground, trapped in the tiny gaps between rock and soil particles. Called groundwater, this water moves far more slowly than surface water and can stay underground for thousands or millions of years. It helps to keep rivers flowing in dry periods, and it provides more than a fifth of the world's population with water for farming and drinking.

▼ OASIS
In the Sahara Desert, low points in the land allow groundwater to emerge, forming oases. Lake Gaberoun in Libya is fed by water that has been trapped in rock below the dunes for thousands of years. Evaporation has made the lake's water too salty to drink, but desert travelers can reach drinkable water from nearby wells.

A sand sea (erg) surrounds the oasis.

The water in Lake Gaberoun is five times saltier than seawater. Bathers can float in the salty water without swimming.

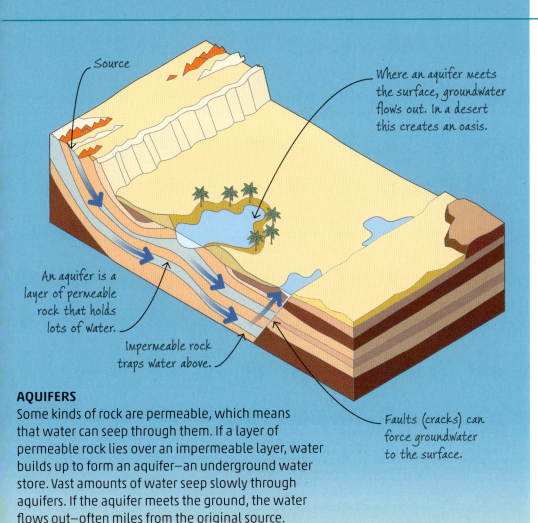

Source

Where an aquifer meets the surface, groundwater flows out. In a desert this creates an oasis.

An aquifer is a layer of permeable rock that holds lots of water.

Impermeable rock traps water above.

Faults (cracks) can force groundwater to the surface.

AQUIFERS
Some kinds of rock are permeable, which means that water can seep through them. If a layer of permeable rock lies over an impermeable layer, water builds up to form an aquifer—an underground water store. Vast amounts of water seep slowly through aquifers. If the aquifer meets the ground, the water flows out—often miles from the original source.

Date palms flourish around oases in the Sahara.

WATER IN ROCK
Certain kinds of rock have tiny gaps between the solid grains that water can seep into. For a rock to make a good aquifer, it must also have connections between the gaps so that water can flow. Sedimentary rocks such as sandstone and chalk make the best aquifers.

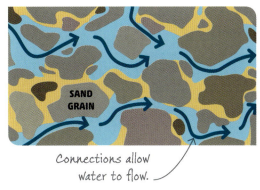

SAND GRAIN

Connections allow water to flow.

WELLS
Wells are deep holes that reach down to groundwater. Water usually has to be pumped out of a well or lifted with buckets. However, some wells have water that spurts upward under its own pressure. These are called artesian wells and form when the hole taps into a confined aquifer that is fed by a water source higher than the well.

UNDERGROUND RIVERS
Not all groundwater is trapped within permeable rock. In limestone areas, the natural acidity in rain eats away at rock minerals to form cavities that eventually grow into caves. Underground rivers flow through these cave systems, in some places forming hidden waterfalls and lakes.

HOW CAVES WORK

Caves are natural underground spaces in rock that are large enough for people to explore. They vary in size from small hollows a person can barely squeeze into to vast caverns with connecting passages that are miles long. Some caves are full of water, while others are dry or dripping with moisture. Caves occur in several rock types, but most form in limestone.

Soda straws are delicate, hollow tubes formed by drips from the cave roof, each leaving a fine ring of the mineral calcite.

Stalactites form when soda straws get clogged and water starts running down the outside, allowing calcite to deposit in a thicker cone shape.

Columns are created when a stalactite and a stalagmite join together.

Stalagmites form from drips that hit the cave floor, building calcite deposits upward over time.

Flowstones are sheets of calcite that form from water flowing down the walls or along the floor of a cave.

- Stream on surface disappears into ground via sinkhole
- Sinkhole
- Dry gallery—the former course of underground stream
- Cracks in limestone allow water to trickle down
- Stalactite
- Limestone
- Stalagmite
- Column
- Underground river
- Underground stream further enlarges cave system

LIMESTONE CAVE SYSTEM
Rain is naturally acidic because it absorbs carbon dioxide from the air. As a result, it reacts chemically with the minerals in limestone, dissolving them in some places to form caves and depositing them in others to form speleothems (stalactites, stalagmites, and so on).

HOW CAVES WORK

◀ INSIDE A CAVE
Harrison's Cave is a limestone cave located in the Caribbean island of Barbados. It contains a variety of geological features, including stalactites, stalagmites, and columns. All these formations grow from mineral deposits left by the groundwater that trickles through the cave.

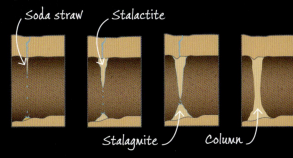

COLUMN FORMATION
Columns form when a stalactite and a stalagmite fuse. This process can take thousands of years. The tallest known column is just over 200 ft (60 m) and is located in a cave in Thailand.

FLOODED CAVES
Water can fill caves quickly when it rains. Cave explorers must check the weather forecast to avoid getting trapped, and many carry diving equipment so they can explore underwater.

CAVE ANIMALS
Many caves are home to their own unique wildlife. Eyes are not needed in the pitch darkness, which is why some species, such as this salamander, have lost them.

FERTILE GROUND
The ground in deltas is mostly silt—a type of sediment that makes rich, fertile soil. The Ganges Delta is one of the most fertile agricultural regions on Earth.

Rivers divide into many branches (distributaries) in a delta.

The dark green areas are natural mangrove forests.

HOW DELTAS FORM
Scientists study how deltas grow by running water through a large tray of artificial, colored sand. The lightweight yellow sand is washed out to sea and builds up in a fan shape, forming new land. As sand piles up in one place, the river is forced to change course and so starts dumping sediment elsewhere. The delta expands, with the river continually changing course and branching as it flows though it.

① EROSION
As a river flows, it erodes the ground and washes particles of sediment downstream toward the sea.

② DEPOSITION
The river slows down as it nears the sea. This causes sediment particles to drop out of the water and build up.

③ FAN GROWS
The sediment forms a fan shape that extends into the sea, creating new land. The river changes position as it forces its way through.

④ DELTA
The river keeps moving and branching, forming new channels. Each channel deposits more sediment, enlarging the delta.

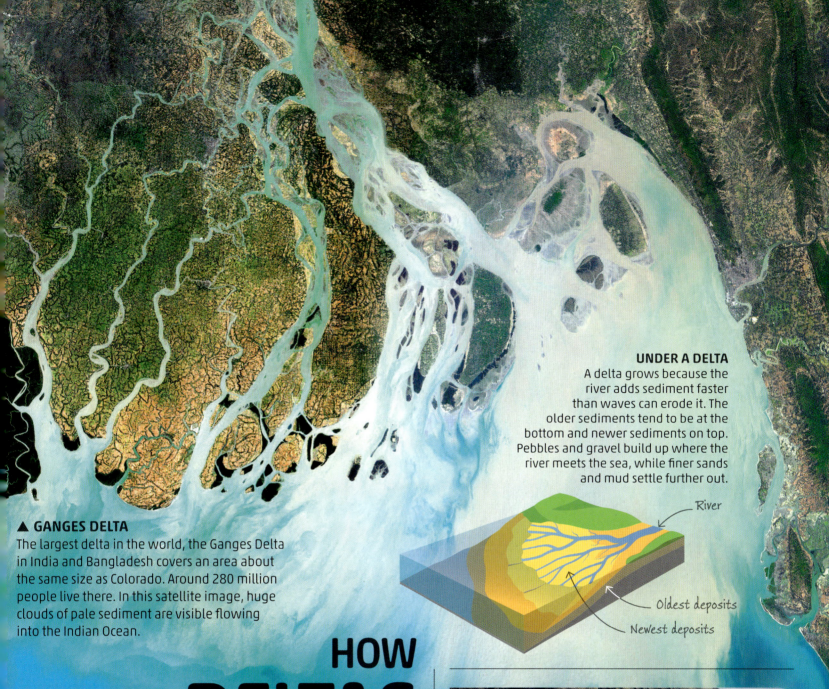

UNDER A DELTA
A delta grows because the river adds sediment faster than waves can erode it. The older sediments tend to be at the bottom and newer sediments on top. Pebbles and gravel build up where the river meets the sea, while finer sands and mud settle further out.

▲ **GANGES DELTA**
The largest delta in the world, the Ganges Delta in India and Bangladesh covers an area about the same size as Colorado. Around 280 million people live there. In this satellite image, huge clouds of pale sediment are visible flowing into the Indian Ocean.

HOW DELTAS AND ESTUARIES WORK

Rivers carry vast amounts of sediment (sand and mud) from land to sea. The largest rivers dump so much sediment at the coast that it builds up to form new land—a delta. Smaller rivers end at wide, muddy mouths called estuaries. Here, the river and tide are in a constant battle to move sand and mud around.

ESTUARIES
In an estuary, mud and sand are pushed inland when the tide rises, but flushed back out by the river as the tide falls. These forces create large channels in between islands of sediment. Estuaries with stronger inward currents become clogged with mud and are bad for ships. Estuaries with stronger outward currents are more stable, with deeper channels.

HOW COASTLINES CHANGE

SHORE PLATFORMS
As a rocky coastline retreats over time, a horizontal or gently sloping rock surface can be left behind. This may have rock pools that get covered at high tide and exposed at low tide.

Coastlines are a constantly changing feature of our planet. The rocky cliffs of many coasts are continuously eroded by pounding waves, carving out caves and weakening cliff faces, which eventually crumble into the sea. Waves also deposit sand and rocks on the coastline, building up beaches that stretch along the shore.

Chalk is a soft sedimentary rock that erodes easily, forming white cliffs.

▶ **ROCKY COASTLINE**
The gradual wearing down of rocky coastlines creates amazing scenery such as these chalk formations, known as Old Harry Rocks, off the Dorset coast in the UK. While the waves erode the cliffs, they also deposit rocks and sand in the bays along the coast.

This sea stack was once connected to the land.

HOW COASTLINES CHANGE 123

BLOWHOLES
A blowhole forms when the roof of a sea cave collapses, leaving a hole in the top of the cliff. When waves gush into the cave, the water is squeezed upward through the hole, creating a fountain of sea water.

SANDY COASTLINES
Beaches form from the buildup of pebbles and sand carried by waves. They constantly change shape. In calm conditions with gentle waves, sand and pebbles slowly pile up, making a beach steeper. In stormy weather, large waves wash sand and pebbles back out, making the beach flatter.

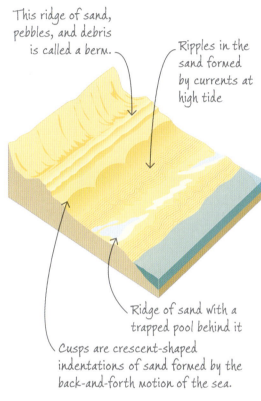

- This ridge of sand, pebbles, and debris is called a berm.
- Ripples in the sand formed by currents at high tide
- Ridge of sand with a trapped pool behind it
- Cusps are crescent-shaped indentations of sand formed by the back-and-forth motion of the sea.

LONGSHORE DRIFT
If waves wash up on a beach diagonally, they push sand and pebbles up the beach diagonally too. However, the water flowing back to the sea (backwash) pulls sand and pebbles straight back down. The overall result is a zigzag movement of sand and pebbles along the beach—a process known as longshore drift. Barriers called groins are often placed on beaches to control erosion by longshore drift.

→ INCOMING WAVES   → BACKWASH

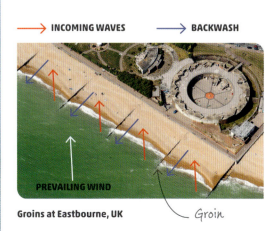

Groins at Eastbourne, UK

HOW A SEA STACK FORMS
The force of waves pounding against cliffs can open up cracks in the rock, which over time get bigger to form caves, and then bigger still to form arches. When an arch collapses it can leave a sea stack—a tall column of rock standing in the sea.

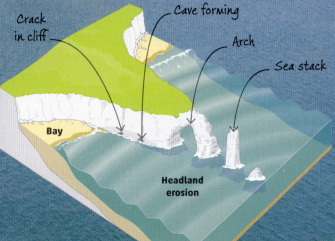

- Crack in cliff
- Cave forming
- Arch
- Sea stack
- Bay
- Headland erosion

HOW WAVES WORK

Ocean waves form when the wind blows over the sea's surface. They can travel thousands of miles, and large waves may arrive at a coastline that's experiencing little wind. Waves transfer the wind's energy—but not the water itself—across the oceans, and this energy is released when waves break at coastlines.

German surfer Sebastian Steudtner holds the world record for the biggest wave ever surfed.

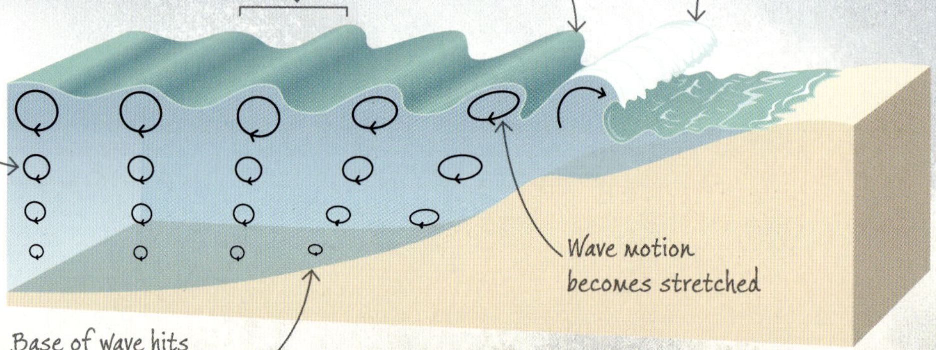

Wavelength is the distance from crest to crest or trough to trough

Crest begins to tip over

Wave breaks on the beach

Circular motion, which becomes smaller at depth

APPROACHING THE SHORE
Out at sea, the surface water forms a circular motion as each wave passes. As the wave approaches shallow water, its circular motions become more stretched, before it breaks on the beach.

Base of wave hits seabed and slows down

Wave motion becomes stretched

HOW WAVES WORK 125

Rescuers on Jet Skis are ready if surfers fall under the waves at Nazaré.

◀ **TOWERING WAVES**
As waves approach land and the water becomes shallower, they slow down and grow taller. At Nazaré on the coast of Portugal, the waves are huge—as tall as 80 ft (25 m)—and attract surfers from all over the world. Energy from incoming surface waves here combines with wave energy from an underwater canyon to create the largest waves ever surfed.

The froth formed by breaking waves is known as spume.

FREAK WAVES
Occasionally, two large ocean waves combine to create a single giant wave called a freak wave. This can happen when two sets of waves collide at just the right angle or when a storm makes waves combine randomly. Freak waves taller than an eight-story building can sink ships.

Rip current   Incoming wave

RIP CURRENTS
On beaches with an uneven floor, the water carried inland by waves may rush back out in a single powerful channel where the sea is deeper. This is called a rip current and can be deadly. Every year, hundreds of unwary swimmers are swept out to sea by rip currents and drown trying to swim back against the powerful flow.

BENDY WAVES
Just as light waves bend (refract) as they pass into glass and slow down, water waves can bend when they hit land. If one end of a wave reaches shallow water first, it slows down and the whole wave bends. Bending affects how waves erode land. Areas of land that stick out into the sea are hit by the fast ends of waves and are eroded, while slower ends of waves tend to deposit sand, forming beaches.

Look closely at a rock and you can sometimes see hundreds of tiny interlocking **crystals**. These are **minerals**—the solid, crystalline chemicals that are Earth's building blocks. Minerals crystallize into their solid form in various ways, such as when **molten rock** cools down and solidifies. They vary from tiny flecks of dull gray grit to glittering **gemstones** with brilliant colors.

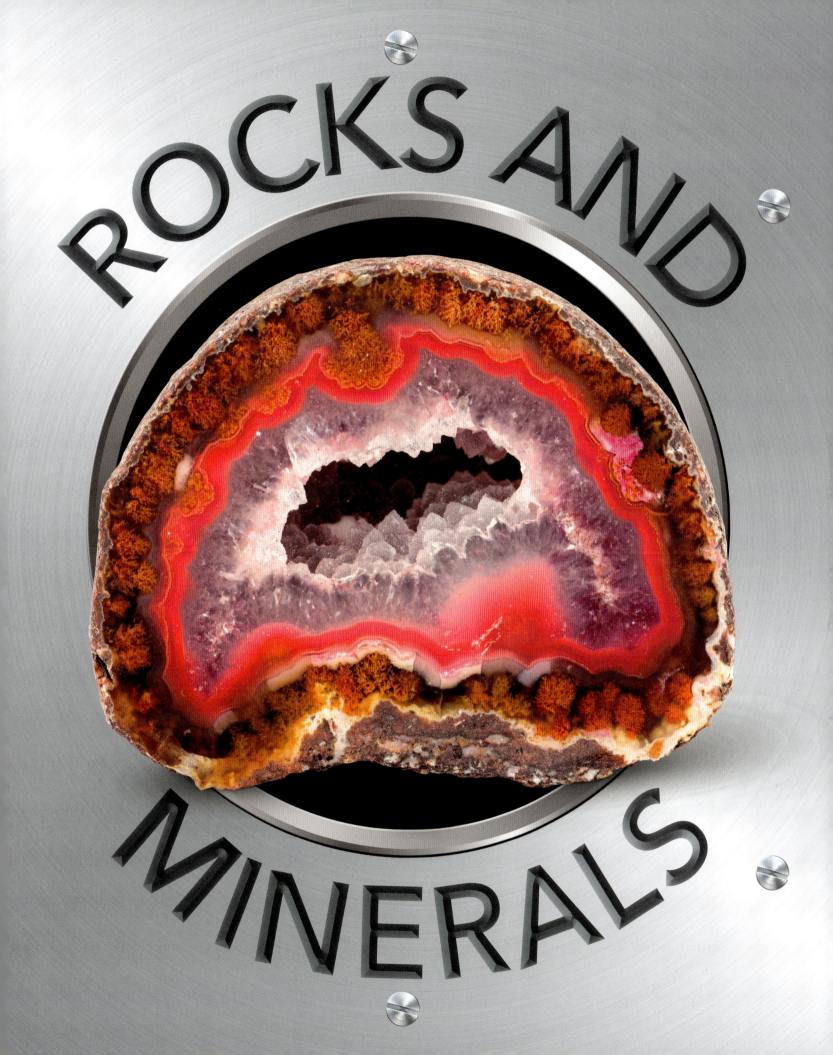
ROCKS AND MINERALS

HOW THE ROCK CYCLE WORKS

Earth's rocky crust has been around for more than 4 billion years, but it's rare to find a rock this old. Rocks are constantly being broken down and recycled in a process known as the rock cycle. Each rock, stone, and pebble has a different story to tell.

▶ THE ROCK CYCLE
In the rock cycle, old rocks get transformed into new rocks by erosion, heat, pressure, or a combination of these things. For instance, deep in the Earth's crust, high temperatures and pressure changes melt ancient rocks to form magma, which rises toward the surface and solidifies as it cools. Most changes take hundreds, thousands, or even millions of years.

COMPACTION AND CEMENTATION

WEATHERING AND EROSION

SEDIMENTS

WEATHERING AND EROSION

WEATHERING AND EROSION

HEAT AND PRESSURE

MELTING

MELTING

COOLING

MAGMA

By looking closely at a rock, you might be able to see grains or crystals of the minerals it is made from.

This granite rock contains crystals of several different minerals, including quartz, feldspar, and biotite.

Quartz is made from silicon and oxygen. Its chemical name is silicon dioxide, SiO_2.

IGNEOUS ROCK
If rocks deep underground are heated enough, they melt to form magma. This is less dense than solid rock. It may rise into the upper part of Earth's crust or even erupt onto the surface. Here it cools to form igneous rocks, such as andesite and basalt.

HOW THE ROCK CYCLE WORKS 129

WHERE ROCKS FORM
Sedimentary rocks form on Earth's surface, as layers of sediment build up at the bottom of rivers, seas, and lakes. Metamorphic rocks form deep within Earth's crust, or in other areas of high heat and pressure. Igneous rock forms either underground when molten rock (magma) cools slowly, or on Earth's surface when lava spilled by a volcano cools quickly.

SEDIMENTARY ROCK

METAMORPHIC ROCK

IGNEOUS ROCK

Weathering breaks down rock.

SEDIMENTARY ROCK
Rocks on Earth's surface are broken down by weathering and erosion, forming mud and sand, which settle in layers at the bottom of rivers, lakes, and seas. Over time, the deepest layers are squeezed together and hardened by minerals that form in the tiny spaces between particles of sediment. This forms sedimentary rocks such as sandstone (above) and limestone.

HEAT AND PRESSURE

Rocks do not move through the rock cycle in a particular order. Any type of rock can change into any other type of rock.

SPACE ROCKS
Meteorites are rocks that fall to Earth from space. Most contain lots of iron or nickel, which makes them magnetic and heavy for their size. Many have a smooth black crust of rock that melted as the meteorite zoomed through our atmosphere.

MELTING

METAMORPHIC ROCK
As Earth's crust is changed by tectonic forces, rocks may become buried even deeper. Intense heat and pressure may cause minerals to change without melting completely, forming metamorphic rocks such as quartzite, marble (above), and slate.

HOBA METEORITE NEAR GROOTFONTEIN, NAMIBIA

HOW IGNEOUS ROCK WORKS

Water and weather constantly attack and erode rocks at Earth's surface, yet the crust is not getting thinner. New rock is added all the time as molten rock wells up, cools, and then hardens. Rocks formed by molten rock that cools and hardens is known as igneous rock, meaning "fire born."

IGNEOUS GRAINS
Deep underground, magma cools slowly, and mineral crystals can keep growing for a long time before the rock sets solid. These coarse mineral grains are easy to see in granite.

PLAGIOCLASE FELDSPAR
Feldspars are the most common minerals in granite rock.

BIOTITE MICA AND AMPHIBOLE
Black grains are iron-rich minerals, such as biotite mica or amphibole.

POTASSIUM FELDSPAR
Pink granite gets its color from potassium feldspar.

QUARTZ
At least a fifth of granite is made up of quartz.

Granite is a hard rock that takes a long time to weather and erode.

HOW IGNEOUS ROCK WORKS 131

MINERAL MOSAIC
Looking at a very thin slice of granite under a microscope reveals tiny interlocking mineral crystals. While most rocks are a mixture of two or more minerals, the minerals themselves are pure substances.

◀ GRANITE
Granite is one of the most common igneous rocks. It forms when molten magma cools deep beneath Earth's surface over many years. Granite's main mineral ingredients—quartz and feldspars—are both rich in silica (silicon dioxide). This is a clue that granite forms from shale or sandstone that has melted or partly melted deep underground.

CRYSTAL CLUES
Although all igneous rocks form from magma or lava, there is huge variation in the mineral crystals that make them up. The size of these grains gives igneous rocks different textures and tells you how quickly they cooled.

OBSIDIAN
Glassy obsidian forms when silica-rich lava cools so quickly (within hours) there is no time for mineral crystals to grow.

PUMICE
Pumice forms when the lava from a volcano mixes with water and gases. It cools and hardens quickly, so remains filled with tiny bubbles and rarely has visible crystals.

Blue topaz crystal in pegmatite

PEGMATITES
When magma cools slowly, crystals may keep growing for thousands or even millions of years. Pegmatites are rocks with crystals larger than 0.4 in (1 cm), including minerals that crystallize only at lower temperatures.

IN OR OUT?
Igneous rocks are classified as intrusive or extrusive, depending on where they form. Intrusive rocks, such as granite, form deep inside Earth's crust, often from magma that forced its way in between layers of existing rock before cooling slowly. Extrusive rocks form when magma exits the crust as lava and cools quickly.

LAVA COOLING TO FORM BASALT ROCK ON KĪLAUEA, HAWAII

HOW IGNEOUS INTRUSIONS FORM

▼ DEVILS TOWER (MATO TIPILA)
This giant block of igneous rock in Wyoming is an igneous intrusion that formed deep underground about 50 million years ago, perhaps as a laccolith or a volcanic plug. Over time, the softer sedimentary rock surrounding it wore away, leaving the tough igneous rock standing like a giant monument.

Igneous intrusions are rock formations created by magma that melts its way through Earth's crust but fails to erupt from volcanoes. When erosion wears away the softer rock around intrusions, these masses of hard, resistant rock are left standing proud.

The intrusion towers 866 feet (264 m) above the landscape.

IN OR OUT
An igneous intrusion can take many different shapes. Runny magma may find its way horizontally between layers of rock, and more viscous (gloopy) magma rises more slowly toward the surface, cracking and melting the rock above it.

Stocks are similar to batholiths, but are smaller.

A volcanic plug forms when magma cools in a volcano's vent.

Laccoliths are mushroom-shaped intrusions.

Sills form in horizontal sheets parallel to existing rock layers.

Batholiths are huge and have irregular shapes.

Dikes are sheets that cut vertically through other rock layers.

A xenolith is a rock that gets trapped in the magma while it cools.

HOW IGNEOUS INTRUSIONS FORM

ROCK COLUMNS
The igneous rock of Devils Tower forms spectacular hexagonal (six-sided) and pentagonal (five-sided) columns. Each one is hundreds of meters tall. They formed as molten magma cooled, shrank, and then cracked.

HALF DOME
Half Dome in Yosemite National Park is a batholith with the remains of an ancient magma chamber at its core. It originally formed as a dome but erosion has cut it in half, creating a sheer face on one side.

LA PALMA
Erosion can reveal the shape of a dike within the surrounding rock, like this example on the island of La Palma in the Canary Islands. These frozen moments provide valuable clues about how lava finds its way through Earth's crust.

UNST
This laccolith on the island of Unst in Scotland got its distinctive dome shape when rising magma spread out horizontally between rock layers and pushed up the overlying layer of rock.

FINGER MOUNTAIN
Finger Mountain in Antarctica gets its name from the vast dolerite sill that cuts through the layers of sandstone. Dolerite is a hard, dark rock that forms as magma cools.

Devils Tower consists of an igneous rock called phonolite porphyry.

HOW METAMORPHIC ROCK WORKS

Around 62 miles (100 km) beneath your feet, Earth's mantle becomes hot enough to melt rock into magma. However, rocks much nearer the surface can also find themselves facing extreme conditions. Along the faults where Earth's giant tectonic plates meet, and around magma that is forcing its way to the surface, existing rocks can be heated or squeezed so much that they change into new forms without melting completely. We call rocks that form this way metamorphic.

① SHALE
Shale is a sedimentary rock that is fine-grained due to being formed from compacted layers of clay and silt.

Slate is usually gray, but can also be green, purple, or red.

② SLATE
Close to Earth's surface where the temperature isn't very high, shale is transformed into slate. This low-grade metamorphic rock is brittle with fine grains.

③ PHYLLITE
Slightly higher temperatures and pressures can transform slate into phyllite. Its tiny, neatly arranged mica crystals reflect light, giving phyllite a glossy sheen.

▶ **GRADES OF METAMORPHIC ROCK**
When rock such as shale is heated by superhot magma and squeezed with enough force, it changes into metamorphic rock. Some rocks go though multiple transformations, changing from one metamorphic rock type to another. The grade tells you how much the rock has changed—the higher the grade, the greater the transformation.

UNDER STRESS
Stripes, folds, or waves are often the first clue that you are looking at metamorphic rock. These patterns may be microscopic or enormous. Largest of all are the metamorphic rock formations that develop within mountain ranges as colliding tectonic plates squeeze and crumple Earth's crust.

Dark bands often contain heavy minerals, such as hornblende.

Pale bands are often rich in silica minerals, such as quartz and feldspars.

HOW METAMORPHIC ROCK WORKS   **135**

4 SCHIST
At even higher temperatures metamorphism goes further, transforming phyllite into medium-grade schist. The mineral grains in schist are large enough to see.

5 GNEISS
At very high temperatures and pressures, shale transforms into high-grade gneiss, which often has stripy patterns.

TRANSFORMATION
Metamorphic rocks may be altered slightly or transformed so much that it's hard to work out their original forms—rather like butterflies emerging from a caterpillar's cocoon. It's not just their appearance that changes either, as metamorphic rocks often have completely different properties from their parent rocks (protoliths).

SLATE
When shale is transformed by pressure into slate, certain minerals line up at right angles to the direction of the squeeze. This creates flat layers that flake apart easily, making slate a popular material for roof tiles.

MARBLE
Marble forms when limestone comes under heat and pressure. The mineral calcite recrystallizes to form interlocking crystals, making marble much tougher than limestone.

IMPACTITE
Not all metamorphic rock forms deep underground. The shock of a meteorite strike can change rock, sand, or soil into rocks called impactites. These include rare types of natural glass that were prized as gemstones in ancient Egypt.

ROCKS AND MINERALS

How SEDIMENTARY ROCK works

At Earth's surface, rocks of all kinds are gradually worn away. Over millions of years, weathering and erosion even break mountains into tiny particles of silt, sand, and mud. These are washed into rivers and oceans where they settle to the bottom. Over millions more years, the sediments are squeezed and cemented together as minerals form in the tiny spaces between them. They become sedimentary rock.

DIFFERENT TYPES OF SEDIMENTS
The particles that sedimentary rock forms from—and the way it forms—determine whether the rock will be soft or hard. Many sedimentary rocks contain fossils, and some types consist almost entirely of fossils.

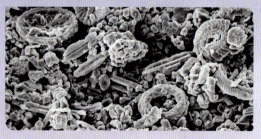

LIMESTONE AND CHALK
Chalk and many types of limestone are made of the fossils of marine organisms. This microscope image of chalk shows fragments of tiny shells made of calcium carbonate.

SANDSTONE
About a fifth of all sedimentary rock is sandstone, which is made of ancient sand grains. Sandstone is often used as a building material as it is durable but easy to carve.

MUDSTONE AND SHALE
Mudstone and shale form when very fine particles of mud and clay are tightly compressed, leaving little room for mineral cement between the grains. This makes these rocks soft and flaky.

CONGLOMERATE
Conglomerate is made from larger bits of rock from grit and gravel to pebbles and even boulders dumped by fast-flowing water. These are all held together by a finer-grained material called a matrix.

FORMATION OF SEDIMENTARY ROCKS
Sedimentary rock tends to form flat layers called strata. As new sediment settles at the top (deposition), its weight squeezes lower layers (compaction). Water seeping through the strata carries dissolved minerals that crystallize between the particles and bind them (cementation). Sedimentary rock can also form chemically when minerals dissolved in water crystallize into solid form.

Rivers wash sediment from land into the sea.

DEPOSITION

COMPACTION

CEMENTATION

Over time, sedimentary rock may be lifted and tilted by the movements of Earth's tectonic plates.

HOW SEDIMENTARY ROCK WORKS 137

▼ LAYER UPON LAYER
Weathering in Argentina's Gorge of the Shells has revealed spectacular layers of sandstone, siltstone, shale, and conglomerate. These layers formed from sediments that were carried by fast-flowing water. As the water emerged from a small gap it fanned out, slowed, and the sediments settled to the bottom.

Most of the layers are sandstone and siltstone. The red and orange colors come from iron that has oxidized (rusted) in the air.

MICROSCOPE VIEW
If you look at sandstone with a microscope, you can see the individual grains along with the matrix that cements them together. Other types of sedimentary rocks, such as mudstone, may also contain microscopic fossils such as pollen grains, which help reveal the rock's age.

Some of the layers are conglomerate, a type of sedimentary rock with large grains.

The green-gray layers are shale.

HOW SOIL WORKS

Soil is the skin that covers Earth's rocky crust. It's made up of particles of rocks and minerals from the crust, mixed with air, water, decaying plants and animals, and countless living organisms too. The soil layer makes up a tiny fraction of the planet, but it provides water and essential nutrients to plants as well as a home to many animals.

SAND, SILT, AND CLAY

Around half of soil is made up of rock particles. The three main types are sand, silt, and clay. Sand particles are largest and help water flow, so sandy soils tend to be drier. Clay particles are smallest and hold on to water, so clay-rich soils can be wet and sticky. They also retain nutrients well and so are more fertile than sandy soil.

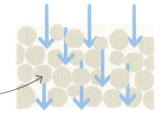

Sand particles help water drain away easily.

FREE DRAINING

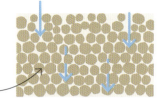

Silt particles are smaller than sand but bigger than clay.

GOOD DRAINAGE

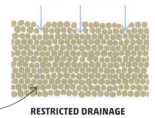

Water clings to tiny clay particles, helping soil retain moisture.

RESTRICTED DRAINAGE

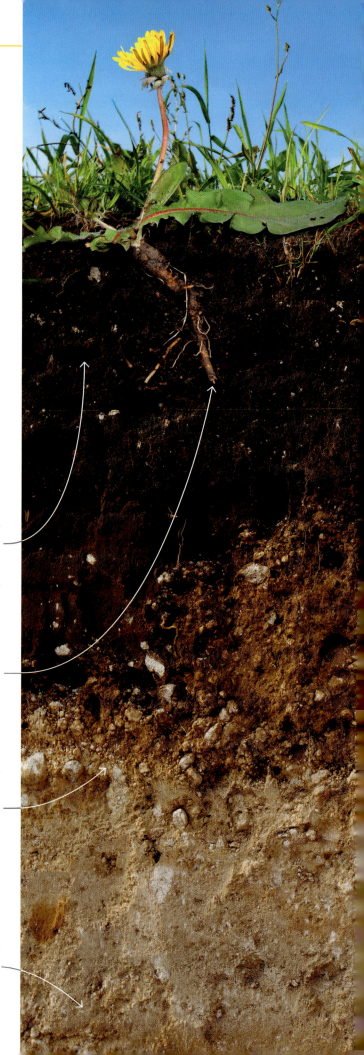

Rich in organic matter, the upper layer of topsoil tends to be darker than the layers below.

As plant roots push down through soil, they create spaces for water and air. As roots grow and expand, they can crack and break down rock.

Soluble substances such as calcium, sodium, and potassium dissolve in water and then leach (drain) away and accumulate in lower layers.

Below the soil is the bedrock of Earth's crust. Moisture and biological activity in soil slowly weather this rock, and break it down into small particles.

HOW SOIL WORKS

BACTERIA
Soil contains countless trillions of microscopic bacteria, which are vital for its health. Among other things, they play a crucial role in nitrogen fixation. This involves taking nitrogen from the atmosphere and converting it into nitrates, which plants need in order to grow.

WORMS
Worms tunnel through soil, eating decaying organic matter, fungi, and bacteria. This helps to recycle the nutrients in soil so that they can be used by plants. The tunnels also help oxygen enter soil and reach the roots of plants.

SPRINGTAILS
Tiny insectlike animals known as springtails live in the top layer of healthy soils. They feed on organic matter, which helps to break down and recycle nutrients. Each square foot (0.1 sq m) of soil contains an estimated 10,000 springtails, which makes these tiny creatures the most numerous and successful animals on Earth.

◀ SOIL HORIZONS
Soils have distinct layers known as horizons. The upper layer of topsoil, called humus ("hyoo-muss"), is rich in dead organic matter. It's also rich in tiny living animals, fungi, and microorganisms. These all help to break down the decaying matter and release nutrients, which plants absorb and recycle. Further down, soil becomes richer in rock particles that are slowly weathering.

SOILS IN DIFFERENT CLIMATES
Soils form gradually, beginning with sediments that have been eroded from a mountain, deposited by water, or carried on the wind. Over time, the local climate, living creatures, and the landscape all play their part in shaping a soil's story.

FROZEN SOIL
Near the poles, and at high altitudes, the water held by soil can stay frozen for years at a time. This "permafrost" pauses the process of decay, which means the frozen soil can store carbon that would otherwise be released as greenhouse gases.

DESERT SOIL
Soil forms slowly in deserts. The dry climate means there is less weathering of the underlying rock, and fewer living things to become humus when they die. However, low rainfall also means nutrients in desert soils are less likely to be leached away. They often collect as a rock-hard, white layer below the surface.

RAINFOREST SOIL
Rainforests have only a thin layer of topsoil and are low in nutrients. High temperatures allow microbes to digest decaying matter in hours, and dissolved nutrients are soon leached away by heavy rain. Only iron and aluminium oxides hang around, giving rainforest soils the red color of rust.

HOW MINERALS WORK

A dazzling display of minerals can rival Earth's most colorful plants and animals. Minerals are the chemical building blocks of rocks. They grow naturally—often deep underground—but they are not alive. A mineral is simply a solid substance made of a specific set of chemical ingredients. Every mineral has a unique set of properties, which come in handy for working out which of Earth's 6,000 or so named minerals you're looking at.

▶ NATURAL TREASURES
Most rocks are made of minerals, but geodes are famous for putting their building blocks on spectacular display. Geodes are roundish, ordinary-looking rocks from the outside, but breaking one open reveals a hollow cavity lined with mineral crystals. These crystals grow from minerals deposited by water and can take thousands of years to form.

Crystals inside a geode grow inward toward the center.

Many geodes are filled with visible crystals of quartz, one of the most common minerals found on land.

AGATE CRYSTALS
Geodes often contain a special form of quartz called agate. Its crystals are too small to see with the naked eye, but they are visible through a microscope. They are colored by tiny traces of other substances and build up in layers, forming wavy patterns called arcs.

HOW MINERALS WORK 141

NEAT AND ORDERED
Minerals are pure substances, so their chemical ingredients can arrange themselves in regular, repeating 3D patterns. These orderly insides give each mineral's crystals a precise geometric shape, which can help identify it.

Atoms of silicon and oxygen in a quartz crystal

The outer part of a geode often consists of volcanic rock.

CLASSIFYING MINERALS
Scientists group and name minerals based on their main chemical ingredients. For example, silicate minerals contain the elements silicon and oxygen, often with metal elements too.

Carbonates
Copper gives malachite its green color, but it's the nonmetal elements (carbon and oxygen) that make it a carbonate.

Silicates
More than a thousand different minerals are classed as silicates, making this the largest group of minerals.

USING MINERALS
Minerals have shaped human history from the Stone Age, when people learned to strike flint with pyrite to create sparks and start fires. Since then, we have found millions of ways to put different minerals to use, including more than 42 minerals used to manufacture a typical smartphone.

MINING MINERALS
Rocks that contain useful minerals are known as ores. We get them from mines with digging machines, though doing so uses lots of energy and can harm the natural environment.

HOW CRYSTALS WORK

Most pure solid substances, from minerals to metals, are made up of crystals. These are often too small to see, but in some rocks they are visible as separate grains or as larger geometric shapes. Crystals form when the atoms or molecules in a substance become arranged in an orderly, repeating pattern. This can happen when the minerals in molten rock (magma) cool and solidify, or when the water around dissolved minerals evaporates.

▼ PYRITE
The shape of a crystal depends on the structure of its atoms and molecules. In the mineral pyrite, iron and sulfur atoms are arranged in repeating units that are cube-shaped, and so the crystals are cube-shaped too. Pyrite is also called fool's gold because it's sometimes mistaken for gold. A good test is to scratch it with a fingernail—this would leave a mark on gold, but not pyrite.

The cubes of pyrite are natural, despite their appearance.

Many repeating cubic structures

ATOMIC CUBES
The iron and sulfur atoms inside pyrite are arranged in repeating cubes, giving pyrite crystals their seemingly unnatural shape.

CRYSTAL SYSTEMS
A crystal begins as a single unit (a group of atoms or molecules). As the crystal grows, more units are added. In perfect conditions, they build up neatly in three dimensions along axes (imaginary straight lines). The shape of a crystal depends on the number of axes, their length, and the angle between them, but all crystals can be grouped into one of seven basic classes called crystal systems.

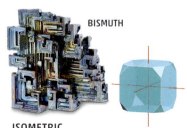

BISMUTH

ISOMETRIC
Three axes of equal lengths are at right angles to each other. Isometric crystals include cubes, octahedrons, or dodecahedrons.

VESUVIANITE

TETRAGONAL
Three axes are at right angles to each other, but one is longer than the other two. Tetragonal crystals include cuboids or square blocks with a point at each end.

TOPAZ

ORTHORHOMBIC
Three axes, all with different lengths, are at right angles to each other. Orthorhombic crystals can look like tetragonal crystals that have been squashed in one direction.

HOW CRYSTALS WORK 143

ALLOTROPES
The exact same atoms can make different crystals in different conditions. At high pressure, carbon atoms form hard diamond crystals with atoms arranged in tetrahedral (pyramid) structures. At low pressure, they form flat layers of soft graphite, with weak bonding between layers. These two forms of carbon are known as allotropes of carbon.

Graphite is soft. It's the substance inside pencils.

Diamond is the hardest mineral on Earth.

GIANT CRYSTALS
In the right conditions and given enough time, crystals can grow to gargantuan sizes, like these crystals of gypsum discovered in the Naica Mine, Mexico.

EMERALD

HEXAGONAL
Three horizontal axes are at 120° to each other, plus one vertical axis. Hexagonal crystals can look like six-sided blocks with a point at each end.

AMETHYST

TRIGONAL
Three horizontal axes are at 120° to each other, plus one vertical axis. This is like hexagonal, except there are fewer lines of symmetry. Trigonal crystals can look like a triangular block with a point at each end.

KUNZITE

MONOCLINIC
Two axes are at right angles to each other, and a third axis is on a tilt. All three axes can be different lengths. Monoclinic crystals have end faces that are tilted to one side.

AMAZONITE

TRICLINIC / RHOMBOHEDRON
Three axes are at different angles and have different lengths. Triclinic crystals are the least symmetrical and can often have a seemingly random shape, despite following a system.

CRYSTAL HABITS

The microscopic building blocks of a mineral's crystals are neat and orderly geometric shapes. However, when crystals build up in nature they can grow into more complex shapes, from fibers and needles to grapelike clusters and flat sheets. These distinctive shapes have special names and are known as crystal habits.

FIBROUS
Silicate minerals can form crystals so long, thin, and flexible that they look more like plant or animal fibers. Asbestos is the most infamous—if breathed in, asbestos fibers can damage people's lungs.

Fine fibers

ACICULAR
Crystals of mesolite grow into long and slender needles, like pins in a tiny pincushion. This habit, called acicular, makes the brittle crystals very fragile.

RADIATING
Wavellite crystals radiate outward from a single point, forming spheres. When cut in half, the tightly packed, fibrous crystals look like sparkling starbursts.

CONCENTRIC
Malachite is usually found with a banded pattern of dark and light green layers, which sometimes grow out from a center and look like circles. Cutting and polishing can reveal these patterns.

Clusters of tiny quartz crystals

BOTRYOIDAL
The name for these clusters of rounded masses means "bunch of grapes." Up close, each grape turns out to be a cluster of tiny crystals with flat geometric faces.

CRYSTAL HABITS

LENTICULAR
"Desert roses" form in dry, sandy places in Mexico when water evaporates and leaves dissolved gypsum behind. The lentil-shaped crystals form clusters like petals in a rose.

LAMELLAR
Lamellar means platelike and describes minerals that form thin, flaky sheets. Mica forms the thinnest sheets of all—about the same thickness as a piece of paper.

AGGREGATE
Two or more types of crystal growing together are described as an aggregate. Here, globular groups of calcite seem to bulge out of a forest of quartz crystals.

TABULAR
Anhydrite crystals typically grow in flat tabular (tablelike) shapes. They sometimes look like small notepads or playing cards clustered together.

Opposite faces remain parallel to one another.

PRISMATIC
When crystals grow slowly with plenty of space, they get the chance to form large, prismatic shapes that show off the inner geometry of their building blocks.

Beryl often forms pencil-like hexagonal crystals.

STALAGMITIC
Clusters of chrysocolla crystals can look like stalagmites but are found inside hollow rocks rather than inside caves. The beautiful blue-green color comes from the element copper.

SCEPTERED
Crystals of "dog-tooth" calcite have sharp points. Sometimes the tips are separate crystals growing on the ends of older ones. This arrangement is called a sceptered habit.

WHY MINERALS GLOW

Never dismiss a dull-looking rock. It might have an extraordinary property known as fluorescence, which makes it light up in glowing colors when lit with an ultraviolet light. The most spectacular glowing rocks contain hundreds of fluorescent grains that sparkle like tiny individual lights, as though lit from deep within.

The cerussite crystals are brownish-white in normal light.

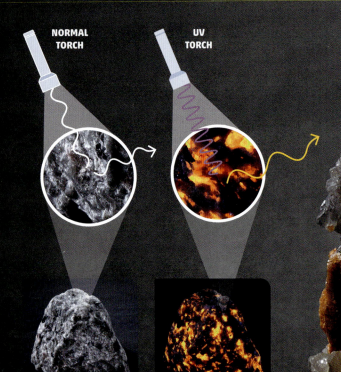

NORMAL TORCH

UV TORCH

SYENITE IN WHITE LIGHT

SYENITE IN UV LIGHT

HOW FLUORESCENCE WORKS
An ultraviolet (UV) torch is needed to see fluorescent minerals glow. UV light has a shorter wavelength but higher energy than normal light and is invisible to our eyes. When it hits a fluorescent mineral, such as this syenite, electrons in certain atoms absorb energy and jump to higher orbits in their atoms. As they fall back to their previous orbits, they emit light of lower energy and longer wavelengths—visible light.

WHY MINERALS GLOW   **147**

▼ GLOW IN THE DARK
This rock contains crystals of the mineral cerussite (lead carbonate). Some cerussite crystals fluoresce with an intense yellow when lit by ultraviolet (UV) light. Geologists aren't sure if this is due to the mineral's high lead content or the presence of impurities such as silver. Fluorescent minerals stop glowing as soon as the UV torch is turned off, but other kinds of mineral have a more persistent glow called phosphorescence.

Cerussite glows bright yellow when lit by UV.

Minerals that aren't fluorescent look dark in UV light.

CALCITE
Calcite is one of the most common fluorescent minerals. Traces of the element manganese make it glow pink-orange.

SPHALERITE
Sphalerite usually glows orange under UV light, but certain specimens light up in a rainbow of colors thanks to a mixture of impurities.

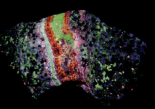

FLUORITE
Fluorescence was named after fluorite, the first mineral discovered to glow under UV light. Not all specimens glow—only those that contain the elements yttrium, europium, or samarium.

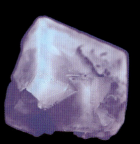

WILLEMITE
The green crystals in this rock are willemite, a mineral rich in zinc. It's one of the brightest phosphorescent minerals, with a glow that lasts a long time after UV light is switched off.

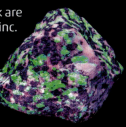

CORUNDUM
Rubies and sapphires are forms of the mineral corundum. Rubies glow bright red in UV light, but green and blue sapphires don't fluoresce.

SODALITE
Some syenite rocks are rich in the fluorescent mineral sodalite. When lit by UV, the sodalite crystals light up with a fiery orange glow.

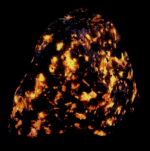

HOW PIGMENTS WORK

Rocks and minerals are among the most important sources of natural pigments—the colorful compounds used to make paints. Cave paintings made by people in the Stone Age show that people have been crushing and heating rocks to make colors for perhaps 100,000 years.

RED FOR DANGER
Cinnabar (mercury sulfide) is a mineral found near volcanoes and hot springs. It was once ground up to make a blood-red pigment called vermilion. This no longer happens because heating cinnabar releases dangerous mercury vapor.

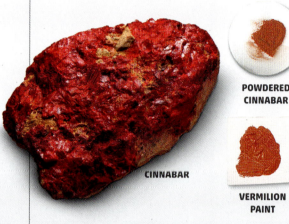

IRON RED
Rocks and minerals containing iron oxides have been used to make pigments for tens of thousands of years. The earthy colors of yellow ocher, red ocher, and brown umber resemble the rocks and soils they're made from. They can also be roasted to make darker pigments.

PRECIOUS BLUE
There are very few blue pigments in nature, so the mineral lazurite was once as precious as gold. It can be polished to make the gemstone lapis lazuli or crushed to create the brilliant blue pigment ultramarine.

PSYCHEDELIC GREEN
Malachite is a copper carbonate mineral and one of the oldest sources of green pigment. It's found in paintings on the walls of Ancient Egyptian tombs.

LETHAL GOLD
The mineral orpiment has a golden sheen that persists even when it's ground and turned into paint. Also called "king's yellow," it was used to decorate medieval manuscripts. There is no gold in orpiment. Instead it contains the deadly element arsenic and was once used to make lethal poisons.

HOW PIGMENTS WORK

CLASSICAL BLUE
Ancient Egyptian artists used a copper carbonate mineral called azurite to make blue pigments. The more finely it's ground, the lighter blue the powder becomes.

AZURITE BLUE PAINT
POWDERED AZURITE
AZURITE

EGYPTIAN ORANGE
The mineral realgar grinds into a bright orange pigment, which was used to decorate papyri and tombs in Ancient Egypt. It's rarely used today because, like orpiment, it contains the toxic element arsenic.

POWDERED REALGAR
ARSENIC ORANGE PAINT
REALGAR

WHITE PIGMENTS
Soft chalk was one of the first minerals to be ground and used as a white pigment. It's found in prehistoric cave art and is still a popular art material today.

CHALK
POWDERED CHALK
CHALK WHITE PAINT

POWDERED MALACHITE
MALACHITE GREEN PAINT

BLACK PIGMENTS
Graphite (a form of carbon) and manganese oxide minerals such as pyrolusite are both sources of black and dark brown pigments.

GRAPHITE
POWDERED GRAPHITE
BLACK PAINT

STREAK TEST
Many minerals vary in color, which can make them tricky to identify. A streak test can be used to find their true color. This is done by dragging the mineral along a white porcelain plate. Minerals harder than porcelain may need to be filed or crushed first.

ORPIMENT
HEMATITE
CROCOITE
CHALCOPYRITE
CINNABAR
MOLYBDENITE

EMERALD
Emerald is one of the different varieties of the mineral beryl. Its deep green color comes from an impurity—the element chromium. Emeralds are rare, which makes them precious. Other types of beryl, such as the pale blue mineral aquamarine, are more common and less expensive.

The symmetrical faces cut into gemstones are called facets.

EMERALD

UNCUT EMERALD IN ROCK

SAPPHIRE
Sapphires are made of a mineral called corundum (aluminum oxide). Their varying colors—from blue and green to yellow and hot pink—come from impurities. Blue sapphires contain traces of iron and titanium in place of some of the aluminum atoms. This allows the crystal to absorb all colors except blue, which is reflected.

BLUE SAPPHIRE

UNCUT SAPPHIRE IN ROCK

RUBY
Rubies are corundum crystals in which up to 1 percent of the aluminum atoms are replaced by chromium. This impurity gives rubies their intense red color. Like sapphires, rubies are very hard and durable, which is ideal for jewelry.

UNCUT RUBY IN ROCK

Cutting a gemstone makes light reflect inside it, enhancing its color, sparkle, and value.

TYPES OF GEMSTONES

Once you learn the secrets of Earth science, every rock feels like treasure. But the rocks that are most treasured of all are gemstones. These crystalline minerals are valued for their sparkling colors. They are usually cut and polished to improve their shape and reflect light, which enhances their beauty.

CUT RUBY

TYPES OF GEMSTONES 151

JADE
The minerals jadeite and nephrite are both sources of the semiprecious gemstone jade, valued for its green color and smooth texture. It is hard but can be carved into intricate shapes.

Gemstones can be polished to smooth pebbles by tumbling them in grit.

UNPOLISHED JADE

POLISHED JADE

GARNET
Garnets are made of silicate minerals. Like sapphires and rubies, they get their color from impurities. Silicates are not rare, so garnets are not as precious as sapphires and rubies.

CUT GARNET

GARNETS IN ROCK

LAPIS LAZULI
Most gems are crystals of a single mineral, but lapis lazuli is a mixture of several minerals, including blue lazurite, white calcite, golden pyrite, and blue sodalite. This rare rock is prized for its intense blue color and is polished into rounded gemstones (cabochons).

POLISHED LAPIS LAZULI

ROUGH LAPIS LAZULI

SUNSTONE
Feldspars are the most common minerals in Earth's crust, but they sometimes grow into large crystals that are used as gemstones. Sunstone is golden with a metallic sparkle caused by flecks of other minerals embedded in the feldspar.

ROUGH SUNSTONE

POLISHED SUNSTONE

MOONSTONE
Moonstone is a feldspar gemstone. It has a pearly color with blue highlights that are iridescent. This means the color shimmers and changes when viewed from different angles, like colors on a soap bubble.

ROUGH MOONSTONE

POLISHED MOONSTONE

OPAL
Opal is made of silica with an added ingredient: water. This makes it a mineraloid rather than a mineral. Opal does not have the ordered inner structure of crystalline minerals. Instead, each opal is a unique substance. The most precious opals have brilliant iridescence, displaying a rainbow of different colors. Black opals are rarer than diamonds and can be more expensive.

RAW OPAL

POLISHED OPAL

HOW DIAMONDS WORK

Every year billions of dollars are traded for tiny pieces of diamond, a mineral made of carbon—the same element as in coal and the graphite in pencils. What makes diamonds so special? For jewelers, it's their rarity and their brilliant sparkle. For toolmakers, it's their extreme hardness. For Earth scientists, it's the story of their explosive journey to Earth's surface.

Impurities in the diamond crystal or exposure to natural radiation produce green diamonds.

INSIDE A DIAMOND
Diamond's hardness comes from the way the atoms bond when carbon crystallizes at high temperatures and pressures. Each atom forms strong bonds with four other carbon atoms in a tetrahedral (triangular pyramid) shape. This shape resists compression in every direction, making diamond very strong.

Tetrahedral shape

Diamond embedded in kimberlite

The mineral olivine gives kimberlite its greenish color.

DIAMOND PASSENGERS
All natural diamonds are very old—a billion years or more—and formed at least 90 miles (150 km) underground. Geologists are still unsure exactly how diamonds form. Most found in mines are embedded in a rock called kimberlite. This rock forms from magma that rises to Earth's surface during volcanic eruptions. On its journey upward, kimberlite carries gemstone passengers, including diamonds.

Bort diamonds are low-quality grainy crystals, usually crushed and used as abrasives in industry.

HOW DIAMONDS WORK 153

▼ ROUGH DIAMONDS
Natural, uncut diamonds come in a range of shapes and colors. Some crystals are octahedral—like two pyramids joined at their square bases—and others are round or irregular in shape. The most common colors are white, yellow, and brown, but diamonds can also be green, orange, red, and blue.

The quality of this octahedral crystal makes it suitable for being cut into a gemstone.

DIAMOND DRILL
Diamond is the hardest natural substance, which makes it ideal to cut or drill into other hard substances, such as rocks, metals, and gemstones, including other diamonds. The diamond-tipped drill bit shown here is polishing metal.

CUTTING DIAMONDS
Like other gemstones, diamonds are cut into a range of symmetrical shapes with lots of facets (flat faces). The facets reflect light inside the jewel, making it sparkle. Diamonds are so hard that they can only be cut and polished using tools coated in diamond.

CUSHION **ROUND BRILLIANT** **BAGUETTE** **MIXED CUT**

MARQUISE **SQUARE** **STEP** **PENDELOQUE** **OVAL**

DIAMOND FIRE
Diamond refracts (bends) light more powerfully than glass. As a result, light bounces around inside a cut diamond and splits into a rainbow of colors as it leaves. This gives diamonds a colorful sparkle known as diamond fire.

BRILLIANT-CUT DIAMOND

HOW NATIVE ELEMENTS WORK

The chemical elements are the building blocks of matter, each consisting of a unique kind of atom. Most of the matter around us consists of compounds—substances in which atoms of different elements are bonded together. However, a small number of elements can be found in their pure form in Earth's crust. These are known as the native elements.

▼ **NATIVE SILVER**
Silver is classed as a "precious metal" because it is relatively rare. It has long been used as a form of money and in ancient times was more highly valued than gold. Today both metals are important in electronics as they are good at conducting electricity. Silver is also "ductile," which means it can be drawn into wires. These can be so fine that a single gram of silver can stretch 1.2 miles (2 km).

Silver tarnishes (loses its shine) because it reacts with sulfur in the air to form silver sulfide. This coating can be polished off to make silver bright again.

The vertical columns are called groups.

The horizontal rows are called periods.

PERIODIC TABLE
The periodic table is a chart that lists all the elements in order of their atomic number (the number of protons in an atom's nucleus). Elements that fall in the same column have similar chemical properties. Every element has a unique chemical symbol. For instance, carbon is C, gold is Au, silver is Ag, and copper is Cu.

HOW NATIVE ELEMENTS WORK   155

When native silver crystallizes in hollows, it forms amazingly varied shapes, from flakes and plates to finely branched crystals and long, curly wires.

Native silver can have a filiform (wirelike) habit.

GOLD
As gold doesn't react easily with other elements, it doesn't tarnish and keeps its shine. Along with its rarity and color, this makes it one of the most precious metals.

PLATINUM
Rarer even than gold, platinum is more valuable. It also has a higher melting temperature and so platinum ornaments were traditionally hammered into shape.

COPPER
The world's third most-used metal, copper is used to make electric wires. Around 5,000 years ago, people found they could make a stronger metal by mixing it with tin, which triggered the Bronze Age.

SULFUR
Crystals of pure, bright yellow sulfur can be found in rocks near volcanoes. Although it is famous for forming stinky compounds, pure sulfur has no smell.

CARBON
In the forms of coal, diamond, and graphite, carbon has been used for thousands of years. Only in the 1700s did chemists realize that these are all different forms of the same element.

ORES
Iron and many other useful metals are found in rocks as chemical compounds rather than native elements. These metals are extracted from their ores (rocks) by melting, roasting, or chemical reactions.

SULFUR PONDS

One of the most alien places on Earth is the Danakil Depression in Ethiopia. Here, hot springs stained yellow and orange by the elements sulfur and iron sit among active volcanic vents belching the stench of rotten eggs. The magma-heated spring water is close to boiling, saturated with salts, and incredibly acidic, yet strange forms of microorganisms have been found thriving in this scalding chemical soup.

BIOMINERALS

While most minerals are found as rocks, a small number can be found inside living creatures. These biominerals are created by their hosts for support, defense, as sensors, or to store useful substances. More than 60 different biominerals have been found, in microbes, plants, animals, and fungi. It's even thought that mineral crystals played a starring role in getting life started in the first place.

PLANT PROTECTION
Crystals of calcium oxalate are found in plants of all shapes and sizes. Needle-shaped crystals form in leaves and stems to deter plant-eating insects, by damaging their mouthparts. Some plants have stinging spines or hairs tipped with calcium oxalate to defend against grazing herbivores.

VIRGINIA CREEPER

CALCIUM OXALATE NEEDLES

JEWELS OF THE SEA
The surface waters of the sea teem with trillions of tiny, plantlike microorganisms called phytoplankton. Many of these single-celled organisms protect themselves with shells made of the minerals silica or calcium carbonate. Diatoms have such ornate silica shells that they are sometimes called the jewels of the sea.

DIATOMS

CHALK
When phytoplankton die, their remains sink to the sea floor. Over millions of years, deep layers of phytoplankton shells can build up and turn into rock. Chalk is a rock formed from broken bits of calcium carbonate that once formed the shells of organisms called coccolithophores.

COCCOLITHOPHORE

CHALK CLIFFS, UK

Nacre's iridescent shimmer is prized by makers of jewelry, furniture, and musical instruments.

PEARLS
As well as coating their shells with nacre, oysters and mussels sometimes cover flecks of dirt with the mineral too. After several months or years, the nacre can build up to form a pearl. These shiny blobs of waste have been used by humans as jewelry for centuries.

MOTHER-OF-PEARL
Some molluscs toughen their shells with a lining of nacre (mother-of-pearl). This shimmering mineral is a special form of calcium carbonate also known as aragonite. It is laid down in tiny plates, sandwiched with stretchy protein to prevent cracks. It makes the shell very resilient to crabs or fish.

PEARL IN PACIFIC OYSTER

The calcium carbonate shell is left behind after the mollusc dies and decays.

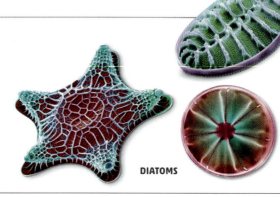

SPIRAL SHELL
Many molluscs, from land-living snails to their marine relatives, build shells from aragonite to protect their soft bodies from predators and from drying out. The mineral is laid down in layers and extended as the mollusc grows. This gives some seashells and snail shells their spiral pattern.

BIOMINERALS 159

SUITS OF ARMOR
A crab's exoskeleton begins as a bendy scaffold made of protein and carbohydrate. As gaps in the scaffold are gradually filled with the mineral calcite (a type of calcium carbonate), the shell hardens into formidable armor.

REEF BUILDERS
Coral reefs are built by tiny, jellyfishlike creatures called polyps. Each one builds a tough calcium carbonate shelter, popping out its tentacles to gather food. When polyps die, a new generation of skeletons forms on top of the old one. In this way, coral reefs slowly grow over millions of years.

CORAL SKELETON

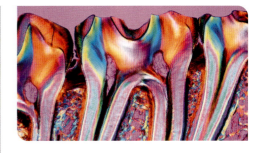

BONES AND TEETH
The building blocks of human bones and teeth are tiny crystals of apatite, a calcium phosphate mineral also found in rocks. Running throughout every bone is a network of living cells that control how apatite crystals are arranged. The enamel on teeth is 95 percent apatite, making it the toughest substance in the body.

IN BALANCE
Otoliths (ear stones) are tiny crystals of calcium carbonate that form deep inside your inner ears. Each time your head moves, the crystals move a tiny amount in their bed of gel. This sends signals to your brain, which tells your muscles how to adjust your position so you stay balanced.

UNWANTED MINERALS
Certain illnesses are caused by mineral crystals growing in the wrong place in a person's body. For example, kidney stones grow from dissolved salts in urine. This microscope image shows the microscopic crystals of calcium oxalate sticking up from the surface of a kidney stone.

NAUTILUS SHELL

Life on Earth would not exist if our planet did not have an **atmosphere**. This thin blanket of **gases** protects us from the fierce glare of the Sun and the freezing vacuum of outer space. It gives us breathable air, a stable **climate**, and a steady supply of fresh water in the form of rain and snow.

HOW THE ATMOSPHERE WORKS

The atmosphere is a thin blanket of air that surrounds our planet. If Earth had no atmosphere, animals wouldn't be able to breathe and plants wouldn't be able to grow. Without a warming layer of air above it, Earth's surface would be freezing and all the world's water would turn to ice. There would be no wind, clouds, or rain—in fact, no weather at all, but just the Sun rising and setting every day.

OZONE LAYER
The air in the atmosphere consists mostly of two gases: nitrogen (78%) and oxygen (21%). Oxygen makes air breathable. It also shields us from the Sun's harmful ultraviolet radiation, which is absorbed by a form of oxygen called ozone. This gas is found in the stratosphere (second layer of the atmosphere).

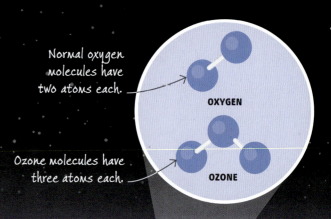

Normal oxygen molecules have two atoms each.

Ozone molecules have three atoms each.

OXYGEN

OZONE

▼ **EARTH'S ATMOSPHERE FROM SPACE**
In this picture, the atmosphere shows up as a blue haze that gradually gets darker with height. There is no clear edge to the atmosphere—the air just gets thinner until there is nothing but empty space.

Earth's horizon

Most clouds stay in the lowest layer of the atmosphere—the troposphere.

HOW THE ATMOSPHERE WORKS 163

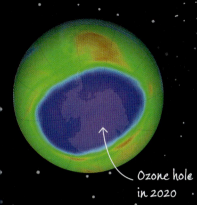
Ozone hole in 2020

THE OZONE HOLE
In the 1970s, scientists discovered that the ozone layer was very thin over Antarctica. This "ozone hole" was caused by chemicals called CFCs, used in fridges and aerosol cans. After CFCs were banned, the hole began to slowly heal.

STRATOSPHERIC CLOUDS
The stratosphere usually has no clouds. However, multicolored clouds of glittering ice crystals occasionally form in cold polar regions. They are best seen just after sunset when the sky darkens but the high clouds catch the last rays of light.

LAYERS OF THE ATMOSPHERE
The atmosphere is divided into five layers, mainly defined by how the temperature changes within them.

EXOSPHERE
440–6,200 miles (700–10,000 km)

The outer edge of the atmosphere, where it fades into space, is called the exosphere.

THERMOSPHERE
50–440 miles (80–700 km)

In theory, this is the hottest layer of the atmosphere as the intense sunlight can warm air molecules to 2,700°F (1,500°C) in the daytime. However, there are so few air molecules here that a human visitor would find it freezing cold. The International Space Station and many satellites orbit Earth in this layer.

MESOSPHERE
31–50 miles (50–80 km)

The mesosphere is the coldest layer, with temperatures falling as low as –120°F (–85°C) at night. Meteors colliding with Earth burn up in the mesosphere, creating shooting stars.

STRATOSPHERE
7–31 miles (12–50 km)

Planes and weather balloons fly in the stratosphere, which is usually cloud-free. The temperature rises with height in this layer because of ozone gas, which absorbs energy from the Sun.

TROPOSPHERE
0–7 miles (0–12 km)

This thin layer is where we live. It is the warmest and densest part of the atmosphere and is rich in water vapor from the oceans. Nearly all clouds and weather systems occur here.

WHAT IS AIR MADE OF?

What looks like empty space around us is actually full of matter: air. The air in Earth's atmosphere is a mixture of colorless and odorless gases. We can't see or smell them, but we feel them every time the wind blows on our skin. Air is essential to life on Earth. It keeps the climate stable, and it provides the oxygen that living things need to release chemical energy from food.

▶ **THE AMOUNT OF OXYGEN IN AIR**
This experiment shows how much of the gas oxygen is in air. Wet iron wool is placed in an inverted glass tube with a dish of water at the bottom. When iron is exposed to oxygen, a chemical reaction takes place. The iron reacts with oxygen to form rust. This removes oxygen from the air.

NITROGEN 78%
OXYGEN 21%
ARGON 0.93%
CARBON DIOXIDE 0.038%
NEON 0.0018%
HELIUM 0.0005%
KRYPTON 0.0001%
HYDROGEN 0.00005%
XENON 0.000009%

WHAT GASES MAKE UP AIR?
Two gases make up 99 percent of the air in Earth's atmosphere: nitrogen (78 percent) and oxygen (21 percent). The remaining 1 percent includes tiny amounts of many other gases. Among them are carbon dioxide, which acts as a greenhouse gas, keeping Earth warm enough for life, and ozone, which protects life on Earth from harmful ultraviolet rays from the Sun.

The iron wool is soaked in water to encourage rusting.

1 SETTING UP
At the beginning of the experiment the water level in the tube is the same as that in the dish. The iron wool hasn't started to rust.

Glass tube containing air

Water

WHAT IS AIR MADE OF? 165

The iron wool has rusted, using up all the oxygen gas in the tube.

② TWO DAYS LATER
The water has risen because all the oxygen gas in the tube has turned into rust. The water level is about 21 percent higher as air is 21 percent oxygen.

The water has risen up the tube by about 21 percent.

RUSTY IRON
Reddish brown in color, rust is scientifically known as iron oxide (Fe_2O_3). Water acts as a catalyst, speeding up the chemical reaction between iron and oxygen.

WHAT ELSE IS IN AIR?
Gases aren't the only things in the atmosphere. Water in liquid or solid form and tiny particles such as dust, soot, and ash float around. Living things can be found in the air too.

WATER
Clouds are made of liquid water droplets or ice crystals that drift in the air. Our eyes can't see the individual drops and crystals, but there are many billions of them in even a very small cloud.

AIRBORNE PARTICLES
Dust and other airborne particles have many sources. Volcanoes spew out vast amounts of ash; strong winds whip up grains of sand into the air; and factories release soot from their chimneys.

AERIAL PLANKTON
Tiny life forms float in the air. Known as aerial plankton, they include viruses, bacteria, pollen grains (above), and seeds. Some baby spiders travel hundreds of miles in the air, using a silk thread to catch the wind and find new homes.

HOW AIR PRESSURE WORKS

The air in Earth's atmosphere is not weightless. Pulled by gravity, it exerts a force on the planet's surface. This force is called air pressure. When we measure air pressure, we are weighing the air in the atmosphere all the way up to the edge of space. Every square centimeter of Earth's surface has about 1 kg of air pressing on it.

▼ **CRUSHING POWER**
The force that air pressure exerts around us can be shown in this simple demonstration. The air pressure inside a sealed bottle is lowered by cooling until the bottle's walls can no longer withstand the power of the air pushing on the outside.

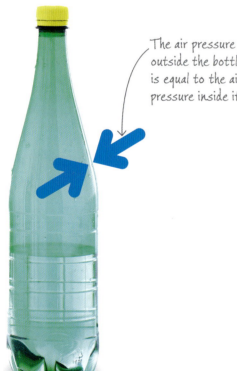

The air pressure outside the bottle is equal to the air pressure inside it.

① ADDING WARM WATER
A plastic bottle is half-filled with hot water and left to stand for a minute so the air inside it warms up. The bottle is then sealed. The warm air inside the bottle is less dense than air outside but the pressure is equal.

Air pressure is now weaker inside the bottle than outside.

Water vapor condenses into droplets, reducing the amount of gas in the bottle.

② COOLING THE BOTTLE
The bottle is plunged into a bowl of ice. This cools the air inside the bottle, which reduces the pressure. Water vapor condenses, reducing the pressure further.

HOW AIR PRESSURE WORKS 167

The difference in air pressure is now so great that the sides of the bottle are crushed.

③ CRUSHED BOTTLE
Air pressure continues to fall inside the bottle as it sits in the ice. Eventually, the bottle's sides cannot withstand the air pressure from outside and the bottle is crushed.

PRESSURE AND ALTITUDE
Air pressure falls as height above sea level increases. On mountains, the pressure may be less than half its value at sea level, which makes breathing difficult. That's why mountaineers sometimes carry oxygen tanks.

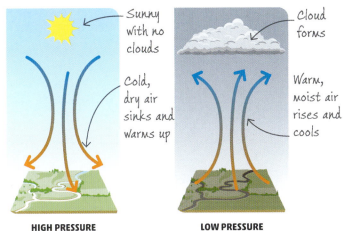

PRESSURE AND WEATHER
When air pressure is high, it usually means that cold, dry air is sinking from high in the sky. This prevents clouds forming and so brings fine weather. When air pressure is low, warm air near the ground rises and cools. Water vapor in the air condenses to make clouds and perhaps rain. Low air pressure usually means bad weather.

WEATHER MAPS
Weather maps used in forecasts often show the air pressure as this tells us what the weather will be like. Black lines called isobars join points of equal air pressure. Areas of very high pressure are indicated by the letter **H**, and very low areas by **L**.

BEAUFORT SCALE

Long ago there were few scientific instruments to measure wind speed. So in 1805 the Beaufort Scale was devised to describe wind strength based on its effects on trees, buildings, and waves. The scale is still used today, with added wind speeds.

CALM
Smoke rises vertically.
Wind 0 mph (0 kph)

LIGHT AIR
Smoke drifts with the wind.
1–3 mph (2–5 kph)

LIGHT BREEZE
Wind felt on face.
4–7 mph (6–11 kph)

GENTLE BREEZE
Leaves and small twigs move.
8–12 mph (12–19 kph)

MODERATE BREEZE
Fallen leaves lifted from the ground.
13–17 mph (20–28 kph)

HOW THE WIND BLOWS

Wind is air moving around in the atmosphere. The air flows from areas of high air pressure to areas of low pressure, similar to the way rivers flow from high ground to lower ground. The direction of winds is also strongly influenced by the rotation of Earth.

▶ **WANDERING WINDS**
In most parts of the world the wind direction is very variable. Over the tropical oceans, however, the winds most often blow from east to west. In the days of sailing ships, these reliable easterly winds were known as the trade winds because they helped sailors move cargoes around the world.

Sails catch the wind to propel the ship forward.

HOW THE WIND BLOWS 169

5 FRESH BREEZE
Small trees begin to sway.
18-23 mph
(29-38 kph)

6 STRONG BREEZE
Large branches move.
24-30 mph
(39-49 kph)

7 HIGH WIND
Whole trees move.
31-38 mph
(50-61 kph)

8 GALE
Twigs break off trees.
39-46 mph
(62-74 kph)

9 STRONG GALE
Slight damage to roofs.
47-54 mph
(75-88 kph)

10 STORM
Trees uprooted; buildings damaged.
55-63 mph
(89-102 kph)

11 VIOLENT STORM
Lots of damage to buildings.
64-72 mph
(103-117 kph)

12 HURRICANE FORCE
Devastating damage.
73+ mph
(118+ kph)

HARNESSING THE WIND
For centuries, people harnessed the wind to grind wheat into flour in windmills. Today, wind turbines are used to generate electricity. They work best in windy places, such as hilltops or the sea.

JET STREAMS
About 6-9 miles (10-15 km) above Earth's surface are narrow bands of very strong winds called jet streams, which can exceed 150 mph (240 kph). Aircraft use these winds to speed up their journeys.

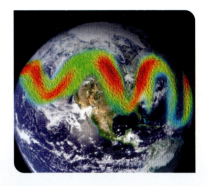

CORIOLIS EFFECT
Earth's rotation deflects winds flowing along the surface. This deflection is known as the Coriolis effect, and you can demonstrate it with a spinning globe.

1 Spin the globe counterclockwise to represent Earth's rotation. Then use a pen to quickly draw a line vertically down from north to south.

2 The line is not straight. It's deflected to the west as the globe rotates, creating a curve. The same thing happens to Earth's trade winds, which is why they blow from east to west.

PREVAILING WINDS
Some winds tend to blow in a particular direction across Earth's surface. These are called prevailing winds and influence the local climate. Westerlies, for example, come from the west and are warm and damp. Surface winds are linked to circulation cells that cycle air high in the atmosphere.

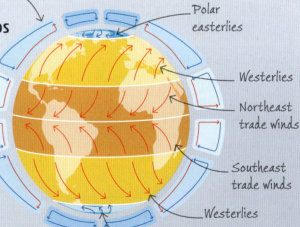

Circulation cell
Polar easterlies
Westerlies
Northeast trade winds
Southeast trade winds
Westerlies
Polar easterlies

HOW HOT AND COLD CLIMATES WORK

Some places are scorching hot all year round, others are always freezing, and some places have warm summers yet chilly winters. Such long-term weather patterns are known as climates. We get different climates because of Earth's spherical shape and the way it receives heat from the Sun.

▶ **AVERAGE TEMPERATURES**
This globe shows the temperatures across Earth, averaged for the whole year. The warmest parts are in the tropical regions, near the equator. The coldest areas are at the poles.

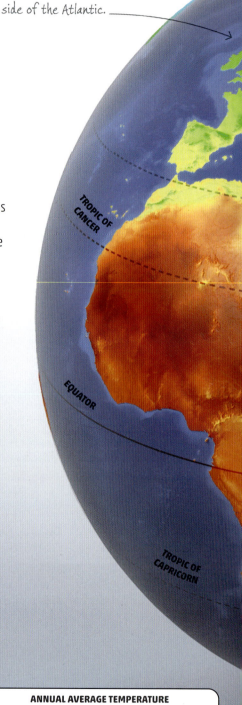

A warm ocean current keeps northwestern Europe warmer than Canada on the other side of the Atlantic.

UNEVEN WARMING
Because Earth's surface is curved, heat from the Sun is spread over a much larger area near the poles than at the equator. So climates are warmer near the equator, where the same amount of solar energy is focused on a smaller area.

The Sun's rays strike the equator straight on.

The Sun's rays strike polar regions at a shallow angle because Earth's surface curves away.

CLIMATE ZONES
Earth can be split broadly into four climate zones in each hemisphere. These different zones are separated by imaginary circles drawn round Earth. Tropical regions, for example, lie between the Tropics of Cancer and Capricorn.

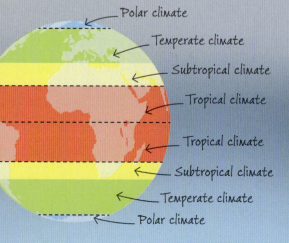

- Polar climate
- Temperate climate
- Subtropical climate
- Tropical climate
- Tropical climate
- Subtropical climate
- Temperate climate
- Polar climate

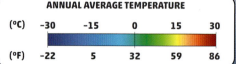

ANNUAL AVERAGE TEMPERATURE

| (°C) | -30 | -15 | 0 | 15 | 30 |
| (°F) | -22 | 5 | 32 | 59 | 86 |

HOW HOT AND COLD CLIMATES WORK 171

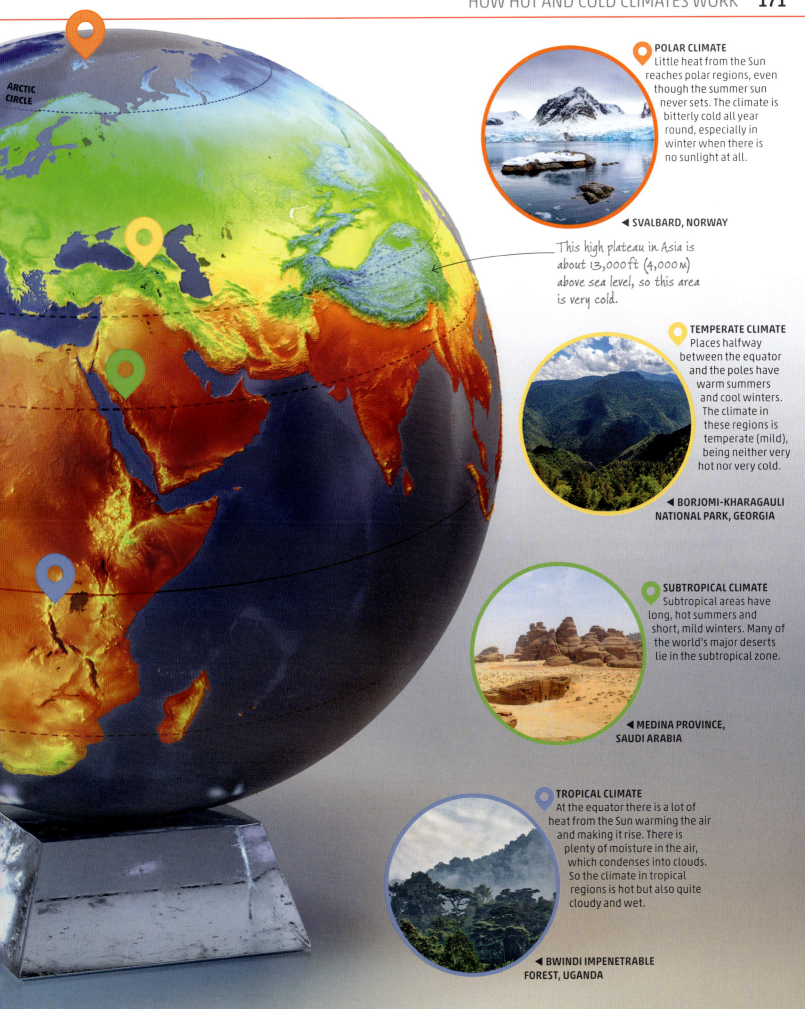

POLAR CLIMATE
Little heat from the Sun reaches polar regions, even though the summer sun never sets. The climate is bitterly cold all year round, especially in winter when there is no sunlight at all.

◀ SVALBARD, NORWAY

This high plateau in Asia is about 13,000 ft (4,000 m) above sea level, so this area is very cold.

TEMPERATE CLIMATE
Places halfway between the equator and the poles have warm summers and cool winters. The climate in these regions is temperate (mild), being neither very hot nor very cold.

◀ BORJOMI-KHARAGAULI NATIONAL PARK, GEORGIA

SUBTROPICAL CLIMATE
Subtropical areas have long, hot summers and short, mild winters. Many of the world's major deserts lie in the subtropical zone.

◀ MEDINA PROVINCE, SAUDI ARABIA

TROPICAL CLIMATE
At the equator there is a lot of heat from the Sun warming the air and making it rise. There is plenty of moisture in the air, which condenses into clouds. So the climate in tropical regions is hot but also quite cloudy and wet.

◀ BWINDI IMPENETRABLE FOREST, UGANDA

HOW WET AND DRY CLIMATES WORK

The winds that blow around Earth pick up moisture from the oceans, and then dump it as rain or snow over land. Not all regions receive the same amount of rainfall, though. Deserts get very little rainfall, while some regions receive more rainfall in a single day than deserts receive in a year.

▶ WET AND DRY

This globe shows average annual rainfall in different parts of the world. The wettest places (dark blue) are near the Equator. Deserts, on the other hand, which are the driest places (light blue), are mostly just north or just south of the wet zones, along the Tropics of Cancer and Capricorn.

ANNUAL PRECIPITATION					
MM	0	2,500	5,000	7,500	10,000
IN	0	98	197	295	394

WHY IS IT WET NEAR THE EQUATOR?

Air cycles known as Hadley cells cause wet regions at the Equator and dry regions around it.

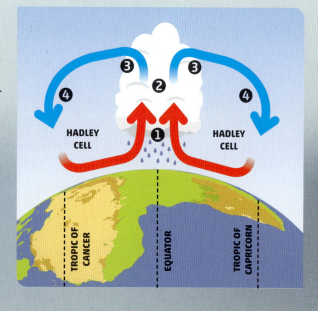

1 Moisture-laden trade winds converge at the Equator. The warm climate heats the humid air and makes it rise.

2 As the air rises, it cools and water vapor condenses to create clouds and rain, which falls back to Earth.

3 Having cooled and lost its moisture, the air is now dry. It travels away from the Equator, spreading north and south.

4 The cool, dry air sinks back over the Tropics of Cancer and Capricorn, giving these areas a dry climate. The air then flows back to the Equator and the cycle repeats itself.

HOW WET AND DRY CLIMATES WORK

DESERTS
Deserts have an annual rainfall of less than 10 in (25 cm), and they can go for months or even years without any rainfall. Animals and plants need special adaptations to survive in deserts.

RAINFORESTS
Around the Equator, it rains nearly every day, and annual rainfall can exceed 79 in (200 cm). The warm climate and plentiful rain are perfect for plants, so rainforests flourish around the Equator.

WET AND DRY SEASONS
Tropical areas between the desert zone and the Equator tend to have distinct wet and dry seasons. Plants die or become dormant in the dry season, and the land turns dry and dusty. When rain returns, the landscape turns green again.

DRIEST DESERT
Not all of the world's deserts are in hot places. Antarctica is considered a "polar desert" because it gets only about 2 in (50 mm) of precipitation a year. This falls as snow and piles up without melting because it's so cold. The South Pole is 9,285 ft (2,830 m) above sea level, but this is mostly just a thick sheet of ice.

RAIN BELT
A permanent belt of cloud and rain wraps around the Equator. Humid trade winds that blow across the oceans, flowing toward the Equator, constantly add moisture to this belt. Because Earth's axis is tilted, the rain belt shifts north in the northern summer, and south in the northern winter, creating a cycle of wet and dry seasons that repeats every year.

HOW OCEAN CURRENTS WORK

The oceans play an enormous role in Earth's climate, absorbing heat from the Sun and moving that heat around in flows of water called currents. These currents are much slower than winds, typically traveling less than 1.5 ft (0.5 m) per second at the surface, and even less than that further down.

▼ **THE GULF STREAM**
This image, created from satellite data, shows a current of warm water called the Gulf Stream flowing out of the Gulf of Mexico and toward Europe, carrying heat northward. The current is driven by wind and by the sinking of cold, salty ocean water near the North Pole. Because of the Gulf Stream, northwestern Europe has a relatively mild climate for its latitude.

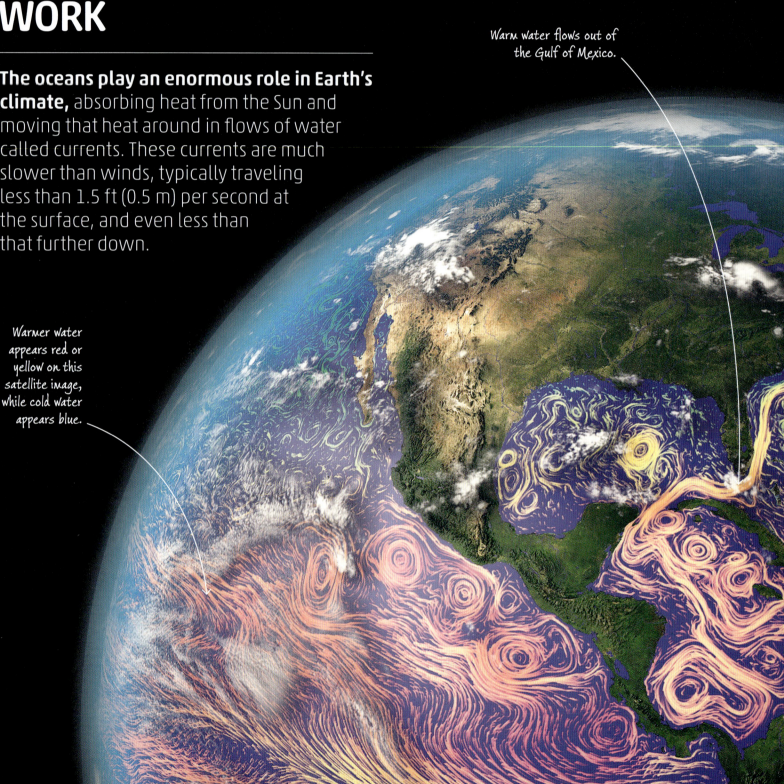

Warm water flows out of the Gulf of Mexico.

Warmer water appears red or yellow on this satellite image, while cold water appears blue.

HOW OCEAN CURRENTS WORK

GLOBAL CURRENTS

The map shows the ocean currents around the globe. The largest oceans have circulating currents called gyres, caused by surface winds. The gyres flow clockwise in the northern hemisphere and anticlockwise in the southern hemisphere. A cold current also flows all the way around the southern hemisphere, uninterrupted by land. It's powered by strong westerly winds called the Roaring Forties, which blow between 40° and 50° latitude.

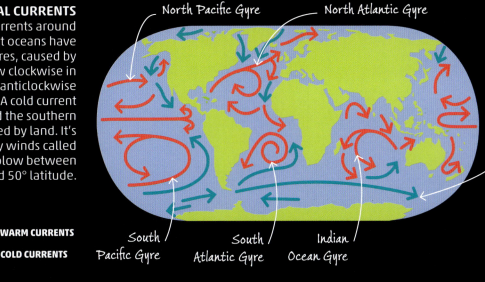

- North Pacific Gyre
- North Atlantic Gyre
- South Pacific Gyre
- South Atlantic Gyre
- Indian Ocean Gyre
- The Antarctic Circumpolar Current flows around the globe, driven by the Roaring Forties.

WARM CURRENTS
COLD CURRENTS

- The water cools as it moves north.
- These swirling currents are called eddies.

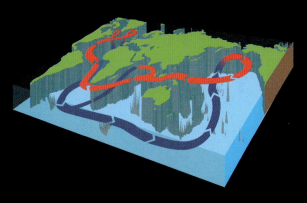

GLOBAL CONVEYOR BELT

Surface currents combine with deep underwater currents to make a "global conveyor belt" of water, which connects all the world's oceans. The conveyor belt is slower than wind-driven currents, taking about 1,000 years to complete a full cycle. The underwater currents start near the North Pole, where cold, salty water sinks down and begins its slow and winding journey around the world.

FLOATING GARBAGE

The "Great Pacific Garbage Patch" is a vast area of floating trash that has been slowly trapped inside the swirling currents of the North Pacific Gyre. It contains large discarded items, like fishing nets and plastic packaging, as well as trillions of tiny plastic particles that are too small to see (microplastics).

DEBRIS WASHED UP ON BEACH, HAWAII

Thin, high clouds form first as a cold front approaches.

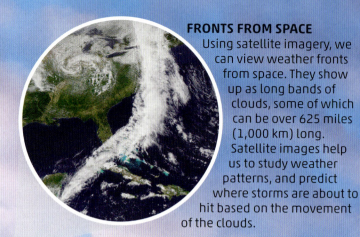

FRONTS FROM SPACE
Using satellite imagery, we can view weather fronts from space. They show up as long bands of clouds, some of which can be over 625 miles (1,000 km) long. Satellite images help us to study weather patterns, and predict where storms are about to hit based on the movement of the clouds.

HOW WEATHER FRONTS WORK

The air in Earth's atmosphere is not evenly mixed. Sometimes, a huge volume of air collides with another volume of air that's warmer, colder, wetter, or drier. The boundaries between these colliding air masses are called weather fronts, and they are like battlegrounds. They often bring bad weather, including clouds, rain, snow, and thunderstorms.

▲ **COLD FRONT**
An approaching cold front brings dramatic changes. Thin, high clouds form first, as warm air is pushed upward. The clouds soon grow thicker and darker, as they block out more light from the Sun. This is a sign that rain is on the way.

HOW WEATHER FRONTS WORK

WEATHER MAPS
Weather maps use colored symbols to show weather fronts, and lines called isobars to show areas of equal pressure. Areas of high pressure bring settled and dry weather. Areas of low pressure, on the other hand, bring unsettled weather that's often wet and windy.

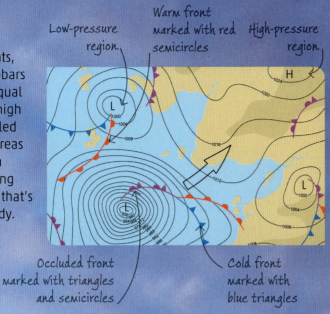

Low-pressure region.
Warm front marked with red semicircles
High-pressure region.
Occluded front marked with triangles and semicircles
Cold front marked with blue triangles

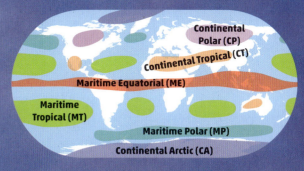

PRINCIPAL WORLD AIR MASSES

AIR MASSES
Whether air masses are warm, cold, dry, or wet depends mainly on where they come from. Polar air masses are cold, while tropical air masses are warm. Air over the ocean (maritime air masses) is humid, while continental air is dry. The map above shows the usual pattern of major air masses.

TYPES OF WEATHER FRONTS
There are three main types of weather fronts, and each one causes a particular kind of weather.

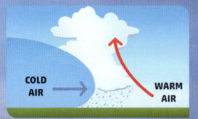

Cold front
As cold, dense air moves forward, it pushes the lighter, warmer air upward, making a band of thick cloud with often heavy rain.

Occluded front
At an occluded front, a mass of warm air is squeezed upward by two colder air masses coming in from either side. Clouds form in the rising warm air.

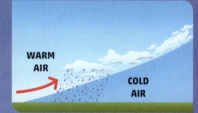

Warm front
Warm air moving forward will rise above a colder, denser air mass, forming a wide band of cloud with rain and drizzle.

Darker, thicker clouds mean rain is on the way.

HOW HURRICANES WORK

Hurricanes are swirling masses of deep clouds, heavy rain, and extremely strong winds. They produce some of the most destructive weather on Earth. Hurricanes occur in the tropical regions and always form over the ocean. In the Atlantic and east Pacific they are called hurricanes but in the west Pacific they are known as typhoons, and over the Indian Ocean they are known as cyclones.

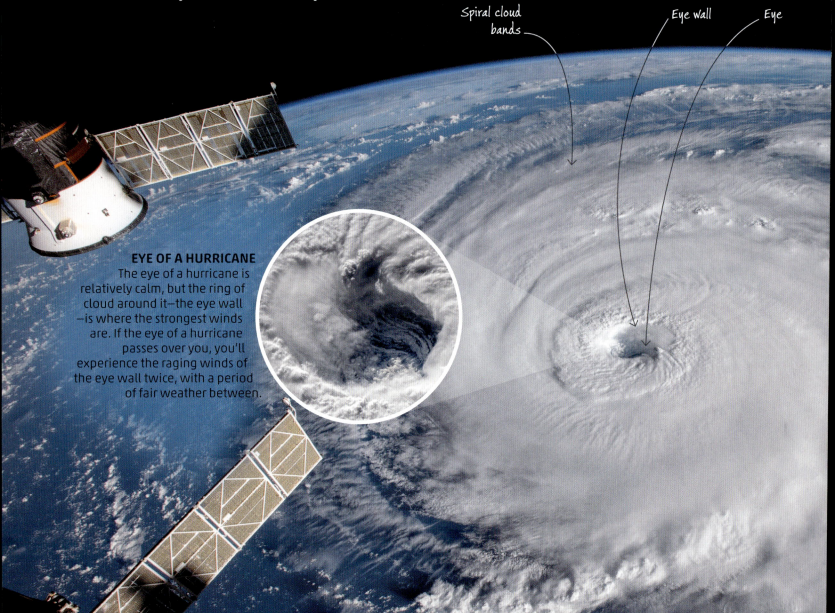

Air spins around the eye in the center.
High in the atmosphere, wind spirals around the storm.
Bands of cloud and rain form where warm air rises.
Air is drawn in, producing strong winds.

INSIDE A HURRICANE
Hurricanes are fueled by heat from the ocean that causes rapidly rising air and very strong winds. Air is sucked toward the center of the storm just above the ocean surface, rises in bands, and spirals out at the top.

Spiral cloud bands — *Eye wall* — *Eye*

EYE OF A HURRICANE
The eye of a hurricane is relatively calm, but the ring of cloud around it—the eye wall—is where the strongest winds are. If the eye of a hurricane passes over you, you'll experience the raging winds of the eye wall twice, with a period of fair weather between.

HURRICANE DAMAGE
Hurricanes can cause catastrophic damage in three main ways: through violent winds, through storm surges from the sea, and from torrential rain.

STRONG WINDS
A category 5 storm can produce gusts of over 157 mph (252 kph). The winds in a category 5 storm can flatten buildings, trees, and power lines.

STORM SURGE
Low air pressure at the center of a hurricane causes the sea level to rise beneath it, leading to huge waves and coastal flooding.

HEAVY RAIN
Hurricanes produce huge amounts of rain. The winds weaken if the storm moves inland, but the heavy rain can still cause severe flooding.

▼ HURRICANE FLORENCE
This photograph, taken from the International Space Station in 2018, shows Hurricane Florence raging over the Atlantic Ocean. The Atlantic hurricane season starts at the beginning of June and finishes at the end of November, with an average of six hurricanes developing each year. In the Atlantic, the names of the hurricanes go from A to Z through the year. They alternate between male and female names, with Q, U, X, Y, and Z left out as there are few names starting with those letters.

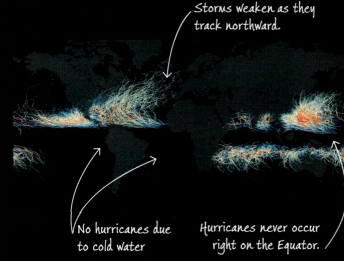

Storms weaken as they track northward.

No hurricanes due to cold water

Hurricanes never occur right on the Equator.

WHERE DO HURRICANES HAPPEN?
This map shows the track of every hurricane from 1848 to 2013. The region with the most storms is the west Pacific. There are no hurricanes in the southeast Pacific and only one in the South Atlantic because the water there is usually too cold. The track of each hurricane is shown as a line, with the color showing the strength of the storm.

HURRICANE SCALE
The strength of a hurricane is rated on the Saffir-Simpson scale, which is based on wind speed. Category 5 hurricanes are rare, with only four making landfall in the US between 1935 and 2018.

1 74–95 mph (119–153 kph)
Weak trees fall, roof tiles blown off

2 96–110 mph (154–177 kph)
Houses damaged, trees snapped

3 111–129 mph (178–208 kph)
Trees uprooted, major damage to homes

4 130–156 mph (209–251 kph)
Roofs blown off; no water and electricity

5 > 157 mph (>252 kph)
Catastrophic damage; area uninhabitable

HOW TORNADOES WORK

▼ **FURIOUS FUNNEL**
Just as water spirals around as it drains through a plughole, the air rushing up into a tornado forms a violent, spinning vortex. A newly formed tornado consists of tiny water droplets and is usually white or gray, but the base changes color as it picks up earth and other debris.

A tornado is a whirling funnel of cloud and wind that can hurl a car into the air and destroy a building in seconds. The average tornado touches the ground for a matter of minutes, but it can leave a trail of devastation in its wake.

HOW TORNADOES FORM
Tornadoes are rare as they form only under certain specific conditions. They develop from powerful storm clouds called supercells.

❶ CLOUDS FORM
For a tornado to form, the air near the ground must be hot and humid, with cooler air above. The hot air rises, forming towering thunderclouds several kilometers tall.

❷ ROTATION BEGINS
Air drawn into the cloud begins to rotate. At first the rotating air moves horizontally.

❸ TOUCHDOWN
Strong winds and heavy rain concentrate the rotating air into a tight funnel and turn it upright. When this funnel hits the ground a tornado has formed.

Base of thundercloud

HOW TORNADOES WORK 181

TORNADO SCALE
Tornadoes are classified from 0 to 5 using the Enhanced Fujita (EF) Scale, which is based on how much damage they do.

EF0: GALE TORNADO
Some damage to chimneys. Branches snapped off trees.

EF1: MODERATE TORNADO
Tiles blown off roofs and cars pushed off the road.

EF2: SIGNIFICANT TORNADO
Roofs detached from houses and trees snapped or uprooted.

EF3: SEVERE TORNADO
Considerable damage to buildings. Cars lifted off the ground.

EF4: DEVASTATING TORNADO
Trucks lifted off the ground. Houses completely flattened.

EF5: INCREDIBLE TORNADO
Significant damage to large buildings. Cars lifted high in the air.

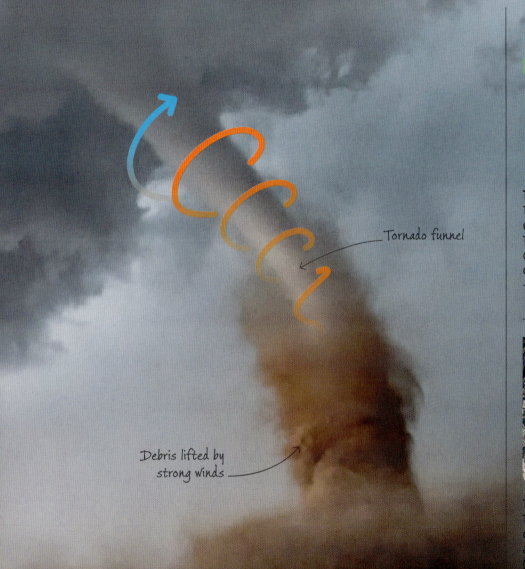

Tornado funnel

Debris lifted by strong winds

TORNADO ALLEY
Tornadoes are rare events, but some places experience far more tornadoes than others. The US has more tornadoes than any other country. Tornadoes are most common in the central states, with Texas receiving the most —an average of 136 a year.

THE TORNADO SWATH
The track of damage caused by a tornado is called the swath. The pale line across the image above shows a swath that is around 1.5 miles (2.5 km) wide at its widest point.

HOW CLOUDS FORM

Clouds may bring bad weather, but without them there would be no fresh water on Earth and life would not exist. As well as watering the land, clouds help regulate the climate. They cool Earth by reflecting sunlight back into space but can keep us warm at night by acting like a blanket to trap heat near the ground.

PRECIPITATION

Clouds release precipitation (rain, snow, or hail).

▶ **THE WATER CYCLE**
Clouds perform a vital job in Earth's water cycle—the movement of water on, below, and above the planet's surface. Water that evaporates from the ocean surface rises and cools until it forms clouds. These clouds are blown across land, where they produce rain or snow that feeds lakes and rivers and waters vegetation.

Some water seeps into the ground and slowly flows back toward the sea.

HOW RAIN CLOUDS FORM
Rain clouds form when warm, moist air rises. The rising air cools, making water vapor condense into droplets. There are three main ways that large masses of air can be lifted, creating rain clouds.

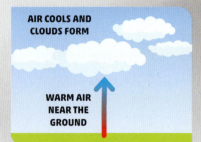

❶ **CONVECTIVE CLOUDS**
When Earth's surface is warm, it heats the air above it, making it rise. This process is called convection. Convective clouds are common in summer and in the tropics. They produce brief showers or thunderstorms.

❷ **OROGRAPHIC CLOUDS**
When wind blows over a hill or a mountain, the air rises and cools, causing clouds to form. Most of the rain from the clouds falls on the windward side of the mountain, with the far side in a dry "rain shadow."

❸ **FRONTAL CLOUDS**
When two large air masses collide, the warmer air mass rises over the colder, denser air and forms a large layer of cloud. The boundaries between large air masses are called fronts, and the rain produced by frontal clouds can be persistent and drizzly.

HOW CLOUDS FORM 183

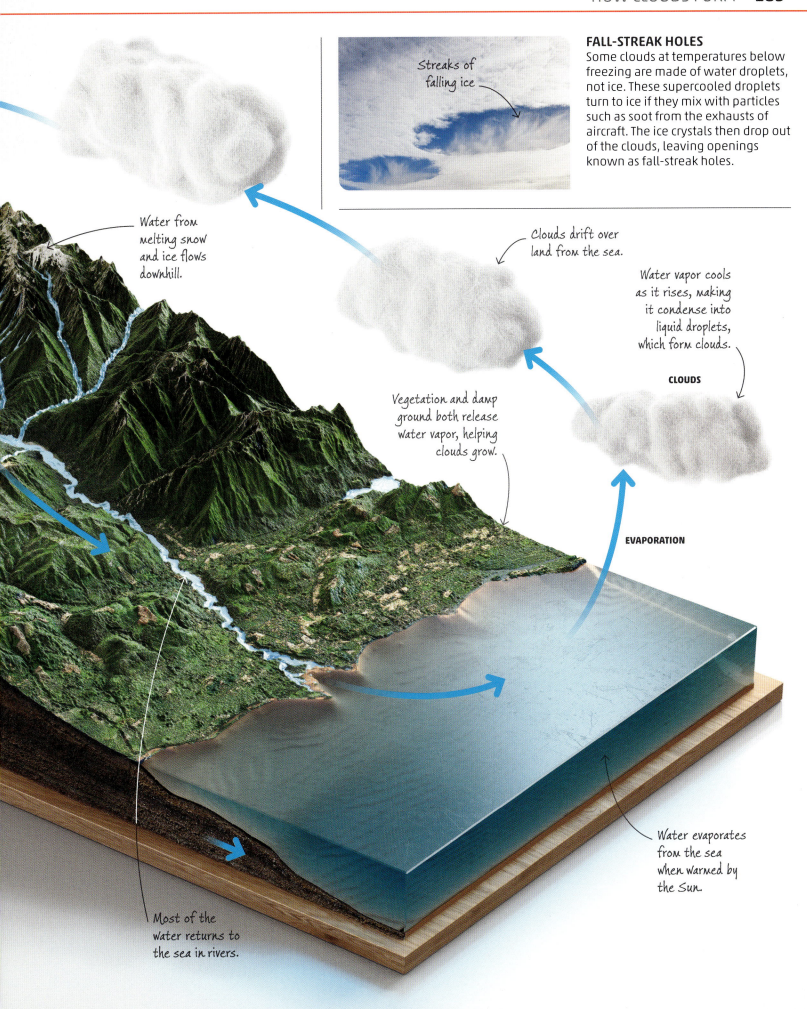

FALL-STREAK HOLES
Some clouds at temperatures below freezing are made of water droplets, not ice. These supercooled droplets turn to ice if they mix with particles such as soot from the exhausts of aircraft. The ice crystals then drop out of the clouds, leaving openings known as fall-streak holes.

Streaks of falling ice

Water from melting snow and ice flows downhill.

Clouds drift over land from the sea.

Water vapor cools as it rises, making it condense into liquid droplets, which form clouds.

CLOUDS

Vegetation and damp ground both release water vapor, helping clouds grow.

EVAPORATION

Water evaporates from the sea when warmed by the Sun.

Most of the water returns to the sea in rivers.

TYPES OF CLOUDS

White and fluffy, thin and wispy, or dark and heavy, clouds are a good indicator of what is happening in the atmosphere. Their shape depends on how high they are and how much water they contain. The ten main cloud formations are divided into three groups according to their level in the atmosphere: low clouds, medium clouds, and high clouds.

CIRRUS
Cirrus are high, wispy clouds made of ice crystals. They appear in fair weather but also tend to form ahead of a warm front, which means rainy weather may be on the way.

CUMULONIMBUS
These towering clouds can reach 12 miles (20 km) tall and often spread out flat at the top. They produce torrential rain, hail, and thunder. One cumulonimbus cloud can store as much energy as 10 atom bombs.

Updraughts of warm, moist air carry the cloud high into the atmosphere.

ALTOCUMULUS
Altocumulus are mid-level clouds that form a variety of shapes, including small towers and flying saucers. They contain more water droplets than ice crystals, which makes them gray.

TYPES OF CLOUDS   185

HIGH LEVEL: 20,000–40,000 FT (6,500–12,000 M)

CIRROCUMULUS
These bouncy little clouds that spread across the sky sometimes resemble the scales of a fish, earning the nickname "mackerel sky." They contain ice crystals and supercooled water, and are usually associated with fair weather.

CIRROSTRATUS
Covering much of the sky, cirrostratus clouds hang high in the air like a transparent veil. They sometimes create circular haloes around the Sun, occasionally with bright spots called sun dogs on either side. Their presence usually indicates the arrival of rain or drizzle the next day.

Sun
Sun dog

ALTOSTRATUS
When the sky looks pale gray and flat, it is probably covered by altostratus clouds. The Sun can be seen weakly through these clouds, but it does not cast shadows. They signify that bad weather is on the way.

NIMBOSTRATUS
These occur when altostratus clouds deepen and thicken as they meet a warm air mass. They darken because of the large water droplets they contain, which eventually fall as rain, often for several hours.

MEDIUM LEVEL: 6,500–20,000 FT (2,000–6,500 M)

CUMULUS
Cumulus clouds are the cauliflower-shaped clouds with fluffy white tops that you often see on sunny days. They form when warm air rises from the ground and cools, the water vapor condensing into droplets. Cumulus clouds occasionally produce light showers.

STRATOCUMULUS
Stratocumulus clouds are the most common type of cloud. They are clumpy gray or white shapes with flat bottoms and spaces between them. Although usually associated with rain, they rarely produce more than drizzle.

STRATUS
These flat clouds cover the sky like a blanket and may be gray and featureless or ragged and broken. They are the lowest clouds and sometimes touch the ground to create fog or mist.

LOW LEVEL: BELOW 6,500 FT (2,000 M)

SUPERCELL

Most tornadoes form in supercells—the most powerful kinds of thunderstorms. Supercell clouds can develop a rounded shape at the base as powerful updraughts spiral around inside them. These updraughts can reach speeds of 90 mph (140 kph), which is fast enough to suspend hailstones the size of grapefruits. As the rising air cools, its moisture condenses and releases heat energy, adding to the storm's power.

HOW RAIN WORKS

Rain can be a nuisance, but it's vital to life on Earth, providing fresh water to plants and animals. Rain forms when invisible water vapor in air rises and cools enough to condense into tiny droplets. If these droplets grow larger than around 0.04 in (1 mm) wide, they begin to fall.

RAINY SEASON
In many parts of the world, almost all the rain falls in one season. Rain pours down on Africa's savanna grassland during the wet season. But in the dry weather that follows, plants turn brown and shrivel, rivers and lakes dry up, and the parched earth cracks. Vast herds of zebras and wildebeests migrate in search of water and food. However, when the rain begins again, plants and trees revive, seeds germinate, and animals return.

WET SEASON

DRY SEASON

❶ NEW RAINDROP
Tiny, newly formed raindrops are shaped into a sphere by a force called surface tension, which acts in the droplet's skin.

❷ GROWING WIDER
When droplets become more than about 0.04 in (1 mm) wide, they start to fall. The force of the air pushing under them makes them lose their spherical shape.

❸ BUN SHAPE
The raindrop speeds up, falling at around 12 mph (20 kph). It forms a bun shape as air pushes into it. A cavity forms in the bottom but the top stays rounded thanks to surface tension.

❹ EXPANDING DROPLET
The force of the air pushing under the droplet continues to stretch it, increasing the size of the cavity too.

HOW RAIN WORKS 189

MEASURING RAIN
Rain is measured in millimeters or inches using a rain gauge. The simplest gauges are a measuring tube with a funnel or a wider opening at the top. The gauges show you how much rain falls on an area of land over a certain period of time.

CLOUDBURSTS
Occasionally, storm clouds dump a week's or a month's worth of rain in a matter of minutes. This is called a cloudburst and can cause flash floods. Cloudbursts often occur when thunderclouds pass over mountains. They are especially common in the Himalayas during the monsoon season.

DRY STORMS
Sometimes rain falls from a cloud but it doesn't reach the ground. It hits warm or dry air and evaporates. These dry storms can be seen in the distance as streaks descending from the base of a cloud.

◀ **THE LIFE OF A RAINDROP**
A raindrop begins to form when water vapor in the air condenses around a dust particle. Small and spherical at first, the droplets collide and grow into larger drops. When these become heavy enough to start falling, they begin to change shape, but they never form a teardrop shape. If a raindrop grows larger than 0.2 in (4–5 mm) wide, it splits into spherical drops again.

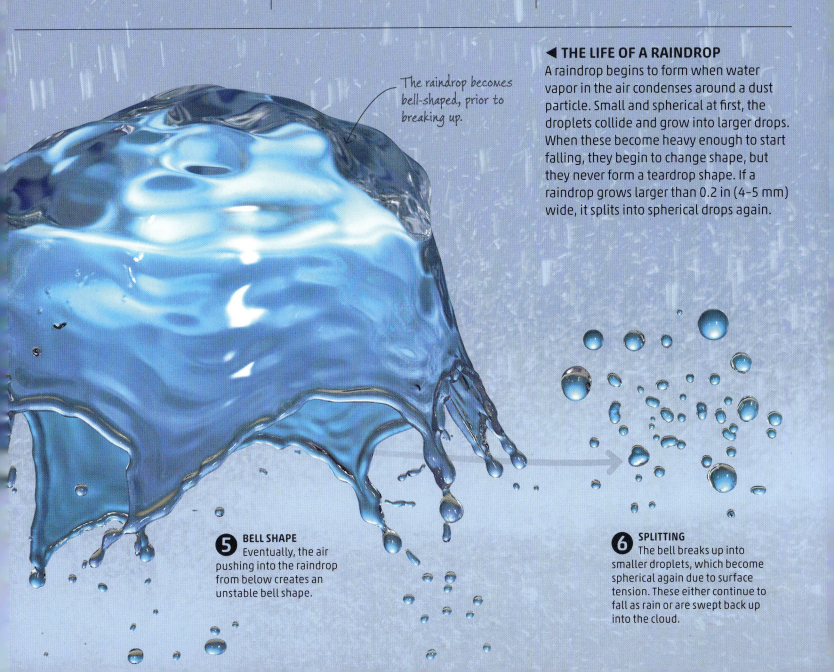

The raindrop becomes bell-shaped, prior to breaking up.

5 BELL SHAPE
Eventually, the air pushing into the raindrop from below creates an unstable bell shape.

6 SPLITTING
The bell breaks up into smaller droplets, which become spherical again due to surface tension. These either continue to fall as rain or are swept back up into the cloud.

THE ATMOSPHERE

▶ **SPLITTING COLORS**
Sunlight is white to our eyes, but in reality it's a mixture of all the colors of the rainbow: red, orange, yellow, green, blue, indigo, and violet. When sunlight passes in and out of raindrops, these colors bend by different amounts and separate to form a rainbow.

① LIGHT ENTERS RAINDROP
When sunlight enters a raindrop, it bends (refracts). The different colors that make up white light bend by varying amounts. Blue bends the most and red the least, with other colors in between.

SUNLIGHT

HOW RAINBOWS WORK

They appear out of nowhere and vanish just as quickly. Rainbows are the most colorful of all weather phenomena and happen when rain is falling but the Sun is shining. But you can only see one if you are standing in the right place at the right time.

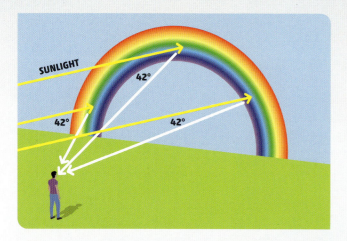

WHY ARCHES FORM
To see a rainbow, you must be standing with the Sun behind you and rain in front of you. The Sun also has to be fairly low in the sky. This is because bright colors are only visible when the angle between light rays hitting raindrops and rays bouncing back to you is around 42°. Raindrops in just the right place to reflect light at this angle form a circular arc. The bottom of the arc is blocked by the ground, so we normally see an arch shape.

③ LIGHT LEAVES RAINDROP
Light is refracted a second time as it leaves the raindrop. This makes the colors spread out even further.

The colors spread out and separate.

REFRACTION

HOW RAINBOWS WORK   191

② REFLECTION
When light hits the back of a raindrop, some of it is reflected back toward our eyes. All the different colors are reflected.

REFLECTION

Raindrops act like tiny lenses, splitting light into colors.

ANGLE OF REFLECTION
Raindrops scatter and reflect light in all directions, but the strongest colors are seen where sunlight bounces back at an angle of 40–42°. Blue is seen at 40° and red at 42°.

SEEING DOUBLE
Look carefully and you might spot a weaker second rainbow above the main one. This happens because some of the light is reflected twice inside raindrops and bounces back to observers at an angle of 50–53°. The second reflection reverses the order of the colors.

FULL CIRCLE
Most rainbows are cut off by the horizon, but if you see one from very high up—such as from inside a plane—you might be lucky enough to see a full circle.

HOW MIST, FOG, AND DEW WORK

If you think clouds are something only birds and planes encounter at close range, you may be surprised to learn that you can walk through them. Mist and fog are simply clouds that have formed at ground level.

Because it contains lots of water droplets, fog is difficult to see through and feels damp.

Dubai's frequent winter fogs are caused by moist sea air flowing inland, where the ground is cold.

▲ SHROUDED IN FOG
The city of Dubai, in the United Arab Emirates, lies swathed in fog on a winter morning. Like their sky-high cousins, ground-level clouds are made of tiny droplets of liquid water suspended in air. It is called fog if you can see less than 0.62 miles (1 km) in front of you. Mist is thinner than fog, so you can see further. Mist and fog clear as the day warms up and the droplets turn back into vapor.

HOW FOG FORMS
Fog can form in lots of different ways, but all involve air cooling down and water vapor condensing into droplets.

Heat radiates from surface

Moisture condenses into fog

Radiation fog
On cold, clear nights, the land radiates (emits) heat it absorbed during the day. As the ground loses heat and cools down, it cools the air above. Water vapor in the air cools and condenses, causing radiation fog.

HOW MIST, FOG, AND DEW WORK

DEW
As objects cool at night, they may cool the air around them enough for airborne water vapor to condense as tiny beads of liquid—dew. A similar thing happens when you take a cold drink from the fridge on a hot day and water forms on the can.

LIFE-SUSTAINING FOG
Redwood trees growing in California rely on fog rolling in from the sea for their survival. The trees—the world's tallest, often exceeding 300 ft (90 m) in height—need huge amounts of water. In the dry summers, their leaves trap droplets of fog and absorb the water.

GHOSTLY ILLUSION
A Brocken specter is a ghostly figure (a specter) that appears in fog or mist. The "ghost" is really just the shadow of the person observing it while standing on a hill and looking into the mist, with the Sun behind them. A rainbow halo may also form around the specter.

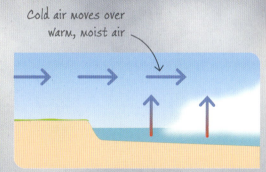

Advection fog
As warm, moist air moves across cold land or water, the air cools and fog forms. This type of fog is called advection fog and is common at sea and along coasts. It also occurs when a warm front passes over snow-covered land.

Valley fog
This type of fog occurs when cold air sinks to the bottom of a valley and gets trapped. Unlike other forms of fog, which often disappear quickly, valley fog may linger for days before clearing.

Evaporation fog
Warm water evaporating from a lake, pond, or moist land warms the air above and causes it to rise. As the warm, moist air mixes with cold air passing overhead, it cools and fog forms.

HOW HAILSTONES FORM

Hailstones are icy pellets that form in towering thunderclouds. Usually the water in thunderclouds falls as rain, but under certain atmospheric conditions it turns to ice and becomes hailstones.

The final coating of ice may be bumpy or spiky as smaller wet hailstones collide with and stick to the large hailstone.

INSIDE A STORM CLOUD
Hailstones form when water in a thundercloud becomes supercooled. This means the water gets down to below freezing point, but instead of turning to ice it stays liquid. Droplets of the supercooled water are swept to the top of the cloud by powerful updraughts and freeze. As they fall back down through the cloud they are coated with more supercooled water, which freezes instantly. After several rise-and-fall cycles, the ice pellets become too heavy to stay airborne and fall.

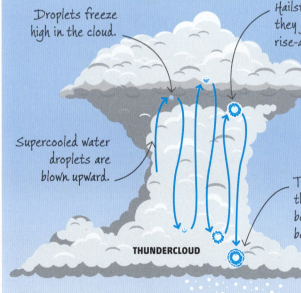

Droplets freeze high in the cloud.

Hailstones grow as they go through rise-and-fall cycles.

Supercooled water droplets are blown upward.

The hailstone falls to the ground when it becomes too heavy to be blown back up.

THUNDERCLOUD

HOW HAILSTORMS FORM

Rings of ice form as a hailstone grows.

Air bubbles get trapped in hailstones if the water freezes very quickly.

◀ HAILSTONE LAYERS
Most hailstones are less than 0.25 in (5 mm) across when they fall, but on rare occasions they can become very large. This happens when they go through many cycles of rising and falling through the cloud. Cutting through a hailstone reveals a number of layers, showing how many times it has completed a rise-and-fall cycle.

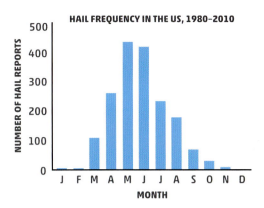

HAILSTORM SEASON
Unlike snow, hail is most common in late spring and early summer. This is when thunderstorms are common but the air temperature isn't high enough to melt the hailstones as they fall. Hailstorms can happen at any time of year in tropical countries, but they tend to occur on mountains where the air is cooler.

GIANT HAILSTONES
Hailstones greater than 4 in (10 cm) across are classed as "giant." The largest on record fell in North Dakota. It measured 8 in (20 cm) in diameter and weighed 1.9 lbs (0.88 kg).

STORM DAMAGE
Large hailstones can hit the ground at 100 mph (160 kph), smashing holes in cars and houses, flattening crops, and injuring animals and people out in the open. Some hailstorms cause billions of dollars' worth of damage.

HOW SNOWFLAKES FORM

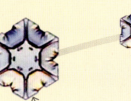

❶ NEW SNOWFLAKE
A snowflake begins as a tiny speck of dust in a cloud. Water vapor from the freezing air solidifies on the speck and begins to grow into crystals.

All ice crystals are six-sided because water molecules arrange themselves in hexagonal patterns as they freeze.

❷ GROWING LARGER
Ice builds up and the snowflake grows larger. It spins as it tumbles about inside the cloud, which keeps its shape symmetrical.

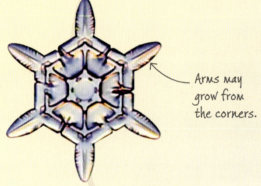

Arms may grow from the corners.

Viewed through a microscope, snowflakes reveal their amazing structure. Snowflakes are simply ice crystals, but no two are exactly alike. That's because ice crystals grow in different shapes as temperature and humidity change, and no two snowflakes experience exactly the same conditions as they tumble through a cloud. When snow finally lands it usually consists of many flakes stuck together, often half melted. However, individual snowflakes as wide as 2 in (5 cm) occasionally float to the ground intact.

❸ CHANGING CRYSTALS
Crystals continue to grow around the edge of the snowflake. As the temperature and humidity in the cloud change, the crystals take new shapes, such as arms, plates, or needles. All are based on an underlying hexagonal symmetry.

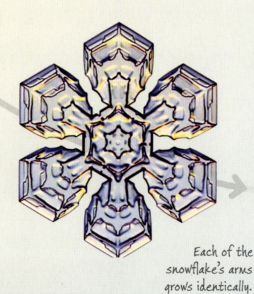
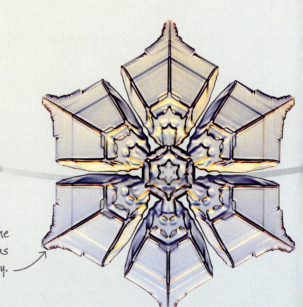

Each of the snowflake's arms grows identically.

HOW SNOWFLAKES FORM 197

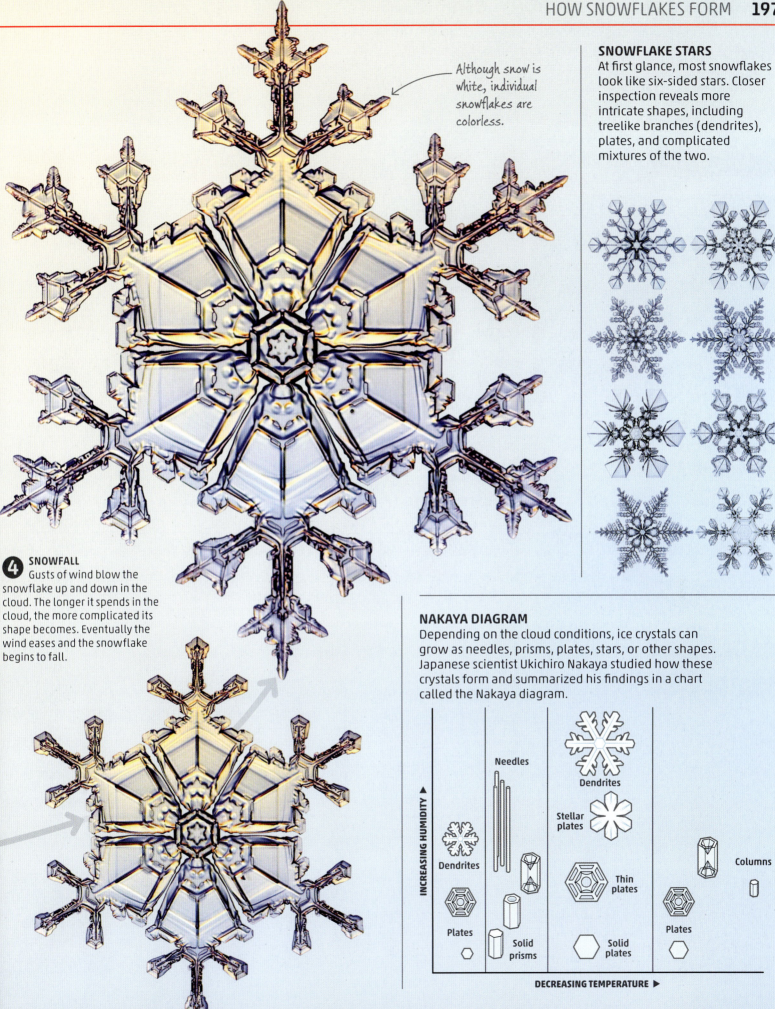

Although snow is white, individual snowflakes are colorless.

④ SNOWFALL
Gusts of wind blow the snowflake up and down in the cloud. The longer it spends in the cloud, the more complicated its shape becomes. Eventually the wind eases and the snowflake begins to fall.

SNOWFLAKE STARS
At first glance, most snowflakes look like six-sided stars. Closer inspection reveals more intricate shapes, including treelike branches (dendrites), plates, and complicated mixtures of the two.

NAKAYA DIAGRAM
Depending on the cloud conditions, ice crystals can grow as needles, prisms, plates, stars, or other shapes. Japanese scientist Ukichiro Nakaya studied how these crystals form and summarized his findings in a chart called the Nakaya diagram.

198 THE ATMOSPHERE

TYPES OF FROST
Frost can take many different forms, from needles and feathers to a smooth layer of glassy ice.

HOAR FROST
The name of this crystalline form of frost comes from the old English word for gray. It has a feathery or sugary appearance and forms from water vapor in the air.

WINDOW FROST
Sometimes frost forms on window panes when the temperature on the outside is below freezing and there is moist, warm air on the inside. Scratches or specks of dirt act as sites for crystals to form. They grow into branching shapes like fern leaves.

GLAZE FROST
Glaze is a transparent covering of ice formed by freezing rain hitting a surface. It's known as black ice on roads as it makes the road look wet rather than icy, which can be dangerous for motorists.

AVIATION HAZARD
Rime ice is a particular hazard to planes. It adds weight, especially to the wings, and increases drag—the force of the air rubbing against the plane's surface and slowing it down. If ailerons (movable parts of the wings) ice up, it can be difficult to control the plane.

HOW FROST WORKS

Frost is a covering of ice crystals on the ground or other surfaces. It appears on clear, cold nights when the ground temperature falls below freezing. Most frost forms when water vapor in the air touches a freezing surface and turns straight into ice crystals without condensing into water first. Other kinds of frost form when dew drops freeze or when fog or mist droplets hit a freezing surface.

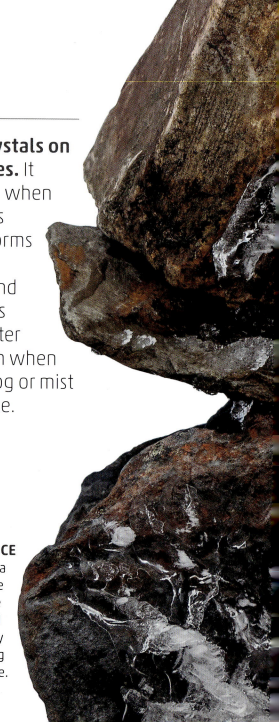

▶ RIME ICE
On windy hills and mountains, a kind of frost called rime ice sometimes appears on the windward side of rocks and trees. Rime ice forms when very cold fog droplets hit a freezing surface and turn instantly to ice.

HOW FROST WORKS   199

DIRECTION OF WIND

FROST POCKETS
Cold air is heavier than warm air, which means it flows downhill and collects in valleys or hollows. This can create frost pockets—low-lying places that become covered in frost while the higher surroundings remain frost-free.

Rime ice builds up on the side of the rock facing the wind.

FROST NEEDLES
Hoar frost is made of crystals that vary in shape, depending on the temperature and humidity. At around 23°F (-5°C), they grow into long needles.

Water vapor turns directly into ice when it touches the cold surface.

Rime ice often looks white and grainy.

Feathery shapes can form as rime ice builds up.

Needle-shaped ice crystals

UNUSUAL TYPES OF LIGHTNING
Some forms of lightning are seldom seen because they happen at very high altitude or are very faint, short-lived, or rare.

SPIDER LIGHTNING
These long, horizontal, spiderlike flashes on the undersides of clouds can cover vast distances as they spread from one cloud to another.

BALL LIGHTNING
In this rare form of lightning, balls of light hover over the ground for about half a minute before disappearing quietly or exploding violently.

SPRITES
Red sprites are weak discharges of electricity over active thunderclouds. Very faint and brief, they may rise 60 miles (100 km) above the cloud top.

VOLCANIC LIGHTNING
Ash particles spewed out by a volcano collide and create static electricity, which generates small bolts of lightning.

HOW LIGHTNING WORKS

Lightning bolts are among nature's most spectacular sights. These sudden, awe-inspiring flashes of light streak from ground to sky, disappearing in a fraction of a second. A bolt of lightning is actually a giant spark of electricity in the atmosphere, usually produced by a thunderstorm.

▶ **LIGHTNING STRIKE**
Powerful charges of static electricity build up in a thundercloud. Eventually, this electricity is discharged as lightning, typically within the cloud or between the cloud and the ground. As lightning surges through the air, it can heat the air around it to more than 54,000°F (30,000°C), causing the air particles to glow and create an instant flash of bright light. The hot air expands so rapidly that it sends out a rumbling shock wave, which we hear as thunder. Lightning often strikes high points, such as tall buildings or—as shown here—trees.

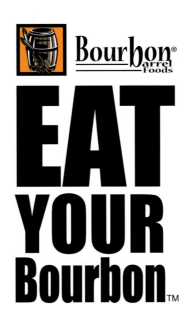

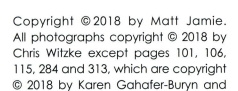

Copyright © 2018 by Matt Jamie. All photographs copyright © 2018 by Chris Witzke except pages 101, 106, 115, 284 and 313, which are copyright © 2018 by Karen Gahafer-Buryn and © 2018 by John Nation page 174.

All rights reserved. No part of this publication may be reproduced, distributed, or transmitted in any form or by any means, including photocopying, recording, or other electronic or mechanical methods, without the prior written permission of the publisher.

Published by Culinary Publishing, Louisville, Kentucky

Printed in the United States of America

Library of Congress Number: 2018910081

Contributions, Food and Prop Styling by Susan Nguyen

Design & Illustrations by Karen Gahafer-Buryn

Photography by Chris Witzke

Interviews & Writing by Josh Moss

ISBN 978-1-889937-32-8

bourbonbarrelfoods.com

CONTENT

The Story	7
Foreword (by Edward Lee)	33

Breakfast & Brunch	**41**
Apps & Snacks	**73**
Soups & Salads	**123**
Dinner & Main Dishes	**161**
Sides	**221**
Baked Goods & Sweets	**249**
Drinks	**289**
Pantry Staples	**319**

Acknowledgments	339
Product Information	342
Index	345

THE STORY

Ten years ago I was in my basement in Louisville, Kentucky, staring at the first batch of soy sauce I'd ever made. It looked nothing like soy sauce. Just a mess of beans and wheat in a five-gallon plastic pail. I was almost scared of it. Nothing I had read online prepared me for this moment. I had no clue how to get the soy sauce out, so I just kept looking at the mash in the bucket. Finally, I shoved a sieve down in there. The soy sauce rushed in over the sides, and I was like, "Wow! I fucking made soy sauce!" I tried it. Pure, unpasteurized, raw soy sauce. It tasted like I had struck gold.

My background involves a lot of quitting. I dropped out of college in Illinois during my senior year. After finishing my undergrad in Louisville and moving to Gainesville, Florida, I lasted a year in an exercise physiology Masters program before I quit. One time, through a temp agency, I got a job in a tissue bank's receiving area. These were organ and tissue donors, so I was pulling legs out of coolers. I'd have jobs for two years and leave or get fired — most of the time fired.

Then I got a job at Mildred's Big City Food, one of the best restaurants in Gainesville, and realized I had a passion for cooking, a natural ability with food and flavor. I'd waited tables before — at everything from Mexican restaurants to Jack Fry's, a Louisville fine-dining institution — but the chef at Mildred's, who had worked in five-star restaurants, gave me classical French training. He encouraged me to take a class at the Culinary Institute of America in Napa Valley with the Certified Master Chef who wrote the garde manger chapter in the CIA's cookbook. I learned how to make foie gras and sweetbreads. In the kitchen, I couldn't get enough of that rush in the middle of the night when you've got nothing but tickets in front of you. I was in my early 30s and had finally found something I loved. But I knew I wasn't going to be at Mildred's much longer because my wife at the time was pregnant with our son, and the plan was for me to stay at home while she finished a medical fellowship.

On Wednesday nights my friend Tom Wurzbach and I would always go to this oyster bar called Calico Jack's near the University of Florida. Total dive. Bikini contests, wet T-shirt contests. They had a cement counter and trough, college kids just popping dozens of oysters at a time. It was down to a science: If I ordered two dozen, they knew I wasn't going to eat all of them at once, so they'd pop me six, move down the line. One night in 2003, Tom and I were drinking longneck Budweisers there, and he asked me, "So what do you think you're gonna do?"

I said, "I think I might brew soy sauce."

I'm not a deep-thinker. I'm really not. I had seen an article in *Food & Wine* about Maytag Blue Cheese, with pictures that almost romanticized it. I wanted to do something interesting like that. The whole "craft" movement was taking off: olive oil, balsamic vinegar, hot sauce. For some reason I got stuck on soy sauce. I told Tom I didn't want to do something that had already been done, that I didn't think anybody was micro-brewing soy sauce in the U.S. A month went by and Tom said, "You know, I've been thinking about that idea. You should really look into it."

I was like, "What are you talking about?"

"The soy sauce idea. I think it's gold."

I became a stay-at-home dad, and when Max would sleep, I would research how to make soy sauce. My daughter Madeline was born in 2005 and after we moved back to Louisville, all I did with any free time I had was work on this business idea.

I downloaded a business plan on the Internet. My dad, who helped with the spreadsheets, actually carries it in his briefcase to this day. He says, "It's an important document!" I'm like, "You're such a nerd." Not only had I never started a business, but I didn't know anything at all about making soy sauce or food manufacturing in general. I knew how to cook on a line in a kitchen. So I asked myself every question I could think of: "OK, I need to buy a kettle. What size? How do I get the beans out of there? How big are the bottles gonna be?" Anybody I thought could help me, I'd call them out of the blue. I reached out to an entrepreneurship program at the University of Louisville; Heine Brothers' Coffee in Louisville to see if I could retrofit a coffee roaster for wheat; a dude in Texas who had retrofitted a peanut roaster for sesame seeds to make tahini; a local venture club. Of course I met people who would say, "This will never work." Plenty of 'em. But I had a blind passion. Nobody was going to tell me I couldn't do it. I used to buy myself a new tie every time I gave a presentation. I don't wear ties anymore.

In the beginning, I didn't even know that dozens of different soybean varieties existed. I thought there was, you know, a soybean, and that's what you used. Well, there's food-grade, feed-grade, seed-grade and different varieties of each of those. The soybean expert with the University of Kentucky's Department of Agricultural Economics told me I needed food-grade, which led me to a guy named Chris Kummer in Marion County, about 45 miles from Louisville. He's not some hippie out in the country. It's a large operation that grows non-GMO soybeans for the Japanese soy sauce and miso markets. He'd just ship his soybeans to Japan and never see the end product. I called him and he was like, "Cool idea."

Mind you, I hadn't made anything yet. It was just an idea. My wife said, "You don't even know if you can make it." I told her I knew I could. "Well then, just do it," she said.

I made that first batch with a pound of soybeans, a pound of wheat and like two gallons of water. I roasted the wheat, shaking it back and forth in a cast-iron skillet and scratching our glass-top stove. I boiled the soybeans, which are pretty sour-smelling. The whole house reeked. Only two strains of yeast will make soy sauce. I ended up having some shipped from a place in Fort Bragg, California. I poured the mash, called "koji," into that five-gallon bucket I got from a beer-supply store. It fermented for six months. I still have that first batch hidden away in the warehouse.

Early on, I started to notice parallels between the distilling and aging of bourbon and the brewing and aging of soy sauce. Not only in process but in history and heritage. The fermentation process is thousands of years old and originated in China, but hundreds of years ago a monk took this knowledge from China to Japan. The Japanese are known for perfecting everything. A monk built a temple in Wakayama and started making soy sauce. Soy sauce is hundreds of years old in Japan; bourbon is the only spirit native to America. The clouds fucking parted, like: I'm supposed to do this. You could do this anywhere in the U.S., but it makes the most sense here in Kentucky. In Japan, many soy sauce breweries are located near or on limestone-filtered natural springs. Distilleries have done the same thing in Kentucky Bourbon Country. At Bourbon Barrel Foods we get our limestone-filtered water from a spring in Bardstown, Kentucky, the same one that bourbon distillers use. We buy our wheat from the guy who also grows it for Maker's Mark. Not all bourbons are wheated, but those that are use a soft red winter variety, which is what they grow for us.

I had started the habit of Googling soy sauce every day and had read almost everything I possibly could about it. But I came across an article by Mark Bittman in *Condé Nast Traveler* about "Japan's liquid gold." He worked at the *New York Times*, so I called the paper and asked the receptionist if I could speak to him. "Sure, one minute." He picked up the phone, and I said, "Mr. Bittman, you don't know me, but—" He replied, "Call me Mark." He shared all of his notes and photos and was adamant that I needed to age the soy sauce in bourbon barrels. "It completes your story," he said. And he was right. Not to mention that I had been considering spending $4,000 on a 1,500-gallon fermentation tank from the company that makes them for Woodford Reserve. One of bourbon's rules is that the charred, white oak barrels can be used only once. Barrels were free when I started. Now they cost about $200 apiece, but we'll reuse them until the salt starts to oxidize the iron hoops.

I went from my basement straight to six 50-plus-gallon bourbon barrels in a 1,000-square foot section of warehouse in the Butchertown neighborhood, named for its history of butchers and stockyards. That was the next step, going from five gallons to 300. What the hell could go wrong?

One batch is 63 pounds of beans, 63 pounds of wheat. If you imagine the size of a wheat berry, we'll crack those into eight to ten pieces to make a coarse flour. We essentially pan-roast the wheat in a tilt skillet, and boil the soybeans in a kettle for four to five hours to make them soft enough for the yeast to penetrate. The 60-gallon kettles we use were both made in Louisville in the '70s. I bought one out of a prison, the other out of a school in Indiana. They're freaking workhorses. The guys who service them love it because they don't make 'em like this anymore.

After the beans cool, we mix them with the wheat in large bins and introduce yeast. That koji goes into cedar boxes my dad made. The koji increases in temperature as the yeast starts to grab hold of the soybeans and wheat, and takes on the green color of the yeast. It looks like pistachios that have been snowed on. After three days, the koji goes from the boxes into barrels containing limestone-filtered water and sea salt. The Japanese call this brine "moromi." With bourbon, it's "the mash." In my warehouse down the street I have more than 200 barrels aging right now, each one for a year. All of them stirred by hand, every day for the first six weeks, then once or twice a week. In the summertime, when it was 100 degrees, I think I made a couple of high school kids cry.

We buy our wheat from the guy who also grows it for Maker's Mark. Not all bourbons are wheated, but those that are will use a soft red winter variety, which is what they grow for us.

We get our limestone-filtered water from a spring in Bardstown, Kentucky, the same one that bourbon distillers use.

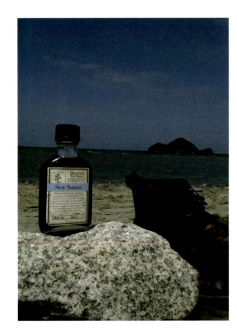

ON A JOURNEY

We develop flavor by keeping everything moving around; a sharp palate will taste the flavor notes from the barrel. The soy sauce is probably done at six months, but premium soy sauce in Japan is aged between 12 to 18 months. A lot of soy sauce makers over there say, "It's done when it's done." My friend Edward Lee, a Louisville chef, brought back a bottle of soy sauce that had aged seven years. It was so in-your-face that we didn't know what to do with it.

My dad made the original press, which we named after him: Ken was a tub of laminated particleboard with holes drilled in it so the soy sauce could get out. He plumbed it to a bucket. Well, I say "plumbed," but it was a freaking plastic hose. Our "press boards" were oak planks over the muslin cloth that held the mash. I was probably the only guy in town who had the Jo-Ann Fabric app on his phone. We'd go in there and buy bolts of muslin for half-off. To press the mash, you just cranked down on the bottle jack. The more liquid in there, the more likely that it would explode all over you. It clogged up so fast the first time I tried it that soy sauce sprayed my face. I had to go to the eye doctor and tell him something salty got in my eye. I said, "No, really, it was soy sauce." It would take us seven days to press a barrel, to get 24 gallons of soy sauce, and as we got busier and busier I'd have to come in at night just to put pressure down on the bottle jack. I found the next press, Big Ken, at an industrial graveyard. It was a perfectly square stainless-steel tub with a slight pitch to it so liquid could make it to the drain and out the spigot. We could press a barrel in three or four days. Now, our custom-built press, Ken 2.0, is made of iron I-beams and pharmaceutical-grade stainless steel. It's a freaking tank. Probably a little overkill, but we had never built one before. It can do an entire barrel in a day and a half.

I saw bourbons named after creeks or a family name, but that was almost too specific for what I was doing. One day I was driving to Bardstown and I called my dad and said I had the perfect name: Bluegrass Soy Sauce. I don't think anybody would have been surprised if somebody from Napa Valley came out with a soy sauce. But the fact that some blond-haired dude in Kentucky developed a soy sauce aged in used bourbon barrels was a head-scratcher.

You'll never see the words Bourbon Barrel Foods in my original business plan. But as a sort of stopgap, I needed to figure out how to make money while my soy sauce aged. One day I was walking down the aisle at Whole Foods and noticed a Chardonnay-smoked fleur de sel. I was like, "I'm in Kentucky. We need to do a bourbon-smoked sea salt." I bought a box of kosher salt and turned my Weber grill into a smoker by burning some barrel staves. Then I started thinking of other bourbon-smoked products: paprika, pepper, chili powder, sugar, sesame seeds, garlic salt. I outsourced that first batch of smoked salt to fill a $10,000 order for a local law firm. I remember that Christmas driving to my parents' house to pack 500 tins of salt. We did all the filling, labeling, packaging, gift-wrapping, boxing and shipping labels by hand. I honestly don't know what I would have done without my mom and dad. Soon after, I bought an industrial smoker from Southern Pride BBQ Pits & Smokers in Alamo, Tennessee, then a second one. Each smoker can hold 1,400 pounds of pork butt. I could have a hell of a barbecue operation if my business goes under.

The bourbon industry was spiking in the mid-2000s, but I don't think anybody thought it would last as long as it has. In 2007, when I went to file the articles for incorporation for Bourbon Barrel Foods in the Secretary of State's office in Frankfort, Kentucky, they were like, "I can't believe this name's available." Now we have 50 products, including a barrel-aged Worcestershire, a teriyaki named Kentuckyaki and the Southern sweetener called sorghum, which we get from a farmer named Danny Ray Townsend in Montgomery County in eastern Kentucky. We went from buying 100 gallons of sorghum a year to — well, now he grows more than 100 acres for us. Two years in, he said, "I don't know what you're doing, but I like it."

I'll never forget that first story about us in the *New York Times*, in the Wednesday food section in 2008. My publicist at the time voiced concern, saying, "I don't know if you're ready for this." That day I was going through the drive-thru at Taco Bell and my phone started blowing up with Internet orders. Suddenly, I was digging boxes out of a dumpster to ship stuff to people.

Chefs started calling. At Husk in Charleston, South Carolina, chef Sean Brock doesn't let anything into the kitchen that wasn't made in the South. He said, "The fact that you make soy sauce in Kentucky is awesome." Since then we've been on the TV shows *How It's Made*, *FoodCrafters*, *The Today Show* with Matt Lauer and *Bizarre Foods America* with Andrew Zimmern.

In the beginning it would take me a day to cook the beans, mix in the wheat and yeast, put them in the koji room. Then I'd start the next batch in the morning. I was constantly making soy sauce. I smelled of roasted wheat when I picked up the kids from school. That first year, I was buying a couple thousand pounds of wheat and soybeans. Ten years later? More than 20,000 pounds of each. Now I have 25 employees and a 30,000-square-foot facility, plus a barrel warehouse and retail store. We did everything by hand until about three years ago. Now a six-headed bottle filler churns out more than 4,000 bottles a month. My dad, though, he unfurls an entire roll of labels and writes the batch and bottle number by hand.

I went to Japan for the first time in 2016. The producers of a show over there had reached out and said, "You have no idea how long we've been looking for you." I said, "Really? If you Google 'white guy making soy sauce' I'm pretty easy to find." The show had no subtitles, other than English-to-Japanese, so I don't know what the hell they're saying about me. But during filming I met a soy sauce maker, Toshio Shinko, and he says it's all good things.

On YouTube, Toshio saw how the drill I was using to stir the mash was actually a cement mixer. "Too violent," he said. Now we use what looks like a stainless-steel oar. Toshio stirs his soy sauce in 7,500-gallon cypress tubs with bamboo tools. They bow and pray before mixing the moromi. Very ritualistic, almost like being in a monastery. It's not quite like that here, but we take it very seriously. When Toshio saw the muslin we were using as press cloth, saw how much soy sauce it was soaking up, he got us some cloth specific to the soy sauce industry, cut to the size of our press. "Parachute cloth," was the best English he could muster. The newly purchased cloth cut our press time in half. We do two barrels a day with it. It cost $400 for 20 pieces and should last ten years, versus $15,000 for a second press.

When I told Toshio we threw out the water used for boiling the beans, through a translator he said, "No. That's flavor. Save it and make your brine with it." While filming in Japan, I was texting my office in Louisville: "Change the way you're doing shit right now." We're getting ready to harvest the first soy sauce since we changed our methods. I can't wait to taste it.

One of the things Toshio told me was that our limestone-filtered water is too hard, but I mentioned how the spring it comes from is part of our story. "I get that," he said. "The most important part is that it's your story. If you had come here to study, you'd be making something we already know." He visited Louisville and held my koji in the warehouse. He said, "Japanese soy sauce producers would be proud."

I've been doing this for only ten years but my struggle is the same as Toshio's: soy sauce awareness outside Japan. Nobody really knows there's something other than Kikkoman, which is the Budweiser of soy sauce. Kikkoman has a 96 or 97 percent market share of an almost $6 billion-a-year industry. Even a percent of one percent isn't a bad living. Outside Japan, I'm the only person micro-brewing soy sauce, although people from all over — Argentina, Sweden, the Netherlands — have started to reach out for advice.

You know how bourbon has moved out of Kentucky and the South and become a global product? I don't want it to sound all kumbaya, but Toshio and I are trying to educate the world about soy sauce. I want to be able to say I'm big in Japan.

In Wakayama, Toshio and I hiked to the Kokokuji Temple, which was built by the monk who brought fermentation, and soy sauce, to Japan over 750 years ago. A monk in his 30s just looked at me like, "What the hell's this guy doing here?" We walked down what's called Soy Sauce Avenue, where you can see and smell all the soy sauce breweries. Somebody else might be like, "What the hell is that smell?" But it's familiar to me. Toshio even took me to a soy sauce museum. I left a bottle of Bluegrass Soy Sauce on a shelf inside.

I hope you'll find that the recipes in this book show the broad use of the products we make.

Yes, there's a lot of the South in here. But I don't want this book to be pigeonholed as Southern, which is why we've included recipes from Japanese chefs, Korean chefs, Mexican chefs. No matter what you decide to make, here are six of my kitchen rules:

1. My favorite tool is a spatula. Have a drawer full of them. You've put the effort into making a dressing or a dish or a dessert, so getting every last bit out of the bowl is important. Unless you're trying to save some to lick out of the bottom.

2. Own a cast-iron skillet.

3. And a lot of bowls.

4. I have fresh herbs growing on my counter: cilantro, flat-leaf parsley, basil. I have a rosemary plant that I'm trying to shape like a Bonsai tree. I clipped it all the way back, and it's just starting to grow. I guess I'll just have to be patient.

5. I keep a basket full of towels on a shelf in my kitchen, and I go through them like they're paper towels.

6. Have at least one knife you're comfortable with and can do everything with. I have a French knife, which tends to be lighter than, say, a German knife but doesn't hold an edge as well, so I have to sharpen it often. In Japan I was gifted a sushi knife with my name engraved in kanji. I have it out because it's cool, but I don't use it a lot.

TOWNSEND SORGHUM MILL

TALK TO ME AND YOU'LL SURMISE I'M SOMEWHAT OF A REDNECK

My dad made the original press, which we named after him: Ken was a tub of laminated particleboard with holes drilled in it so the soy sauce could get out. He plumbed it to a bucket. Well, I say "plumbed," but it was a freaking plastic hose.

BATCH	BOTTLE NUMBER
217-15	186

Matt's Dad, Ken

EAT
YOUR
Bourbon

"Oysters and beer. A symbiotic relationship."
– Daniel Christie

FOREWORD
By Chef Edward Lee

I had been in Louisville for a short time when I heard about a guy making soy sauce in the Butchertown neighborhood. I was curious to say the least. As a newcomer to the Bluegrass State, I was discovering a new culinary language of sorghum and country ham and bourbon. Soy sauce was the last thing I would have expected to find. But I secretly craved something to link this Kentucky world back to the Asian foods I love to cook and eat. Soy sauce was that rare ingredient, at once the ubiquitous condiment of Asia but also an everyday pantry item for indoctrinated American chefs. But I had never heard of anyone brewing small-batch soy sauce. Then I saw an article in the local paper about Matt Jamie, and I was astounded. A white guy? Making soy sauce? I may have even rolled my eyes.

Tradition is a controversial thing. It is part history and conservation, all the things that make me who I am both as a person and as a chef. Tradition is a necessary and worthy pursuit. But it can also limit us into a belief system that is stifling and outdated. I have always known that I was destined for something more than the traditional Korean food I grew up eating. As much as I embraced my childhood, I knew I would have to distance myself from it to find my own voice within the contemporary American landscape of food. I live by the all-things-are-possible mantra. That same guiding principle that allows me to reinterpret the traditional foods of the American South also gives credence to a Kentucky native brewing small-batch soy sauce in bourbon barrels. Even before I tasted it, Matt's soy sauce meant more to me than just another gourmet ingredient. It was a symbol, a metaphor of what is possible in America when limitless creativity replaces cultural inhibitions. I was scared to try his soy sauce. What if it was no good? It is rare that a story lives up to its hype. But life has a funny way of surprising you at just the right time.

Matt's soy sauce immediately identifies itself as something different. Less salty than commercial soy sauce, it has an umami flavor that is instantly recognizable, almost broth-like. You wouldn't want to rinse your mouth with commercial soy sauce, but this? The mouthfeel is dense and savory, a pleasant salinity that is deceptively mellow. It adds a haunting depth to dishes that is not easily identifiable, but once you get a feel for the soy sauce you definitely know it's there. It captures you in an addictive umami spell. Matt's soy sauce is the best soy sauce I have ever had.

The culinary world is in flux. Soy sauce is not purely an Asian ingredient anymore. No more than Parmesan occupies a space called Italian. As chefs look forward to a cuisine without strict borders, we open our minds to accepting different sources of flavor. Take sodium, for example. Occidental cuisines have historically added salinity to dishes in the form of sea salt. That has been the backbone of its cuisine from the very beginning. Only recently have chefs opened their world to the idea of combining salinity with umami in the form of soy sauce, miso or fish sauce — items that have been in the Asian lexicon for centuries. And if the soy sauce has been mellowed by the tannins and toast of bourbon barrels, well then, all the better. This soy sauce transcends the narrow categories that once defined ingredients that had an ethnic identity. This soy sauce is as American as apple pie.

The first time I met Matt was on a road trip to Virginia. Along the way, we stopped off in Winchester, Kentucky, to meet up with Danny Ray Townsend, who was making a prize-winning sorghum syrup that Matt wanted to bottle. He had this vision of bringing sorghum to the world. It was on this trip that I realized how nuts Matt is. Like most chefs, Matt is a dreamer, an innovator, a salesman and a scholar. It was on that trip that I found out he had once been a chef, that he had yet to travel to Asia, that he was, like myself, guided by a force that required us to throw a healthy amount of caution into the wind. Naturally, we got along just fine.

Over the years, I have watched him grow his company from a small room with his dad into a full-blown warehouse operation. From his sorghum to bourbon-smoked sugar to sassafras bitters, he has tackled every new ingredient with the same fearlessness and obsession for perfection that got him started a decade ago. Each new product line assures me of two things: It will taste delicious and there will be an element of surprise. Through his many television appearances and write-ups, in everything from the *New York Times* to *Esquire*, I've seen the gastronomic cognoscenti celebrate the gospel of his Bourbon Barrel Foods line. I have witnessed hoards of Japanese foodies confounded by how delicious his soy sauce is. And I have seen a barrelful of imitators — the best form of flattery. I am fortunate that he was in Louisville at the same time I was starting out. I like to say that I knew him before he was famous. I am also now happy to call him a friend.

His warehouse is not far from my restaurant, and sometimes I'll stop by on a whim. I like standing there in the heart of Butchertown, with the faint smell of dead swine mixing with the bourbon aroma billowing from Matt's smokers. As I get closer, I pick up the waft of hundreds of barrels of sweet soy sauce. The air is thick with the slow evaporation. It is dizzying and intoxicating. It is the smell of a pipe dream turned into a success story.

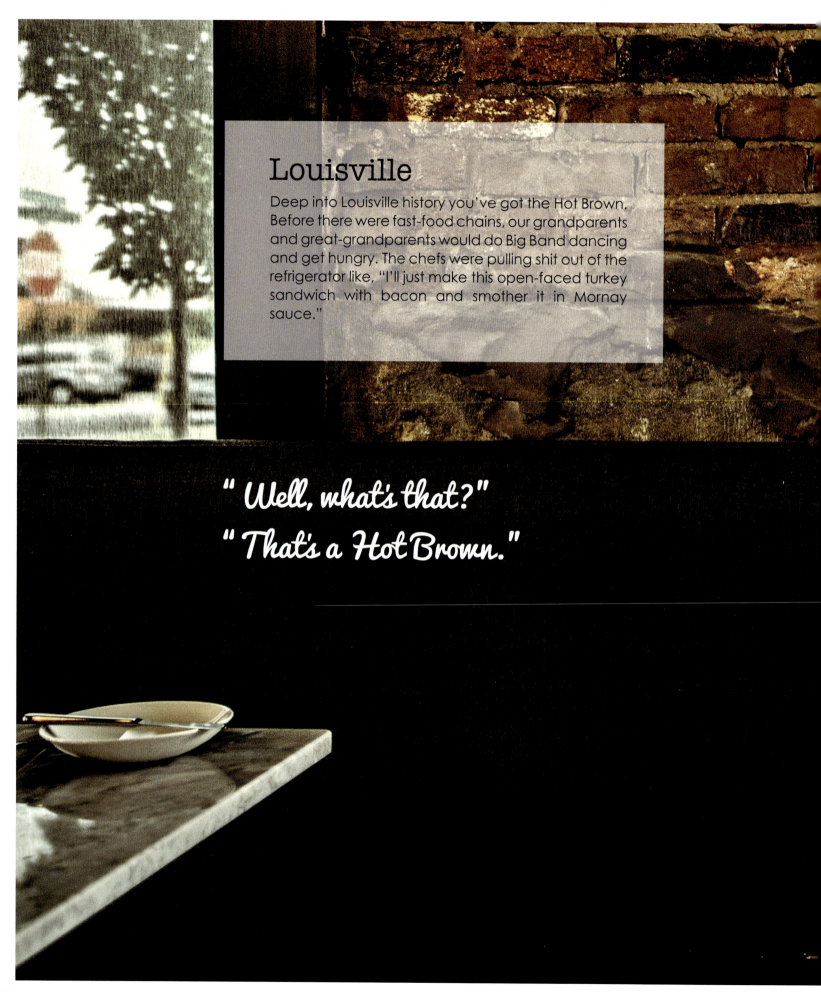

Louisville

Deep into Louisville history you've got the Hot Brown. Before there were fast-food chains, our grandparents and great-grandparents would do Big Band dancing and get hungry. The chefs were pulling shit out of the refrigerator like, "I'll just make this open-faced turkey sandwich with bacon and smother it in Mornay sauce."

"Well, what's that?"
"That's a Hot Brown."

BATCH 217-15 | BOTTLE NUMBER 186

BREAKFAST & BRUNCH

Who wouldn't want to be

surprised with French toast in the morning?

Madeline's Pancakes

There's nothing special about these other than my daughter Madeline and I like making them together. Our secret ingredient is no secret: my Bourbon-Madagascar Vanilla Extract. Honestly, Madeline likes the batter in the bowl more than the actual pancakes. These are cake-like. If we ever forget something, the recipe is always taped to the inside of a kitchen cabinet.

Makes 8 pancakes

¾ cup whole milk

2 tablespoons white vinegar

1 cup (125 grams) all-purpose flour

2 tablespoons Bourbon Vanilla Sugar

1 teaspoon baking powder

½ teaspoon baking soda

½ teaspoon salt

1 egg, slightly beaten

4 tablespoons butter, melted and divided

1 tablespoon Bourbon-Madagascar Vanilla Extract

Bourbon Barrel Aged Pure Cane Sorghum or maple syrup, for serving

1. Combine milk with vinegar and set aside for 5 minutes to "sour". Whisk together flour, vanilla sugar, baking powder, baking soda and salt in a large bowl. Add egg, 2 tablespoons of the melted butter, and vanilla into soured milk. Pour the wet ingredients into the dry ingredients and whisk just until large lumps are gone. Do not over mix or pancakes will be tough.

2. Heat a large skillet or griddle pan over medium high heat and brush lightly with melted butter. Pour ¼ cup of batter for each pancake and cook until bubbles appear on the surface and edges seem dry. Adjust heat as needed if the pan is too hot. Flip with a spatula and cook until browned on the other side. Repeat with remaining batter. Serve immediately with sorghum or maple syrup.

Variations:

Blueberry or Blackberry Lemon Poppy Seed Pancakes

Add: 2½ teaspoons of poppy seeds, 1 teaspoon of lemon juice, and the zest of 1 lemon to batter. After pouring pancakes onto skillet, dot each pancake with fresh or frozen blueberries or blackberries. Proceed as directed.

Brûléed Banana, Coconut Pancakes

Add: ½ cup coarsely mashed banana and ¼ cup sweetened coconut flakes to batter. Slice a large banana into slices and sprinkle with Bourbon Vanilla Sugar. Using a blowtorch, carefully brûlée the banana slices until sugar is caramelized. Garnish the finished pancakes with brûléed bananas and syrup.

In the kitchen...

The Joy of Cooking is my favorite cookbook. When Maddie and I used to make a recipe, we would write down the date. If we made it more than once, we'd date it again. Biscuits, chicken piccata, chocolate cake. Maddie, she's not afraid to get her hands dirty in the kitchen. She'll touch raw meat, chop stuff and then she'll make a point of saying, "We made everything for dinner tonight. Nothing was frozen." She's competitive, too. For Thanksgiving last year, we needed to wash and halve five pounds of Brussels sprouts and chop bacon. Maddie wanted to race her brother Max.

Max's Smoothies (3 ways)

It's not that my son Max isn't into cooking. He'd rather just eat. If I gave him a mango he wouldn't know what to do with it because he's only eaten it puréed. In the morning, all he wants is a smoothie. I'll buy a bunch of bananas and as they brown, I'll chop them up and freeze them in a bag. Same with strawberries and mangoes. These smoothies are a great way to get your kids to eat different fruits. I like to sneak healthy stuff in there.

Strawberry, Banana, Orange Smoothie

Makes 2 cups

1 cup fresh or frozen strawberries, hulled and quartered

½ fresh or frozen banana, sliced

½ cup orange juice

1-2 tablespoons Bourbon Smoked Sugar

1 tablespoon lime juice

½ cup ice cubes

Mango, Peach, Ginger Smoothie

Makes 2 cups

1 cup fresh or frozen mango, sliced

½ cup fresh or frozen peaches, sliced

½ cup plain Greek yogurt

1 tablespoon fresh ginger, coarsely chopped

1-2 tablespoons Bourbon Smoked Sugar

½ cup ice cubes

Chocolate, Raspberry, Oat Smoothie

Makes 3 cups

1 cup milk (or milk alternative, such as almond milk)

1 cup rolled oats

¾ cup fresh or frozen raspberries

1 tablespoon cocoa powder

1 tablespoon Bourbon Barrel Aged Pure Cane Sorghum

1-2 tablespoons Bourbon Smoked Sugar

½ teaspoon cinnamon (optional)

½ cup ice cubes

For all Smoothies

Combine all ingredients in a blender. If using frozen fruit, you will not need to use ice. Blend until completely smooth. Add more juice, milk, or water if smoothie is too thick. Pour into glasses and serve immediately.

In the kitchen...

I always thought shucking oysters would be the perfect job for Max in college. I want to have parties where he shucks oysters for everybody. "But Dad, my hands are all bloody."

Sorghum and Pomegranate Molasses Granola

Sorghum is one of the most popular chef ingredients of the last few years, especially in Kentucky, which is the leading producer of it. There's a lot of romance to it. You're taking something people were used to having generations ago and introducing it in a more modern way. The breakfast table sweetener of the South is becoming more of a gourmet condiment.

— Recipe by Chef Jenn Louis, executive chef/owner of Lincoln in Portland, Oregon

Makes about 6 cups

¼ teaspoon fennel seeds

¼ teaspoon coriander seeds

2½ cups rolled oats

1¾ cups coconut flakes

½ cup Spanish peanuts, with skin on

¼ cup Bourbon Smoked Sesame Seeds

¼ cup extra virgin olive oil

¼ cup Bourbon Barrel Aged Pure Cane Sorghum

2 tablespoons butter, melted

1 tablespoon light brown sugar

2 teaspoons Bourbon Smoked Sugar

2 teaspoons Bourbon Smoked Sea Salt

1 tablespoon pomegranate molasses

⅓ cup Bourbon Smoked Cacao Nibs

2 cups golden raisins

1 Preheat oven to 350 degrees. Place fennel and coriander seeds in a small frying pan over medium heat. Stirring constantly, toast until seeds are fragrant. When cool, grind seeds finely in a spice grinder. Set aside.

2 In a large bowl, combine rolled oats, coconut flakes, Spanish peanuts and smoked sesame seeds. In a small bowl, combine ground spices, olive oil, sorghum, melted butter, brown sugar, smoked sugar, smoked salt and pomegranate molasses. Whisk to combine. Pour over oat mixture and stir to combine. Spread in an even layer on a rimmed baking sheet. Bake for 25-30 minutes, stirring once or twice, until granola is golden and toasted.

3 Remove from oven and add cacao nibs and golden raisins. Stir to incorporate. Allow to cool completely before storing in an airtight container for up to two weeks.

"The products are so different than what I use in my region. We don't have sorghum up here, so that was a whole different world for me."

— Chef Jenn Louis

Shakshuka with Eggs and Spiced Bread

These are eggs cooked in a spicy, tomato-y sauce. You eat it with bread. Maybe I'm crazy, but I think it'd be perfect camping food.

Serves 4 (or 2 very hungry people)

For the Spiced Bread:

12 naan breads or pitas

1 tablespoon olive oil

½ teaspoon Bourbon Smoked Sesame Seeds

¼ teaspoon Bourbon Smoked Paprika

¼ teaspoon Bourbon Smoked Sea Salt

¼ teaspoon Bourbon Smoked Togarashi

For the Shakshuka:

1 small onion, diced

2 tablespoons olive oil

1 garlic clove, minced

1 teaspoon Bourbon Smoked Paprika

½ teaspoon Bourbon Smoked Chili Powder

1 (14.5-ounce) can diced tomatoes

¼ cup water

½ teaspoon Bourbon Smoked Sea Salt

¼ teaspoon Bourbon Smoked Pepper

4 eggs

¼ cup cilantro, roughly chopped

1. Preheat oven to 350 degrees. Brush breads on one side with vegetable oil. Sprinkle sesame seeds, smoked paprika, smoked salt and smoked togarashi on oiled bread. Place on baking sheet and set aside.

2. Heat a medium-sized skillet over high heat. Add olive oil and diced onions. Sauté for 5 minutes. Add the garlic and sauté for 1 minute more. Add the smoked paprika and chili powder and cook for 1 minute. Add the diced tomatoes, water, smoked salt and smoked pepper. Bring to a boil and simmer on medium heat for 2-3 minutes. Using a large spoon, create four wells in the sauce and crack an egg in each well. Cover pan with a lid, lower heat to medium-low, and cook for 4-6 minutes or to your preference, based on how you like your eggs cooked.

3. As the eggs are cooking, bake the spiced breads for 5-7 minutes or until toasted. Cut into slices. Garnish the eggs with cilantro and serve from the pan, with spiced breads on the side for dipping.

French Toast with Blackberry and Cherry Sauce

Any time you cook something for somebody else it's a special thing, especially when it's a surprise. Who wouldn't want to be surprised with French toast in the morning?

Serves 2

For the French Toast:

1½ cups milk

2 teaspoon Bourbon-Madagascar Vanilla Extract

1 egg

2 tablespoons Bourbon Smoked Sugar

6 slices baguette, 1-inch thick

1-2 tablespoons butter, for cooking

For the Fruit Sauce:

1 tablespoon butter

1 cup blackberries

½ cup cherries, pitted and cut in half

1 tablespoon Bourbon Smoked Sugar

1. In a small, shallow pan, whisk together the milk and vanilla. In another shallow pan, whisk together the egg and sugar. Add the bread slices to the milk mixture. Allow the bread to soak into the milk for 5 minutes, turning the slices once.

2. While the bread is soaking, make the fruit sauce. In a medium skillet, heat the butter on high heat until sizzling. Add the fruit and sauté for 2 minutes. Add the sugar, toss and cook for 1 minute more. Remove from heat and set aside.

3. Heat a large skillet on medium-high heat and add the butter. Lift the bread from the milk, allowing it to drain slightly, and drop into the sizzling butter. Lower heat to medium, if needed. Cook both sides for about 5 minutes, or until golden brown.

4. Divide French toast between two plates. Spoon fruit sauce over each serving and serve immediately

Monkey Bread

It's best right when it comes out of the oven.

Serves 10-12

1 cup plus ½ cup Bourbon Vanilla Sugar, divided

1 teaspoon cinnamon

¾ cup (1½ sticks) unsalted butter

1 tablespoon Bourbon-Madagascar Vanilla Extract

2 (16.3 ounce) cans large, refrigerated biscuits

½ cup pecans, coarsely chopped

1 Preheat oven to 350 degrees. Grease or spray a 12-cup Bundt pan. In a medium bowl or plastic bag, combine ½ cup vanilla sugar and the cinnamon. In a small saucepan over medium-high heat, melt butter and add the remaining 1 cup vanilla sugar. Stir until most of the sugar is dissolved. Remove from heat and add vanilla extract.

2 Pop open cans of biscuits and cut each biscuit into four pieces. Toss the pieces in the cinnamon sugar mixture, coating well. Arrange the pieces in the Bundt pan, adding the pecans in layers. Pour over the vanilla sugar and melted butter. Bake for 30 minutes or until golden brown. Cool in the pan for 10 minutes. Place a serving plate on top of the Bundt pan and carefully invert, releasing monkey bread onto the plate. Cool until you can handle with fingers. Serve warm, allowing guests to pull apart.

Monkey Bread for Big Kids

Serves 10-12

¾ cup Bourbon Smoked Sugar

1 teaspoon cinnamon

4 slices bacon, cooked and roughly chopped

¾ cup (1½ sticks) unsalted butter

½ cup Bourbon Barrel Aged Pure Cane Sorghum

2 tablespoons bourbon

2 (16.3 ounce) cans large, refrigerated biscuits

½ cup pecans, coarsely chopped

1 Preheat oven to 350 degrees. Grease or spray a 12-cup Bundt pan. In a medium bowl or plastic bag, combine sugar, cinnamon, and bacon. In a small saucepan over medium-high heat, melt butter and add sorghum and bourbon. Turn off heat and stir to combine.

2 Pop open cans of biscuits and cut each biscuit into four pieces. Toss the pieces in the sugar mixture, coating well. Arrange the pieces in the Bundt pan, adding the pecans in layers. Pour in melted butter and sorghum over the pecans. Bake for 30 minutes or until golden brown. Cool in the pan for 10 minutes. Place a serving plate on top of the Bundt pan and carefully invert, releasing monkey bread onto the plate. Cool until you can handle with fingers. Serve warm, allowing guests to pull apart.

Spanish Omelette
(Tortilla Española)

I hear from people who are vegetarian and miss the flavor of meat. Our Bourbon Smoked Paprika gives them some of that taste they miss.

Serves 4-6

6 eggs, well beaten

¼ cup plus 2 tablespoons olive oil

1 cup yellow onion, thinly sliced

2 large waxy potatoes, peeled and thinly sliced

1 teaspoon Bourbon Smoked Sea Salt

½ teaspoon Bourbon Smoked Pepper

½ teaspoon Bourbon Smoked Paprika, plus extra for garnish

1. Whisk eggs in a medium bowl. Heat a 10-inch, oven-safe skillet with ¼ cup olive oil on medium-high heat. Add onions and potatoes and cook over moderate heat, stirring frequently, until potatoes are tender, but not browned, about 15 minutes. Remove potato mixture with a slotted spoon and stir into the beaten eggs, along with the smoked salt, pepper and paprika. Cover and let sit for 10 minutes. The mixture should thicken a bit.

2. Preheat oven to broil. Pour out oil and wipe out the skillet. Heat pan over high heat. Add 2 tablespoons fresh olive oil to the pan. Pour the egg mixture into the pan. Reduce heat to medium. Cook for 3 minutes to set the eggs on the bottom. Place pan in oven and broil for 3 minutes or until eggs are just set and slightly brown. Loosen edges with a rubber spatula or knife. Place a serving plate on top of the skillet and carefully, but quickly, invert pan, dropping the omelette onto the plate. Remove skillet. Dust the top with a little more smoked paprika and cut into slices. Serve warm or at room temperature.

Madeline's Quick Scrambled Eggs

Maddie makes these for her mom a lot. The peppercorns give them some texture and the paprika gives them some smoke. Maddie has always been a company girl. She wants to put as many products as possible into these eggs.

Serves 2

4-5 eggs

1 teaspoon Bourbon Smoked Sea Salt

¼ teaspoon Bourbon Smoked Pepper

1 dash Bourbon Barrel Aged Worcestershire Sauce

1 dash Chef Edward Lee's Sambal Hot Sauce

2 tablespoons butter

Bourbon Smoked Paprika, for garnish

Parsley, chopped, for garnish

1. Heat a medium non-stick skillet over medium heat. Crack the eggs into a bowl and add the smoked salt, smoked pepper, Worcestershire sauce and hot sauce. Whisk well to combine. Add the butter to the skillet. When the butter is melted, add the eggs to the pan. Using a heat-proof spatula or wooden spoon, gently stir the eggs in the pan until curds begin to form. Once large, wet curds form, remove from heat. Eggs should still be a little undercooked, as they will continue cooking off the heat.

2. Divide between two plates and garnish with the smoked paprika and parsley.

Cinnamon Rolls

Your kids will love you. Trust me.

Makes 15 rolls

For the Dough:

¾ cup lukewarm water

2¼ teaspoons active dry yeast

½ cup Bourbon Vanilla Sugar

¼ cup buttermilk, room temperature

1 egg

⅓ cup vegetable oil

½ teaspoon Bourbon Smoked Sea Salt

4½ cups all-purpose flour, divided; plus more, if necessary

For the Filling:

1¼ cups light brown sugar

2½ tablespoons cinnamon

2 tablespoons cornstarch

½ cup (1 stick) unsalted butter, softened, plus extra for greasing the pan

For the Frosting:

¼ cup (½ stick) unsalted butter, softened

12 ounces cream cheese

1 teaspoon Bourbon-Madagascar Vanilla Extract

1 teaspoon lemon juice

1¼ cups powdered sugar

1. In the bowl of a stand mixer, add the lukewarm water, yeast and 1 tablespoon of the vanilla sugar. Stir to combine and set aside. In a small bowl, whisk together buttermilk, egg and oil. Once the yeast is frothy, add the buttermilk mixture to the yeast, along with the remaining vanilla sugar, and smoked salt. Stir to combine.

2. Using the dough hook attachment, pour in 2 cups of the flour and stir on low speed until the flour is incorporated. Add the remaining flour, one cup at a time, until the dough pulls away from the bowl. It should be slightly sticky. If dough is too wet, add another ¼ - ½ cup flour. Transfer dough to an oiled bowl and cover with plastic wrap. Set aside in a warm place to rise for 1 hour or until doubled in size.

3. Prepare the filling. In a small bowl, combine the brown sugar, cinnamon and cornstarch. Butter an 11 x 15-inch baking dish. Once the dough has risen, flour a large work surface. Punch down the dough and transfer it to the floured surface. Roll the dough out into a large rectangle, roughly 20 x 30-inches wide. Spread softened butter over the dough, leaving the edge farthest away from you unbuttered.

4. Evenly sprinkle the filling mixture over the butter. Starting with the edge closest to you, gently roll up the dough into a tight log. Slightly pinch the unbuttered edge into the log to seal. Trim off uneven ends. Score the log every 2 inches with a knife, then using those marks, cut into rolls. Place rolls into the buttered dish and cover with plastic wrap. Leave to rise again for another hour or until doubled in size.

5. Bake in a preheated 350 degree oven for 15-17 minutes or until tops start to brown. Do not over bake. While rolls are baking, prepare the frosting. In the bowl of a stand mixer, beat together butter and cream cheese. Add vanilla and lemon juice. Beat to combine. Add the powdered sugar and mix on low speed just until incorporated. Slowly increase speed to high and beat for 5 minutes until frosting turns white.

6. After removing the rolls from the oven, spread half the frosting over the rolls. Cool rolls for 15 minutes. Spread remaining frosting. Serve warm.

Doughnut Holes and Toppings

When I told Maddie chocolate is made from cacao nibs, she immediately shoved a handful into her mouth and I'm like, "No, no, no, no, no!" They're kind of bitter.

Makes 32 doughnut holes

Vegetable or canola oil, for frying

1 (16.3 ounce) can large, refrigerated biscuits, refrigerated biscuits

Topping Combinations:

¼ cup Bourbon Vanilla Sugar + 1 teaspoon cinnamon, combined

¼ cup granulated sugar + 1 teaspoon cardamom, combined

Smoked Salt Caramel Sauce (See recipe on page 332) + 1 teaspoon Bourbon Smoked Sea Salt

Chocolate Ganache (See recipe on page 331) + 2 teaspoons Bourbon Smoked Cacao Nibs

Powdered sugar

1. Prepare toppings in small bowls. Heat 3 inches of oil to 350 degrees in a medium saucepan over high heat. Cut each biscuit into 4 pieces. When the oil is hot, carefully drop dough pieces into the oil. Do not crowd the pan. Lower heat to medium if doughnuts are cooking too quickly. Fry doughnuts on each side for 1 minute or until very golden brown. Remove with a slotted spoon and drain on paper towels.

2. For sugar and spice toppings, roll doughnuts in spiced sugar while still very hot. For caramel sauce, ganache, or powdered sugar, allow doughnuts to cool for 5 minutes before dipping into sauce or rolling in powdered sugar. Sprinkle smoked salt on caramel doughnuts. Dip ganache doughnuts in cacao nibs. Serve immediately.

Asparagus and Country Ham Frittata

Country ham elevates just about everything and asparagus is one of my favorite vegetables. Usually I'll do a frittata when I have things left over from the night before.

Serves 4-5

1 tablespoon butter

⅓ cup asparagus, cut into 1-inch pieces

½ cup country ham, chopped

6 eggs beaten

½ teaspoon Bourbon Smoked Pepper

½ teaspoon Bourbon Barrel Aged Worcestershire Sauce

¼ teaspoon Bourbon Smoked Sea Salt

⅓ cup grape tomatoes, halved

½ cup smoked Cheddar or Gouda cheese, grated

1 tablespoon parsley, chopped

1. Preheat oven to broil. In a 10-inch oven-safe skillet, melt butter over medium-high heat. Add the asparagus and ham and sauté for 2-3 minutes. In a medium bowl, whisk together eggs, pepper, Worcestershire sauce and smoked salt. Pour egg mixture into pan, along with the grape tomatoes, and stir with a rubber spatula. Cook for 4-5 minutes, reducing heat to medium, until the egg mixture begins to set on the bottom. Sprinkle with the grated cheese.

2. Place pan into the oven and broil for 2-3 minutes, until lightly browned and puffed. Remove from pan, garnish with parsley and cut into 6 servings. Serve immediately.

Superfood Cocoa and Banana Smoothie

Max plays soccer and Maddie's a swimmer. I'll make them this smoothie while they're training.

Makes 2 servings

1½ cups almond milk (or any milk you prefer)

2 tablespoons chocolate protein powder

1-2 tablespoons Bourbon Barrel Aged Pure Cane Sorghum

2 teaspoons cocoa powder

1 teaspoon cinnamon, plus extra for garnish

⅛ teaspoon cayenne pepper (optional)

3 frozen bananas

½ cup ice

2 teaspoons Bourbon Smoked Cacao Nibs, for garnish

Fresh banana slices, for garnish

1. Blend everything together, except the cacao nibs and fresh banana slices, until smooth. Divide between two serving glasses and garnish with sliced bananas, a dusting of cinnamon and the smoked cacao nibs. Serve immediately.

BATCH	BOTTLE NUMBER
217-15	186

APPS & SNACKS

Grilled Oysters with Bourbon, Brown Butter and Soy Vinaigrette

I've included a lot of Ed's recipes in the book. For this one, he has an outdoor pizza oven in the courtyard of his wine studio across the street from 610 Magnolia. He'll put the oysters in his oven and they pop. You barely have to open them. He's got butter that's been browning with a little bit of garlic then he adds some of our soy sauce. It's one of the best things I've ever eaten.

— Recipe by Chef Edward Lee, 610 Magnolia, Louisville, Kentucky

Makes 1 dozen oysters

4 tablespoons unsalted butter

1 garlic clove, lightly smashed

1 tablespoon Bluegrass Soy Sauce

2 teaspoons Kentucky bourbon

2 teaspoons rice vinegar

¼ teaspoon Bourbon Smoked Sea Salt

⅛ teaspoon Bourbon Smoked Pepper

12 oysters, scrubbed and rinsed

 In a small saucepan, melt butter over high heat. Drop in garlic clove, reduce heat to medium and cook butter until it looks brown and starts to smell nutty and fragrant. Remove from heat. Spoon the clear brown butter into a small bowl, leaving the milk solids behind. Add the soy sauce, bourbon, rice vinegar, smoked salt and smoked pepper. Whisk well to combine. Set aside.

 Preheat a grill or grill pan on high. Grill oysters directly on grill until they pop open, about 5-8 minutes. Remove the top shell, being careful to reserve juices. Place on serving plate. Drizzle with the brown butter vinaigrette. Serve immediately.

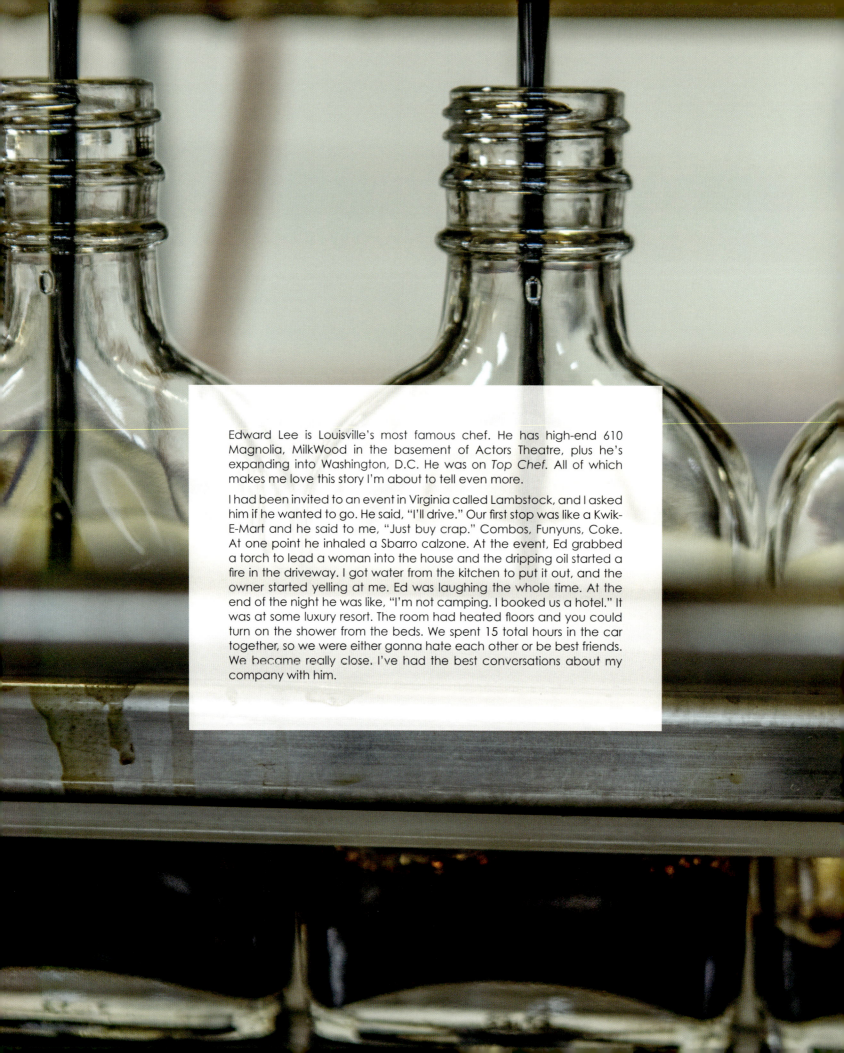

Edward Lee is Louisville's most famous chef. He has high-end 610 Magnolia, MilkWood in the basement of Actors Theatre, plus he's expanding into Washington, D.C. He was on *Top Chef*. All of which makes me love this story I'm about to tell even more.

I had been invited to an event in Virginia called Lambstock, and I asked him if he wanted to go. He said, "I'll drive." Our first stop was like a Kwik-E-Mart and he said to me, "Just buy crap." Combos, Funyuns, Coke. At one point he inhaled a Sbarro calzone. At the event, Ed grabbed a torch to lead a woman into the house and the dripping oil started a fire in the driveway. I got water from the kitchen to put it out, and the owner started yelling at me. Ed was laughing the whole time. At the end of the night he was like, "I'm not camping. I booked us a hotel." It was at some luxury resort. The room had heated floors and you could turn on the shower from the beds. We spent 15 total hours in the car together, so we were either gonna hate each other or be best friends. We became really close. I've had the best conversations about my company with him.

"A white guy? Making soy sauce? I may have even rolled my eyes."

— Chef Edward Lee

Edward Lee with Matt

Bluegrass Soy Steamed Mussels

One of Louisville's best chefs, Anthony Lamas, cooks Latino food with Southern ingredients, and his place is packed night after night. It's probably the busiest, most consistent restaurant in town. Last time I was in there, Bluegrass Soy Sauce was an ingredient in so many dishes that the menu looked like the side of a racecar I had sponsored, and I felt honored.

— Recipe by Chef Anthony Lamas of Seviche, A Latin Restaurant, Louisville, Kentucky

Serves 4

1 cup water

½ cup Bluegrass Soy Sauce

2 tablespoons fresh ginger, grated on a microplane

2 tablespoons sesame oil

1-2 tablespoons Chef Edward Lee's Sambal Hot Sauce (to taste)

2 garlic cloves, chopped

Juice of 4 limes

1 tablespoon vegetable oil

2 pounds fresh black mussels, scrubbed, beards removed

1 small bunch cilantro, chopped, for garnish

1 lime, cut into wedges, for serving

Crusty bread, grilled, for serving

1. Whisk together the water, soy sauce, ginger, sesame oil, sambal hot sauce, garlic and lime juice. Set aside.

2. Heat an 8-quart pot over medium-high heat with the vegetable oil until smoking. Remove pot from heat and add mussels. Cover and put back on heat for 1 minute. Carefully add the soy mixture to the pot. Cover and bring to a boil. Steam mussels until they are fully open and meat is exposed, about 2-4 minutes. Divide mussels and broth between 4 bowls and top with cilantro and lime wedges. Serve with grilled bread.

"*Sometimes soy sauce can be too salty – too soy, if that's possible. Matt's is more balanced. I can take a teaspoon and sip it.*" — Chef Anthony Lamas

Anthony Lamas & Matt

I've done a lot of TV interviews and Andrew Zimmern was the most affable TV host ever. I ran into him in New York, and he was like, "Hey, Matt." I said, " I gotta tell ya, man, I feel like I'm pretty forgettable, so it means the world to me you remember my name."

MilkWood Wings with White Barbecue Sauce

These were amazing. Anything Edward Lee does has such a unique flavor, which is probably something I'll say a bunch throughout this book. It just amazes me what he does. Ed is not only one of the best chefs I know but just one of the smartest guys. I go to him for advice all the time. I asked him, "Hey, you think anybody would get mad at me if I started calling my sesame seeds benne seeds instead?" He sends me a long, well-researched response about the difference between benne and sesame seeds, continents of origin, different strains. I said, "So that's a, 'Yeah, they'd get offended'?"

— Recipe by Chefs Edward Lee and Chef Glenn Dougan of MilkWood Restaurant, Louisville, Kentucky

Makes about 30 wings

For the Dry Rub:

Non-stick cooking spray or vegetable oil (for brushing)

⅔ cup Bourbon Smoked Sugar

¾ cup light brown sugar

⅓ cup Bourbon Smoked Paprika

3 tablespoons Bourbon Smoked Sea Salt

1½ tablespoons onion powder

1½ tablespoons cayenne

1½ tablespoons garlic powder

2 teaspoons dry mustard powder

2 teaspoons coriander, ground

2 teaspoons cumin, ground

5 pounds chicken wings (cut between the joints)

For the Honey, Chili, Lime Glaze:

⅔ cup Bluegrass Soy Sauce

2 garlic cloves, minced

2 limes, zested

⅓ cup honey

3 tablespoons fish sauce

2 tablespoons fresh lime juice

1 tablespoon red pepper flakes

For the White Barbecue Sauce:

1 cup mayonnaise

2 cloves garlic, minced

¼ cup apple cider vinegar

2 tablespoons crème fraîche or sour cream

1 teaspoon Bourbon Barrel Aged Worcestershire Sauce

1 teaspoon horseradish

1 teaspoon Dijon mustard

1 teaspoon Bourbon Smoked Smoked Salt

½ teaspoon Bourbon Smoked Pepper

½ teaspoon celery seeds

¼ teaspoon Bourbon Smoked Paprika

For the Garnish:

2 scallions, green parts only, thinly sliced

2 tablespoons Bourbon Smoked Sesame Seeds

1 red chili, thinly sliced (optional)

(continued next page)

1. Cover a large, rimmed baking sheet with aluminum foil or parchment paper. Spray with cooking spray or brush lightly with vegetable oil. Combine all the ingredients for the dry rub in a large bowl. Add the wings and toss to thoroughly coat the wings. Shake off excess and place wings on baking sheet. Leave in refrigerator, uncovered, for 1-2 hours.

2. Combine all the ingredients for the honey, chili, lime sauce in a small bowl. Whisk to combine. Combine all the ingredients for the white barbecue sauce in another small bowl, whisking to combine. Set both aside.

3. Preheat oven to 400 degrees. Bake the wings on lower middle rack in oven for 25 minutes or until golden brown. If wings are browning too quickly, tent with foil.

4. Remove wings from oven and transfer to a large bowl. Pour honey, chili and lime sauce over the wings and toss to coat. Arrange on a serving platter or bowl. Generously drizzle the white barbecue sauce over the wings. Garnish with scallions, smoked sesame seeds and chili slices. Pour remaining white barbecue sauce into a small bowl and serve on the side with the wings.

"The soy sauce is a fulcrum for a discussion about what it is to cook Southern, a reminder of how central soybeans are to agriculture in the South. Whenever anyone asks about what's innovative about agriculture and food in the South, I always bring up Matt Jamie."

— Matt Lee, James Beard Award-winning food and travel writer and co-founder of the *Lee Bros. Boiled Peanuts Catalogue*

Smoked Pickled Grapes

"Pickled grapes look a lot like olives and you can use them a lot like olives, too. Have them in a cold salad, as a cocktail nibble, on a charcuterie plate, by themselves with toothpicks (no dish for pits required!) Their playful, sweet-sour flavor, crispness and gentle chile heat make them super-addictive," the brothers say.

— Recipe by Ted Lee and Matt Lee, food and travel writers and founders of the *Lee Bros., Boiled Peanuts Catalogue*, Charleston, South Carolina

Makes 3 pints

6 cups (about 2 pounds) stemmed, mixed red and green seedless grapes

1½ cups distilled white vinegar or white wine vinegar

1½ cups water

2 tablespoons Bourbon Smoked Salt

2 teaspoons Bourbon Smoked Sugar

3 cloves garlic, crushed and peeled

Leaves from 1 four-inch sprig rosemary

½ teaspoon crushed dried red chile flakes

1. Pack the grapes into three clean, pint size glass containers with lids. Pour the vinegar and water into a saucepan, set it over medium high heat and add the smoked salt, smoked sugar, garlic, rosemary and chile flakes. When the mixture starts to simmer, remove the pan from the heat and divide the hot brine among the pints of grapes. Cover loosely and let cool to room temperature.

2. Cover tightly and chill in the refrigerator for two hours before serving. The pickles will keep in the refrigerator for about two weeks.

Soy Brined Tea Eggs

One of my favorite things to eat is soft-boiled eggs with soy sauce. I wanted a pickled egg in this book because I love *The Simpsons* and Homer Simpson eating those eggs. I love the color on these, which will keep in the refrigerator for two weeks. They're great on salads.

— Recipe by Chef Annie Pettry, Decca, Louisville, Kentucky

5-minute Eggs:

12 eggs

Water, enough to cover eggs

½ cup salt

For the Brine:

2 cups water

1 cup Bluegrass Soy Sauce

½ cup sherry vinegar

¼ cup mirin

1 garlic clove, smashed

1 shallot, sliced

1 clove

1 bay leaf

1 star anise

1 tablespoon Bourbon Smoked Sugar

1 tablespoon Bourbon Smoked Sea Salt

1 teaspoon white peppercorns

½ teaspoon Bourbon Smoked Togarashi

½ cup black tea leaves or 5 tea bags

1. In a large saucepan, cover the eggs with 2 inches of cold water. Add salt. The salt makes the eggs easier to peel. Bring to a boil over high heat. Immediately turn off the heat and cover the pot for 5 minutes. Remove eggs with a slotted spoon and place in a bowl of ice water until chilled. Peel.

2. In a medium saucepan, add the brine ingredients, except the black tea. Bring to a simmer and turn off the heat. Add the black tea and steep for 4 minutes. Strain the brine through a fine mesh sieve. Allow the brine to cool. Place peeled eggs in a large container, then pour over the brine. Cover and brine eggs in the refrigerator overnight. Eggs will keep in the refrigerator for up to 2 weeks.

"Soy sauce was the first seasoning I used as a young cook helping out in the kitchen at home. If I wanted something to have more flavor, I added soy. Even now as a professional cook, with so many ingredients within my reach, I still go for the soy when I want to add a deep and savory pop of flavor – in sauces, dressings, pickle marinades. At home, I drizzle Bluegrass Soy Sauce on sweet potatoes, rice and tofu."

— Chef Annie Pettry

Tuna Seviche

Anthony Lamas' Louisville restaurant is called Seviche, so you know this one is good.

— Recipe by Anthony Lamas, Seviche, A Latin Restaurant, Louisville, Kentucky

Serves 4-6

1 cup coconut milk, unsweetened

½ cup Bluegrass Soy Sauce

1 tablespoon fresh ginger

2 teaspoons sesame oil

Juice of 3 limes

2 teaspoons Chef Edward Lee's Sambal Hot Sauce (or to taste)

2 pounds sushi grade ahi tuna, cut into ½-inch dice

1 jalapeño pepper, diced

1 teaspoon Bourbon Smoked Sesame Seeds

1 teaspoon black sesame seeds

1 scallion, sliced

1 small bunch of cilantro, chopped

1 carrot, julienned

3 radishes, thinly sliced

1. Whisk together coconut milk, soy sauce, ginger, sesame oil, lime juice and sambal chili paste. Refrigerate for at least 1 hour or overnight.

2. In a mixing bowl, combine tuna with enough sauce to generously coat. Gently mix to combine. Divide the tuna between 4-6 bowls and garnish with the jalapeño, smoked and black sesame seeds, scallion, cilantro, carrot and radish. Drizzle a little more sauce over the top, if desired. Serve immediately.

Soy Braised Shiitake Mushrooms
(Fukume'-ni)

Few foods have that umami flavor. Soy sauce is one, shiitake mushrooms are another. When I was in Tokyo, this is one of those comfort foods I had. It can be served as an appetizer or as an accompaniment to rice. It's also simple to make.

Serves 4

20 dried shiitake mushrooms

2 tablespoons Bluegrass Soy Sauce

1½ tablespoons Bourbon Smoked Sugar

3 tablespoons vegetable oil

1 tablespoon toasted sesame oil

1 teaspoon Bourbon Smoked Sesame Seeds

 Place dried mushrooms in a large bowl and cover with water. Place a plate on top to keep them submerged. Let soak overnight.

 The next day, pour off ½ cup of the soaking liquid and add the soy sauce and smoked sugar. Stir to combine. Drain the mushrooms through a sieve. Remove and discard the shiitake stalks.

 Heat a large frying pan or wok over high heat and add the oil. Add the drained shiitakes and stir-fry for 5 minutes, stirring constantly. Pour the soaking liquid and soy mixture over the mushrooms. Turn heat down to low. Cook until there is almost no moisture left, stirring frequently. Add the sesame oil and remove from heat.

 Leave until cool enough to handle. Slice and arrange on a serving plate. Garnish with smoked sesame seeds and serve.

Note: Mushrooms may also be soaked in boiling water for 2-4 hours. They will be slightly chewier but this method also works.

Bourbon Smoked Spiced Pecans

These became so popular that we started packaging them.

Makes 2 cups

1 egg white

2 cups pecan halves

¼ cup (55 grams) Bourbon Smoked Sugar

1 teaspoon Bourbon Smoked Sea Salt

½ teaspoon Bourbon Smoked Paprika

½ teaspoon cinnamon

½ teaspoon ground ginger

¼ teaspoon cayenne

1. Preheat oven to 350 degrees. Whisk egg white in a medium bowl until foamy. Add pecans and stir. Add the remaining ingredients and stir well to combine. Spread mixture in a single layer on a parchment-lined baking sheet. Bake for 13-18 minutes, or until golden brown.

2. Cool for 15 minutes before breaking pecans apart with your hands. Pecans keep for 5 days in an airtight container, or keep in freezer for up to 1 month.

Benedictine and Shaved Vegetable Canapés

Every city has its own food history, but you never see Benedictine (the cucumber and cream cheese spread) any place other than Louisville. One of my favorite sandwiches is Benedictine and bacon on baguette. Yes, some people put green food coloring in their Benedictine, but that's just gross.

For the Benedictine (makes 3 cups):

2 cucumbers (about 1 pound), peeled and deseeded

2 (8 oz.) packages of cream cheese

½ clove garlic, minced or grated

¾ tsp Bourbon Smoked Salt (more or less to taste)

1-2 drops green food coloring (optional)

For the Canapés (Make as many canapés as needed):

1 loaf soft white or wheat sandwich bread or pumpernickel bread

For the Shaved Vegetables (using a mandolin or vegetable peeler is the easiest):

Radishes, thinly sliced

Cucumbers, thinly sliced

Small beets, thinly sliced

Fresh dill, chives, pea shoots, or microgreens, for garnish

Bourbon Barrel Smoked Salt and Bourbon Barrel Smoked Pepper, for garnish

1. Make the Benedictine. Grate cucumbers with a box grater or with the grating disk of a food processor. Place grated cucumber into a sieve in a bowl. Push down on cucumber with a large spoon to release as much water as possible. Reserve cucumber juice for Cucumber Mint G & T's. (See recipe on page 299. Repeat until cucumber is fairly dry.

2. Put cucumber into a large bowl or into the bowl of the food processor fitted with the blade attachment. Add the cream cheese, garlic, smoked salt and green food coloring, if using. Mix until combined well.

3. Assemble canapés. Stack several slices of bread on top of each other. Trim crusts to make square slices of bread. Spread each slice with benedictine and top with assorted vegetable slices in one layer. Garnish with fresh herbs and a sprinkle of smoked salt and pepper. Cut into 2 rectangles or 4 small squares. Arrange on a serving platter.

Togarashi Snack Mix

When I was in Japan the first time, I noticed condiments on all the tables in ramen bars. Fresh ginger, toasted sesame seeds, soy sauce and togarashi. Togarashi is a traditional Japanese seven-spice blend, but I'm a rule-breaker so ours has way more than seven ingredients, like poppy seeds, lemon peel, pepper, cayenne and sesame seeds. The nori, or dried seaweed, gives it that earthy flavor. This is essentially Chex Mix® with our togarashi and our Worcestershire sauce. Lots of umami flavor.

Serves 24

3 cups Corn Chex® cereal

2 cups Rice Chex® cereal

2 cups Wheat Chex® cereal

3 cups garlic or everything-flavored bagel chips

2 cups mini-pretzels

1½ cups mixed nuts

6 tablespoons butter, melted

2 tablespoons Bourbon Barrel Aged Worcestershire Sauce

1 tablespoon Bourbon Smoked Paprika

2 teaspoons garlic powder

1 teaspoon onion powder

1 teaspoon Bourbon Smoked Sea Salt

1 teaspoon cayenne pepper (optional)

¼ cup Bourbon Smoked Togarashi

1. In a very large, microwavable bowl, combine the cereals, bagel chips, pretzels and nuts. Set aside. In a small bowl, combine the melted butter with the Worcestershire sauce, smoked paprika, garlic powder, onion powder, smoked salt and cayenne, if using. Pour over cereal mixture and toss to combine. Sprinkle the togarashi over the mix and toss again.

2. Microwave, uncovered, for 5 to 6 minutes, stirring every 2 minutes. Spread on two rimmed baking sheets to cool. Store in an airtight container.

Bourbon Barrel Beer Cheese

Several years ago I was on a panel for *Garden and Gun* magazine about the state of Southern food. One of the questions they asked was, "What's always in your refrigerator?" I said, "Beer cheese," and they replied, "What's that?" I sent the editorial staff a care package of beer cheese. Beer cheese is German, but there's a huge German population in Louisville so we've claimed it as our own. You go to the grocery store here and there are a dozen different kinds.

Makes 3½ cups

1 pound sharp Cheddar, freshly grated

1 garlic clove, minced

2 tablespoons sour cream

½ tablespoon Bourbon Barrel Aged Worcestershire Sauce

1 teaspoon Bourbon Smoked Paprika

½ teaspoon hot sauce, or to taste

1 cup amber beer, at room temperature

Bourbon Smoked Sea Salt, to taste

Bourbon Smoked Pepper, to taste

1. Combine the first six ingredients in a stand mixer or in a large bowl with a hand mixer on low speed, until blended. Gradually add in beer and blend on low speed. Increase speed and mix on high for 1 minute, or until creamy. Season with smoked salt and pepper. Serve with toast, crackers, chips or our Soft Pretzels with Bourbon Smoked Sea Salt (see recipe on page 253). Leftover beer cheese will keep in the refrigerator for 1 week.

Makes 18-20 appetizers

For the Shrimp:

½ pound shrimp, peeled and deveined

1 teaspoon Bourbon Smoked Paprika

1 teaspoon Bourbon Smoked Sea Salt

¼ teaspoon Bourbon Smoked Pepper

½ cup all-purpose flour

Vegetable or canola oil, for frying

For the Batter:

1 cup all-purpose flour

1 egg

1 cup yellow cornmeal

1 teaspoon garlic powder

1½ tablespoons Bourbon Smoked Sugar

2 teaspoons baking powder

1¼ cups buttermilk

For the Dipping Sauce:

1 cup mayonnaise

½ lemon, juiced

2 tablespoons Dijon mustard

1-2 tablespoons prepared horseradish

1 teaspoon Bourbon Smoked Paprika

1 teaspoon Bourbon Smoked Sea Salt

½ teaspoon Bourbon Smoked Pepper

Mini Shrimp Corn Dogs

They're a little involved to make but are really fun. Great for a Super Bowl party.

1. In a small bowl, toss shrimp with smoked paprika, smoked salt and smoked pepper. Using skewers, start pushing skewer through the tail end through the entire length of the shrimp, stopping just at the head. Repeat with all the shrimp. Set aside in refrigerator. Make the batter. In a small bowl, combine all the ingredients for the batter. Whisk well to combine.

2. In another small bowl, combine all the ingredients for the dip. Keep refrigerated until needed

3. Pour 3-4 inches of oil in a small-to-medium saucepan and heat over medium-high heat. Heat oil to 350 degrees. To check if oil is hot enough, dip the handle end of a wooden spoon into the oil. If bubbles appear, oil is ready.

4. Place the flour onto a plate. Dip shrimp skewers into the flour to coat evenly. Tap off excess. Dip shrimp into the batter to coat thinly and evenly, allowing excess to run off. While rotating skewer, dip into the hot oil. Hold for the first 10-15 seconds, until the batter becomes solid. Release and fry on one side until brown. Turn and fry the other side. Continue with the remaining skewers. Corn dogs are done when golden brown on all sides. Drain on paper towels. Serve warm, with dipping sauce.

Smoked Pimento Cheese

Most Southern restaurants now have a house pimento cheese. Ours uses a lot of our products. It almost tastes like you've added a little bacon to it.

Makes 4 cups

1½ cups mayonnaise

1 (4-ounce) jar diced pimentos, drained

1 teaspoon red onion, finely grated

1 teaspoon Bourbon Barrel Aged Worcestershire Sauce

¼ teaspoon Bourbon Smoked Paprika

¼ teaspoon Bourbon Smoked Pepper

Dash of hot sauce (optional)

8 ounces (2½ cups) extra sharp Cheddar cheese, shredded

8 ounces (2½ cups) white Cheddar cheese, shredded

1. In a large bowl, combine all the ingredients and stir well to combine. Serve with crackers, bread or pretzels. Pimento cheese keeps for 1 week in an airtight container in the refrigerator.

Hot Pimento Cheese Crostini

Make as many as needed

1 French baguette, sliced in ¼-inch slices to make crostini

Pimento Cheese (See recipe on previous page)

Bourbon Barrel Smoked Paprika, for garnish

Dill sprigs or chopped scallions, for garnish

1. Preheat oven to 400 degrees. On a parchment-lined sheet pan, place crostini in a single layer. Bake for 3-4 minutes, or until just lightly toasted. Cool on baking sheet until cool enough to handle.

2. Spread a heaping tablespoon of pimento cheese onto each crostini. Place on baking sheet and bake for 5-7 minutes, or until cheese is bubbly and golden. Garnish with a dash of smoked paprika and dill or chopped scallions. Arrange on a platter and serve.

Pan-Fried Oysters

I could eat two dozen of these.

Makes 12 oysters

For the Egg Wash:

1 egg

2 tablespoons milk or water

2 teaspoons Bourbon Barrel Aged Worcestershire Sauce

For the Seasoned Flour:

1 cup all-purpose flour

1 teaspoon Bourbon Smoked Garlic Salt

1 teaspoon Bourbon Smoked Paprika

1 teaspoon Bourbon Smoked Pepper

½ teaspoon mustard powder

For the Oysters:

12 medium to large oysters, shucked

Vegetable oil, for frying

Bourbon Smoked Buttermilk Dressing (See recipe on page 321)

1. In a small bowl, whisk together the ingredients for the egg wash. In another bowl, whisk together the ingredients for the seasoned flour.

2. Shuck your oysters. In a medium skillet, add enough vegetable oil to come up 1-inch in the pan. Test oil in pan by dropping a pinch of flour into the oil. It should sizzle right away. Turn heat down to medium high when oil is hot.

3. Dip oysters in egg wash, then roll in the seasoned flour. Shake off excess. Fry oysters for 3-4 minutes on each side, or until golden brown. Drain on paper towel-lined plate. Serve immediately with a side of buttermilk dressing and hot sauce.

(Step-by-step guide on page 109)

Shuck the oysters. Holding one in a kitchen towel, insert the oyster knife into the hinge and open with a twisting motion.

Detach the oyster from the shell using the knife tip.

Prepare the egg wash and the seasoned flour.

Dip oysters in the egg wash, letting excess drip off.

Roll in seasoned flour to lightly coat. Shake off excess.

Fry oysters for 3-4 minutes on each side or until golden brown.

Agedashi Tofu

One of the realizations I had in Japan was that these makers specialize in one thing and become experts. I met several soy sauce manufacturers, but I also met several miso and tofu experts. One of my favorite dishes has always been fried tofu. When it's made right, it's nice and creamy, almost like mozzarella. Frying it gives it that great texture. You've got great variance in the creaminess of the tofu, the crunchiness of the batter. Just know that this is not something you can make ahead of time. Fry it up and eat it immediately, otherwise it'll get soggy.

Serves 4

For the Tofu:

1 package (390-400 grams) soft tofu

Canola or vegetable oil, for frying

¼ cup potato flour or cornstarch

Grated daikon radish, for garnish (optional)

2 scallions, green part only, sliced, for garnish

For the Broth:

2 tablespoons Bluegrass Soy Sauce

2 tablespoons mirin

2 tablespoons sake or dry sherry

2 cups dashi broth (or 2 cups hot water with 1 teaspoon *instant dashi powder)

1. Cut tofu into ten blocks of equal size. Lay a sheet of paper towel on a sheet pan and arrange tofu blocks on top. Cover with another sheet of paper towel and anther sheet pan. Place something heavy like a casserole pan or heavy skillet on top to weight. Leave tofu to press for 20 minutes.

2. In a small pot, combine all the ingredients for the broth. Bring to a boil and stir. Remove from heat and set aside, covered, with a lid to keep warm.

3. In a small frying pan, add about a half-inch of oil. Heat over medium high heat until rippling (350 degrees). Coat the pressed tofu in potato flour or cornstarch. Fry the tofu blocks about 2-3 minutes on each side, until lightly golden brown. Remove from oil and drain on paper towels or a wire rack. Repeat with remaining tofu.

4. Arrange 3 cubes of fried tofu in a small bowl. Pour some hot broth into the bowl. Garnish with grated daikon and scallions and serve immediately.

Note: Instant dashi powder is called "Hon Dashi" and is easily found in Asian grocery stores where Japanese ingredients are sold.

Pork Belly Potstickers

I wish these didn't take so long to make because I like to eat them like potato chips. I'm not gonna say go out and buy frozen ones, but sometimes I do.

Makes about 50 potstickers

For the Potstickers:

2 teaspoons vegetable oil

4 ounces pork belly, cut into medium-size dice

11 ounces ground pork

½ teaspoon baking soda

1 teaspoon cornstarch

1 teaspoon Bourbon Smoked Sugar

1½ teaspoons Bourbon Smoked Sea Salt

¼ teaspoon Bourbon Smoked Pepper

3 tablespoons cold water

2 tablespoons Bluegrass Soy Sauce

2 teaspoons ginger, grated

1 clove garlic, minced

2 scallions, green parts only, thinly sliced

1 package round potsticker or gyoza wrappers, defrosted if frozen

To Cook the Potstickers (for each batch in a frying pan):

¼ cup water

1 tablespoon vegetable oil

For the Dipping Sauce:

3 tablespoons Bluegrass Soy Sauce

2 tablespoons water

2 tablespoons rice vinegar

1 teaspoon sambal chili paste or sriracha sauce (or to taste)

1 teaspoon Bourbon Smoked Sesame Seeds

1 scallion, thinly sliced

1 Combine all the ingredients for the dipping sauce in a small mixing bowl. Set aside. Heat the vegetable oil in a small frying pan on high heat. Add the pork belly and pan-fry until golden and crispy on all sides, lowering heat to medium, if necessary. Drain on a paper towel-lined plate. In a large mixing bowl, add the ground pork, cooked pork belly, baking soda, cornstarch, smoked sugar, smoked salt, smoked pepper, water, and soy sauce. Mix well, in one direction, until the pork looks like it's binding to itself. Add the ginger, garlic, and scallions. Mix well to combine.

2 Fill a small bowl with cold water. Taking one potsticker wrapper in one hand, add a heaping teaspoon of the filling into the center of the wrapper. Avoid getting the filling on the edges or it won't seal well. Using one fingertip like a brush, dip it into the water and wet half of the wrapper, just along the edge. Fold the wrapper in half into a crescent moon shape and press the edges well to seal. Make sure to press out all the air. (To make the traditional potsticker shape, pleats are created on just one side of the potsticker as you fold and seal them. There are lots of videos on the Internet if you need a visual guide.) Repeat with the remaining filling and wrappers. Lay the potstickers in a single layer on a sheet tray.

3. Heat 1 tablespoon of vegetable oil in a large frying pan on high heat. Add the potstickers in a single layer, flat side down. Pan-fry for about 2 minutes or until one side is brown and crusty. Add the water and immediately cover the pan with a lid. Cook for 5-6 minutes or until almost all the water has evaporated. Remove the lid and cook for about 1 minute more. All the water should be gone and the potstickers should lift easily from the pan. Using a spatula, remove the potstickers from the pan. Arrange on a serving platter, golden side up. Continue cooking more potstickers, as needed. Serve with the dipping sauce on the side.

Note: Extra, uncooked potstickers may be frozen in a single layer on a sheet tray. Once frozen, store in a plastic bag in the freezer. They will keep in the freezer for one month. Cook from frozen exactly the same way, adding 2 minutes to cooking time once you add the water.

Goat Cheese and Sorghum Onion Jam Tartlets

These are a staple when we do tastings because they're so easy and bite-sized. You can make your own dough or buy puff pastry.

Makes 24 Tartlets

2 tablespoons olive oil

1 sweet yellow onion, thinly sliced

1 red onion, thinly sliced

1 tablespoon Bourbon Barrel Aged Pure Cane Sorghum

2 teaspoons balsamic vinegar

1 tablespoon fresh rosemary, finely chopped

1 teaspoon Bourbon Smoked Sea Salt

¼ teaspoon Bourbon Smoked Pepper

Flour, for dusting

2 sheets puff pastry

4 ounces crumbled goat cheese

1. Preheat oven to 400 degrees. Heat a large skillet with olive oil on high heat. Add the sliced onions and sauté until soft and caramelized, reducing heat to medium, about 10-15 minutes. Add sorghum, vinegar, rosemary, smoked salt and smoked pepper. Remove from heat and set aside.

2. Dust some flour on your work surface. Lightly flour one sheet of dough and a rolling pin to keep it from sticking. Roll dough out to make it slightly thinner. For the tartlets, you will need 2 mini-muffin tins (for 24 tartlets) and a round cookie cutter slightly larger than the muffin tin. Using the cookie cutter, cut out rounds of dough. Place rounds into the muffin tin, pushing down to create little tartlets. Repeat with remaining sheet of dough.

3. Fill each tartlet with ½ teaspoon of onion jam and top with goat cheese. Bake in the oven for 10-12 minutes until light, golden brown. Allow to cool slightly before removing from pan. Serve warm.

Note: Tartlets may be made a day ahead, covered, and stored in the refrigerator until ready to be baked.

(see next page for step-by-step guide)

Using a round cookie cutter slightly larger than the mini muffin tin, cut out rounds of dough.

Prepare muffin tins by placing cut dough-rounds into the muffin tin.

Press center down into muffin tin to create little tartlets.

4

Top with onion jam.

5

Top with goat cheese and bake.

Deviled Eggs (Two Ways)

I'm single and don't use many eggs. Since good eggs aren't usually sold in six-packs, I have to buy a dozen. A dozen eggs are always close to expiring on me, so this recipe is a good way to use them up.

Makes 16 Deviled Eggs

Base Recipe:

8 eggs

⅓ cup mayonnaise

1 tablespoon Dijon mustard

1 teaspoon white wine vinegar

Variations:

Tomato and Smoked Paprika Deviled Eggs

2 teaspoons tomato paste

1 teaspoon Bourbon Smoked Paprika, plus extra for garnish

Spicy Miso-Soy Deviled Eggs

1 teaspoon Bluegrass Soy Sauce

4 teaspoons miso paste (any variety)

1 teaspoon Chef Edward Lee's Sambal Hot Sauce

Bourbon Smoked Sesame Seeds, for garnish

Sliced scallions, for garnish

1. Place eggs in a large saucepan and cover with water. Bring to a boil over high heat. Cover and remove from heat. Leave for 13 minutes. Place eggs in a bowl of ice water to stop the cooking and cool completely.

2. Once cool, peel eggs and slice in half. Place egg yolks into a medium bowl and add the mayonnaise, Dijon mustard, and white wine vinegar. Mash together with a potato masher or fork, mixing well until very smooth. Divide mixture into two small bowls.

3. Add the variation ingredients to each bowl of egg yolk mixture and stir well to combine. Place the mixture into a piping bag fitted with a nozzle or into a plastic sandwich bag with a small corner cut off. Pipe into the egg white halves.

4. Garnish each deviled egg with the appropriate garnish. Arrange on a platter and serve.

Togarashi Grilled Shishito Peppers

These peppers — they say like one in six is gonna-get-you spicy. I always seem to find it.

Serves 4-6 as an Appetizer

8 ounces shishito peppers, washed

1 tablespoon olive oil

1 tablespoon Bluegrass Soy Sauce

1 tablespoon Bourbon Smoked Togarashi

2 teaspoons toasted sesame oil

1 teaspoon Bourbon Smoked Sea Salt

2 teaspoons Bourbon Smoked Sesame Seeds

1. Heat a grill or grill pan on high heat. In a medium bowl, toss peppers with the olive oil. Grill peppers, turning frequently, until slightly charred on all sides, about 5-6 minutes.

2. Place grilled peppers back in the bowl and toss with the soy sauce, smoked togarashi, sesame oil and smoked salt. Garnish with sesame seeds. Serve.

BATCH	BOTTLE NUMBER
217-15	186

SOUPS & SALADS

Chicken and Smoked Pepper Dumplings

I didn't know what I was doing the first time I made dumplings, but it was fun watching them float to the top. You're essentially cooking biscuits in your stock. I love thicker soups and a good dumpling makes this one.

Serves 6-8

For the Stew:

1 tablespoon olive or vegetable oil

4 carrots, diced

3 stalk celery, diced

1 large onion, diced

2 tablespoons fresh thyme leaves or 2 teaspoons dried

2 garlic cloves, chopped

1 (2½-3 pound) chicken, cut into parts, including the backbone (you can ask your butcher to do this)

2 bay leaves

1 tablespoon Bourbon Smoked Salt

2 teaspoons Bourbon Smoked Pepper

½ cup all-purpose flour

1 cup frozen peas

For the Dumplings:

2 cups all-purpose flour

1 tablespoon baking powder

½ teaspoon baking soda

1 teaspoon Bourbon Smoked Salt

½ teaspoon Bourbon Smoked Pepper

6 tablespoons butter, melted

¾ cup buttermilk

2 tablespoons parsley, chopped, plus extra for garnishing

1 Heat oil in a 5-6 quart dutch oven or pot on high heat. Add the carrots, celery, onion, thyme and garlic to the pot, stirring, until vegetables begin to soften, about 5-7 minutes. Add the chicken, along with the bay leaves, smoked salt, smoked pepper and 10 cups of water. Bring to a boil, cover and reduce heat to low. Simmer for 1 hour. Discard the bay leaves and transfer chicken to a plate; let cool. Pull meat off the bones, shredding chicken. Set aside.

2 In a medium bowl, whisk together the flour and 2 cups of the cooking liquid. Slowly pour this mixture into the pot, whisking continuously, until fully incorporated. Return the chicken back into the pot. Simmer until slightly thickened, about 10-15 minutes. Taste soup and adjust seasoning as needed.

3 While the soup is simmering, make the dumplings. In a medium bowl, whisk together the flour, baking powder, baking soda, smoked salt and smoked pepper. Add the melted butter, buttermilk and parsley. Stir with a large spoon to form dough. With the broth at a slow simmer, drop a scant tablespoon of dough at a time into the soup. Once all the dough is in the soup, cover and simmer gently until dumplings are firm, about 12-15 minutes. Add the peas for the last 2 minutes of cooking. Garnish with chopped parsley and serve.

Bourbon Smoked Chili

I've got a guy I know in Illinois who has worked in the chili powder business for 25 years. He's in charge of making the chili at his neighborhood block party, and his neighbors always seemed to like it but never complimented him on it until he dumped in a can of our Bourbon Smoked Paprika.

Once it starts to get cool outside, I crave chili. It just doesn't make sense in the summertime. Kind of like how I have a hard time drinking red wine in the summer.

Makes 10 Servings

2 tablespoons vegetable oil

1 large onion (about 2 cups), chopped

3 garlic cloves, chopped

1½ pounds ground beef

1 pound ground pork

¼ cup Bourbon Smoked Chili Powder

3 tablespoons Bourbon Smoked Paprika

2 tablespoons cumin

2 tablespoons tomato paste

1 tablespoon Bourbon Smoked Sea Salt

2 teaspoons Bourbon Smoked Pepper

2 teaspoons dried oregano

2 teaspoons cayenne (more or less to taste)

12 ounces amber or lager beer

28 ounces canned, crushed tomatoes (fire-roasted preferred)

2 (15.5-ounce) cans beans (kidney, pinto or black), drained and rinsed

2 tablespoons Bourbon Barrel Aged Worcestershire Sauce

1½ cups water

 Place a large Dutch oven or soup pot on high heat and add oil. Add onions and sauté for 5-7 minutes, or until softened and translucent. Add the chopped garlic and cook for 1 minute. Crumble in ground beef and pork. Cook until meat is no longer pink and is starting to brown. Drain excess fat. Add the smoked chili powder, paprika, cumin, tomato paste, smoked sea salt, pepper, oregano, and cayenne. Reduce heat to medium-high and cook for 2 minutes. Pour in the beer to deglaze the pan and cook for 2 minutes. Add the tomatoes, beans, Worcestershire sauce and water.

 Bring chili to a boil. Reduce heat to low, cover and cook for 1-1½ hours, stirring occasionally. If chili seems thick during cooking, add ½ cup water to loosen. Taste and adjust seasoning, as necessary. Serve with your family's favorite toppings and accompaniments.

Fire Roasted Gazpacho

You really do have to follow the directions for this recipe because everything has been measured out based on how it's going to continue to blossom once you've mixed it up. Robyn says her "chief tasting officer" calls this a "landmark recipe." She says she took the soup to a dinner party down the street and it was a hit. "When tomatoes are in season," she says, "this is a great dish to take advantage of all that yummy tomato goodness."

— Recipe by Food Blogger Robyn Lindars of GrillGirl.com

Makes 2½ quarts

3 pounds small to medium-size tomatoes

2 large cucumbers, sliced into long, thin pieces

1 poblano pepper, cut in half and deseeded

4 garlic cloves, wrapped in foil packet

1 small (8-ounce) bag mini peppers, cut in half and deseeded

1 cup water (or more)

3 tablespoons white or red wine vinegar

2 tablespoons extra virgin olive oil

1 tablespoon Bourbon Smoked Sea Salt

2 teaspoons Bourbon Smoked Pepper

1 teaspoon Bourbon Smoked Sugar

½ cup basil leaves, plus extra for garnish

Avocadoes, diced, for garnish (optional)

1. Preheat a grill for medium direct heat. A gas or indoor grill pan can be used, but you won't get as much smokiness, so use charcoal, if possible. Place tomatoes, cucumbers, poblano pepper, garlic packet and mini peppers on the grill. Grill until everything has nice char marks on all sides. Place everything on a sheet pan and allow to cool slightly.

2. Using a blender or an immersion blender, blend all the vegetables with the remaining ingredients, except the basil and avocadoes. Add more water if you want a thinner consistency. Add the basil at the end and blend to incorporate. Taste and adjust seasoning, as needed. Chill at least 3 hours before serving. Garnish with more basil and diced avocadoes, if desired.

Spinach and Blueberry Salad with Soy-Ginger Dressing

I'm not one for drizzling dressing on salads. You need to get the greens in the bowl and make sure every leaf is coated in dressing.

Makes 4 Servings

For the Dressing:

3 tablespoons Bluegrass Soy Sauce

1 tablespoon maple syrup or honey

1 tablespoon toasted sesame oil

1 teaspoon ginger, grated

1 teaspoon Bourbon Smoked Togarashi

½ teaspoon Bourbon Smoked Pepper

For the Salad:

2 cups baby spinach

2 cups mixed greens, such as mesclun or spring mix

1 cup blueberries, rinsed

1 cup cucumber, diced

¾ cup feta cheese, crumbled

½ cup almond flakes, toasted

1. Combine all the ingredients for the dressing in a small bowl. Whisk well to combine.

2. In a large bowl, combine all the salad ingredients, reserving some feta and almonds for garnish. Pour dressing over the salad and toss lightly to combine. Divide among serving bowls and garnish with reserved feta and almonds. Serve immediately.

Grilled Watermelon and Peach Arugula Salad with Feta

It's kind of our go-to duo — Bourbon Smoked Salt and Bourbon Smoked Pepper. I don't expect everybody to buy all of our products, but if you get the salt you should definitely get the pepper. If you're raised right, they travel together at the dinner table. They're a team; never break them up.

Serves 8-10

For the Vinaigrette:

¼ cup balsamic vinegar

Juice of ½ lime

¼ teaspoon Bourbon Smoked Sea Salt

⅛ teaspoon Bourbon Smoked Pepper

½ cup extra virgin olive oil

For the Salad:

3 large peaches, halved and de-stoned

2½ pounds watermelon, cut into 1-inch-thick slices

¼ cup olive oil, for brushing

5 ounces arugula leaves, washed and dried

Bourbon Smoked Pepper, for seasoning

⅓ cup feta cheese, crumbled

Bourbon Smoked Sugar, for sprinkling

Bourbon Smoked Sea Salt, for seasoning

⅓ cup Bourbon Barrel Spiced Pecans, roughly chopped

1. Heat a grill or grill pan over high heat. In a small bowl, combine the balsamic vinegar, lime juice, smoked salt and smoked pepper. While whisking, slowly pour in the olive oil. Set aside.

2. Brush fruit with olive oil and lightly sprinkle with smoked sugar and a pinch of smoked salt. Place peaches, cut side down, and watermelon slices on the grill. Grill for 30 seconds to 1 minute or just until grill marks appear. Remove to a cutting board. Cut off rind from watermelon and slice into large cubes. Slice peaches into small slices or large dice.

3. Place arugula into a large salad bowl and toss with a little balsamic vinaigrette. Arrange watermelon and peaches on top and season salad lightly with smoked salt and smoked pepper. Scatter the feta cheese and chopped spiced pecans, then drizzle a little extra balsamic vinaigrette over the salad. Serve immediately.

Chicken and Egg Miso Ramen

Making ramen is usually how I'll clean out my refrigerator — leftover corn, eggs, fresh herbs, green onions. Yes, a good ramen broth makes the dish, but all these other things on top are just as important. I just love my soft-boiled eggs runny. If I'm not making my own broth, I do keep some in the cabinet. I found a pretty decent packaged ramen noodle on Amazon that my daughter loves. She likes to slurp.

Serves 4

For the Toppings:

1½ cups leftover roast chicken or rotisserie chicken meat, shredded

2 soft-boiled eggs, halved

1 cup corn, sautéed with butter and salt

4 ounces shiitake mushrooms, thinly sliced and sautéed in oil

3 scallions, thinly sliced

Bourbon Smoked Togarashi

For the Broth:

8 cups water

2 cloves garlic, crushed

1 thumb-sized piece of ginger, sliced

½ pound (8 ounces) ground pork

4 scallions, roughly chopped

3-inch x 2-inch piece of dried kombu

5-6 tablespoons miso paste

2 tablespoons sake

2 tablespoons Bluegrass Soy Sauce

½ teaspoon Bourbon Smoked Sugar

¼ teaspoon sambal chili paste or hot sauce (optional)

2 tablespoons toasted sesame oil

For the Noodles:

9 cups water

2 tablespoons baking soda

12-14 ounces fresh angel hair or thin spaghetti noodles

1. Prepare the toppings and set aside. In a large pot, combine the water, garlic, ginger, ground pork, scallions and dried kombu. Bring to a boil and simmer for 15 minutes. Strain, then pour broth back into the pot. Add the remaining broth ingredients, except the sesame oil, and let it gently simmer on low heat.

2. In another large pot, add the water for the pasta and bring to a boil. Carefully add the baking soda. The baking soda will cause the water to boil rapidly. Add the pasta and cook until al dente according to package directions. Drain and divide between four bowls. Stir the sesame oil into the broth and ladle hot broth over the noodles.

3. Top each bowl with the shredded chicken, half an egg, corn, shiitake mushrooms and scallions. Serve immediately with the smoked togarashi on the side.

Beef and Barley Soup in a Crock-Pot

When we first started working on recipes for the book, we sent out an email asking for people to contribute. Everyone in the office thought this one was great, so we kept it.

— Recipe by Janet Firestone of Sylvania, Ohio (Bourbon Barrel Foods consumer)

Serves 6-8

1 tablespoon vegetable oil

1½ pounds ground beef

2 tablespoons tomato paste

1 medium onion, diced

2 large carrots, diced

2 stalks celery, diced

2 tablespoons Bourbon Barrel Aged Worcestershire Sauce

1 tablespoon Bourbon Barrel Aged Pure Cane Sorghum

2 teaspoons Bourbon Smoked Sea Salt

2 teaspoons dried oregano

1 teaspoon Bourbon Smoked Pepper

1 bay leaf

1 (28-ounce) can diced tomatoes

⅓ cup barley

5 cups beef stock

Grated Parmesan cheese, for serving

1. Heat oil in a large skillet over high heat. Add the ground beef and brown until no longer pink. Add the tomato paste and cook for another 2 minutes. Pour the meat mixture into the Crock-Pot, along with the remaining ingredients, except the cheese, and stir to combine.

2. Set the Crock-Pot on high for 4 to 6 hours or low for 6 to 8 hours. Serve with grated Parmesan cheese on the side for garnishing.

Roasted Broccoli and Wheatberry Salad with Sesame, Miso Dressing

To me, roasted broccoli is almost sweet like candy.

Makes 6 cups

For the Salad:

1½ cups wheatberries

1¼ pounds broccoli, cut into florets, stems peeled and cut into ½-inch pieces

3 tablespoons olive oil

2 tablespoons Bourbon Barrel Aged Worcestershire Sauce

1 teaspoon Bourbon Smoked Sea Salt

½ teaspoon Bourbon Smoked Pepper

1 garlic clove, minced

Zest of 1 lemon

1 red bell pepper, diced

2 scallions, sliced

¼ cup parsley, chopped

For the Dressing:

2 tablespoons white miso

2 tablespoons toasted sesame oil

2 tablespoons vegetable oil

2 tablespoons rice vinegar

1 tablespoon ginger, grated

1 tablespoon honey

Juice of ½ lemon

3 tablespoons water

1 Cook wheatberries according to package instructions. Set aside to cool. Preheat oven to 425 degrees. In a large bowl, combine the broccoli florets and stem pieces, olive oil, Worcestershire Sauce, smoked salt, smoked pepper, garlic and lemon zest. Toss to combine. Spread in an even layer on a rimmed baking sheet. Roast for 20 minutes. Flip broccoli using a spatula and roast for another 10-15 minutes or until nicely charred and crispy. Set aside to cool.

2 In a small bowl, add all the ingredients for the dressing. Whisk well to combine. In a large bowl, combine the wheatberries, broccoli, red bell pepper, scallions and parsley. Pour dressing over the top and toss well to combine. Serve.

Baby Kale Salad with Soy-Sesame Dressing

This has so many great layers of flavor and great textures — like the crispy shiitake mushrooms. It's so colorful and fresh.

Serves 2 as a main dish | 4 as a side

For the Salad:

1 large egg

2 tablespoons olive oil

4 ounces shiitake mushrooms, sliced

5 ounces baby kale (any other salad leaves will also work)

3-4 radishes, thinly sliced

1 tablespoon Bourbon Smoked Sesame Seeds

For the Dressing:

2 tablespoons Bluegrass Soy Sauce

1 tangerine, juiced

1 tablespoon Bourbon Smoked Sesame Seeds

1 tablespoon toasted sesame oil

1 dash hot sauce

1 tablespoon Bourbon Barrel Aged Pure Cane Sorghum

1. Boil a large egg for 6 minutes. Drop in a small bowl of ice water to stop the cooking. Peel egg, reserving just the yolk. Set aside. Heat a large skillet over high heat and add olive oil. Add the shiitake mushrooms and saute' for 8-10 minutes or until crispy, lowering heat as needed. Set aside.

2. In a small bowl, combine the ingredients for the dressing and whisk well.

3. Place baby kale, radishes, sesame seeds and shiitake mushrooms in a large bowl. Spoon some of the dressing over the salad and gently toss to coat. Add more dressing, to taste.

4. Mound salad into a serving bowl or onto individual plates. Garnish with crumbled egg yolk and extra smoked sesame seeds. Serve immediately.

Bluegrass Soy Roasted Tofu and Red Quinoa Salad

Tofu is a tough thing to order for carryout. Either order it at the restaurant or make it yourself. It's not hard.

Serves 5-6

1½ cups red quinoa

2¼ cups water

4 tablespoons Bluegrass Soy Sauce

3 tablespoons coconut oil, melted

2 tablespoons toasted sesame oil

2 tablespoons honey

2 tablespoons white wine vinegar

2 red chilies, chopped

2 teaspoons ginger, grated

1 garlic clove, minced

14 ounces firm tofu, drained and cut into 1-inch dice

1½ cups snow peas, thinly sliced

4 scallions, thinly sliced

2 tablespoons Bourbon Smoked Sesame Seeds

1. Preheat oven to 425 degrees. Place quinoa in a sieve and rinse with water. In a medium pot, bring the water to a boil. Add the quinoa, cover with a lid and reduce heat to low. Cook for 20 minutes. Fluff with a fork and set aside.

2. In a medium bowl, whisk together the soy, coconut oil, sesame oil, honey, white wine vinegar, chilies, ginger and garlic. In another bowl, toss the tofu with half the sauce. Line a baking sheet with parchment paper. Remove the tofu with a slotted spoon and arrange in a single layer on the baking sheet. Add leftover sauce back to first bowl. Bake, stirring occasionally, until golden, about 20-25 minutes. Allow to cool for 10 minutes.

3. In a large bowl, combine cooked quinoa, tofu, snow peas and half the scallions. Toss with the sauce. Pour into a serving bowl or onto platter and garnish with the remaining scallions and sesame seeds. Serve immediately.

Toshio saw how the drill I was using to stir the mash was actually a cement mixer. "Too violent," he said. Now we use what looks like a stainless-steel oar.

Then I started thinking of other bourbon-smoked products: paprika, pepper, chili powder, sugar, sesame seeds, garlic salt. I outsourced that first batch of smoked salt to fill a $10,000 order for a local law firm.

I remember that Christmas driving to my parents' house to pack 500 tins of salt. We did all the filling, labeling, packaging, gift-wrapping, boxing and shipping labels by hand. I honestly don't know what I would have done without my mom and dad.

Soon after, I bought an industrial smoker from Southern Pride BBQ Pits & Smokers in Alamo, Tennessee, then a second one. Each smoker can hold 1,400 pounds of pork butt. I could have a hell of a barbecue operation if my business goes under.

After the beans cool, we mix them with the wheat in large bins and introduce yeast. That koji goes into cedar boxes my dad made.

The koji increases in temperature as the yeast starts to grab hold of the soybeans and wheat, and takes on the green color of the yeast. It looks like pistachios that have been snowed on.

After pressing the moromi, all that's left is a brown, cake-y substance. In Japan it's fed to farm animals.

We were just throwing that cake-y substance out, but new American chefs love to play around with the leftover mash. Levon Wallace, who's at the 21c Museum Hotel in Nashville, crushes it up and sprinkles it on sashimi.

Matt's mom, Carol

BATCH	BOTTLE NUMBER
217-15	186

DINNER & MAIN DISHES

Ken's Favorite Bolognese Sauce

My dad used to send his dad, my grandfather, into the worst neighborhood in Chicago to pick up this spaghetti sauce. I've always remembered that because my mom used to give him hell for it.

One time I was making my dad a Christmas present and I remembered how much he liked that sauce, so I wanted to make him a sauce that was original. I kept thinking of things I could substitute that were more Kentucky, less traditionally Italian. I subbed in unsmoked country fatback instead of pancetta, ground pork instead of ground veal, deglazed with bourbon instead of red wine. We celebrated his birthday the other night and he asked me to make the sauce. He's always asking me to make the sauce.

Makes 4 quarts

- 2 tablespoons extra virgin olive oil
- ¼ pound (4 ounces) country bacon, cubed
- 1 pound mild pork sausage
- 2 medium onions, diced
- 4 celery ribs, finely chopped
- 2 medium carrots, finely chopped
- 5 garlic cloves, thinly sliced
- 2 tablespoons Bourbon Smoked Paprika
- 2 teaspoons Bourbon Barrel Smoked Sea Salt
- 1 teaspoon Bourbon Barrel Smoked Pepper
- 1 cup bourbon
- 28 ounces canned crushed tomatoes
- 1 cup whole milk
- 1 cup water
- ¼ cup parsley, chopped

1. Heat olive oil in a large saucepan or Dutch oven over medium-high heat. Add the bacon and sausage and cook, stirring and breaking up lumps until no longer pink. Add the onions, celery, carrots and garlic, stirring occasionally. Cook until vegetables have softened, about 5 minutes. Add smoked paprika, smoked salt and smoked pepper and cook for 1 minute. Pour in the bourbon and deglaze, scraping the bottom of the pot with a wooden spoon. Cook for 5 minutes to reduce bourbon by half.

2. Stir in crushed tomatoes, milk, water, and parsley. Gently simmer, covered, until sauce is thickened, about 1-1¼ hours. Season to taste with smoked salt and smoked pepper and remove from heat. Serve with fresh pappardelle, tagliatelle or spaghetti pasta. Also great over grits and braised meat.

Note: Sauce may be made up to two days ahead. Cool completely before refrigerating in an airtight container. Sauce may be kept in the refrigerator for one week or frozen for up to one month.

Charcoal Grilled Baby Back Ribs with Kentuckyaki Glaze

This is from Sean Brock, a chef in Charleston, South Carolina, best known for his restaurant Husk. He's one of my oldest restaurant customers. When he opened Husk he was buying our sorghum-sweetened Kentuckyaki retail bottles, which are glass. From working as a chef, I knew that it's not always the best thing to have glass bottles in the kitchen. He was buying so much of it, I said, "If you continue to buy this, I'll put it in gallon jugs." We've been putting it in gallon jugs ever since. Now we can tell when chefs cycle through one of his kitchens because they'll start buying the Kentuckyaki gallons.

— Recipe by Chef Sean Brock of Husk, Husk Bar and McCrady's in Charleston, SC

Serves 4

For the Brine:
8 cups water
¼ cup kosher salt
1 tablespoon Bourbon Barrel Pure Cane Sorghum

For the Ribs:
2 full racks pork baby back ribs
Bourbon Barrel Smoked Salt, to taste
Bourbon Barrel Smoked Pepper, to taste
Bourbon Smoked Sesame Seeds, for garnish
½ cup cilantro, coarsely chopped, for garnish

For the Glaze:
1½ cups Kentuckyaki™ Sauce
½ cup orange juice, freshly squeezed
¼ cup lime juice, freshly squeezed
1 tablespoon ginger, minced
1 tablespoon garlic, minced
2 teaspoons Bourbon Barrel Smoked Salt
2 tablespoons cornstarch
2 tablespoons water

Equipment:
Weber kettle grill
Weber charcoal chimney and enough hardwood charcoal to fill up a starter
1 pack of Bourbon Barrel Grill Wood

1. The night before grilling the ribs, combine the ingredients for the brine. I prefer to brine the ribs using a good quality plastic bag that the rib tips can't puncture. You use a lot less brine this way. Place the ribs in the brine and toss to cover well. Refrigerate overnight.

2. Soak the grill wood in water overnight.

3. Make the glaze. Place all of the ingredients except the cornstarch and water into a medium-size pot and place over high heat. Bring to a simmer. Turn off the heat and allow to steep for 20 minutes. Mix the water and the cornstarch to make a slurry. Bring back to a simmer and whisk in the slurry. Bring to a boil and remove from the heat.

(Recipe continued on next page)

Grilling the Ribs:

1 Fill the Weber chimney with charcoal. Ignite the charcoal and allow it to burn until the coals are evenly lit and glowing. Place the coals in an even layer in the bottom of the kettle grill. Place the rack of the grill as close to the coals as possible.

2 Drain the ribs. Discard the brine. Dry the ribs with a paper towel. Season the ribs with the smoked salt and smoked pepper. Place the ribs on the grill, over the hot coals, in a single, even layer. Char the ribs over the hot fire for 5 minutes on each side. Remove the ribs and hold them at room temperature.

3 Lift the rack from the grill and push the coals to one side. Place the barrel staves on the coals. Replace the rack. After about 2 minutes, place the ribs in a single layer on the side of the grill where there are no coals. Place the lid on the grill with the vents slightly open. Smoke the ribs for 30-45 minutes. It's important to monitor the airflow of the grill. Keeping the vents slightly open will allow a nice, steady flow of subtle smoke.

4 Remove the ribs from the grill. Allow the ribs to rest for 3-5 minutes. Cut them into individual bones. Toss them in the sauce and place them on a platter. Sprinkle with the smoked sesame seeds and chopped cilantro.

" This stuff tastes great on everything!"
– Sean Brock talking about our Kentuckyaki

Max's Chicken Fingers with Sorghum-Mustard Dipping Sauce

My son Max likes anything deep-fried. For these chicken fingers, remember: You've gotta be careful because the salt and pepper is heavier than the flour. To prevent the salt and pepper from falling to the bottom, stir it really well. We give measurements, but it's really to taste. You're not gonna mess these up.

Serves 3-4

For the Dipping Sauce (makes ¾ cup):

½ cup mayonnaise

1 tablespoon Dijon mustard

1 tablespoon Bourbon Barrel Aged Pure Cane Sorghum

¼ teaspoon Bourbon Smoked Sea Salt

For the Chicken Fingers:

2 cups all-purpose flour

1 tablespoon Bourbon Smoked Garlic Salt, plus extra for seasoning

1 tablespoon Bourbon Smoked Paprika

1½ teaspoons Bourbon Smoked Pepper, plus extra for seasoning

1 teaspoon mustard powder

2 eggs

1 tablespoon Bourbon Barrel Aged Worcestershire Sauce

2 tablespoons milk or water

1½ cups panko breadcrumbs

Vegetable or canola oil, for pan frying

1 pound chicken tenderloins

1. Combine all the ingredients for the dipping sauce in a small bowl. Set aside in the refrigerator until needed.

2. Make the breading. In a small, shallow bowl or pie pan, combine the flour, smoked garlic salt, smoked paprika, smoked pepper and mustard powder. In another bowl, beat the eggs and whisk in the Worcestershire sauce and milk or water. In a third bowl, add the panko breadcrumbs.

3. Place a large skillet over medium-high heat. Add about ¾ inch of vegetable or canola oil to the skillet. Season the chicken with a little smoked garlic salt and smoked pepper, if desired. Lightly coat one tenderloin in the seasoned flour, shaking off excess. Dredge in the egg wash, letting excess drip off, then coat in panko breadcrumbs. Repeat with remaining chicken.

4. Test the oil temperature by dropping a breadcrumb into the oil. It should sizzle quickly. Lay the chicken fingers in the oil, but don't overcrowd the pan. Adjust heat to maintain a steady oil temperature. Cook for 2½-3 minutes or until golden brown on one side, then flip. Cook until golden brown on the other side. Remove from oil and drain on a wire rack or paper towel-lined tray. Repeat with remaining chicken fingers. Serve immediately with the sorghum-mustard dipping sauce.

Kentuckyaki L.A. Style Galbi

Now, more and more butchers know what you mean when you ask for "Korean-style" short ribs. I used to ask for "picnic-style." The Kroger by me knows exactly what I want. They're thin and they cook fast. If you're pressed for time, soak them in the Kentuckyaki for 30 minutes, though marinating them overnight is better. I love grilling these for guests.

Serves 6-8

5-6 pounds galbi-style cut beef short ribs (ask for picnic ribs cut ¼ inch thick across the bones, also known as "flanken")

1 bottle Kentuckyaki™ sauce

1 Asian or regular pear, grated

2 scallions, sliced

 In a large bowl or shallow pan, mix the Kentuckyaki with the grated pear. Add the ribs, tossing to coat well. Marinate them in this mixture for 12-24 hours.

 Heat a grill on high heat. Grill the ribs in batches, turning until they are caramel brown and slightly charred around the edges, about 3-5 minutes per side. Cut ribs between the bones. Garnish with scallions and serve.

I have been using and experimenting with Bourbon Barrel Foods products since the beginning, and as their family of spices and sauces grows, I find each new one as interesting and delicious as the ones before. The quality of the ingredients and their integrity in production makes Bourbon Barrel Foods an indispensable part of any well-stocked, fine kitchen.

— Chef Allen Heintzman

Steak au Poivre "Louisville Style"

This riff on the classic dish is by chef Allen Heintzman. Instead of deglazing the pan with brandy, he uses bourbon.

— Recipe by Chef Allen Heintzman,
211 Clover Lane, Louisville, Kentucky

Serves 2

2 beef filets (6-8 ounces each; the best you can afford)

3 teaspoons Bourbon Smoked Sea Salt

1 tablespoon Bourbon Smoked Pepper

2 tablespoons vegetable oil or clarified butter

1 teaspoon shallot, minced

2 tablespoons parsley, chopped, plus extra for garnish

1 clove garlic, minced

¼ cup Kentucky bourbon

¼ cup beef stock

¾ cups heavy cream

1. Pat the steaks dry with a paper towel. Season with smoked salt and allow them to sit uncovered, at room temperature, for 30 minutes. Pour the smoked pepper onto a plate. Press each filet firmly into the pepper, creating a crust on all sides

2. Heat a small sauté pan or cast iron pan on medium-high heat. Add the vegetable oil or clarified butter. Sear filets on each side for approximately 2 minutes, then remove from pan and set aside. Add shallots to the pan and cook for 1 minute, then add the parsley and garlic. Sauté for 1 minute more. Pour in the bourbon to deglaze the pan and simmer for 30 seconds. Add the beef stock and heavy cream. Bring to a simmer. Add filets back to the pan. Allow the filets to simmer in the sauce for 5 minutes for medium rare. Remove from the pan and allow them to rest for 5 minutes. Meanwhile, simmer the sauce to reduce it to your desired consistency. Serve.

Citrus Pepper Chicken with Artichokes, Capers and Angel Hair Pasta

Chicken's kind of bland and is gonna take on any flavor you give it. Our Bourbon Smoked Citrus Pepper has some orange peel, a little bit of fennel and parsley. Our peppercorns are quarter-cracked, which might be a little large for some people; they're really smoky.

Serves 2

- 3 tablespoons all-purpose flour
- 4 thin chicken cutlets (about ¾ pound total)
- 1 teaspoon Bourbon Smoked Sea Salt
- 1 teaspoon Bourbon Smoked Citrus Pepper
- 2 tablespoons olive oil
- ½ cup reduced sodium chicken broth
- ½ (7-ounce) can artichoke hearts packed in water, drained and quartered
- 1½ tablespoons capers, rinsed and drained
- 1 tablespoon butter
- 4 ounces angel hair pasta
- ¼ cup parsley leaves, chopped
- ¼ cup Parmesan cheese, grated
- 2 lemon wedges, for garnish

1. Set a medium pot of salted water over high heat to boil. Place flour in a shallow dish. Season cutlets with smoked salt and smoked citrus pepper. Dredge cutlets in flour, shaking off excess. In a medium skillet, heat 1 tablespoon of oil over medium-high heat. Lay chicken in skillet, cooking until light golden brown on one side and until edges look opaque and cooked, about 3 minutes. Flip, adding remaining oil as needed, and cook for 1 to 2 minutes more. Do not overcook. Transfer to a plate and set aside.

2. Add broth to skillet and bring to a boil. Cook until reduced by half. Add artichokes, capers and the chicken, along with any juices. Gently shake to combine and bring just to a boil. Remove skillet from heat. Swirl in butter and cover to keep warm.

3. Add pasta to boiling water. Cook until al dente as instructed on package. Drain. Divide pasta between two plates. Lay two chicken cutlets and sauce over pasta. Top with parsley and grated Parmesan cheese. Garnish with a lemon wedge.

Note: this recipe easily doubles to make 4 servings.

My family moved from Chicago to Oldham County, right outside Louisville, when I was seven. While our house was being built on the Ohio River, we stayed at a place called the Melrose Inn, a little diner with old-school neon, which helped make chocolate pecan pie an iconic Louisville dessert famous.

Matt grilling with Susan Nguyen.

Wild Alaskan Salmon with Chipotle Sorghum Glaze and Pineapple, Ginger Salsa

I introduced Anthony to sorghum and he loves cooking with it now. The sorghum provides a slightly sweet and earthy flavor.
— Recipe by Chef Anthony Lamas, Seviche, A Latin Restaurant, Louisville, Kentucky

Serves 6-8

For the Salmon and Marinade:

1 cup Bluegrass Soy Sauce

½ cup roasted sesame oil

½ cup fresh ginger, finely diced

6-8 (6 ounce) fillets of salmon, with skin removed

For the Chipotle Sorghum Glaze:

½ cup Barrel Aged Pure Cane Sorghum

1 tablespoon chipotle in adobo (puréed)

1 tablespoon maple syrup

1 tablespoon apple cider vinegar

Juice of 1 lime

For the Pineapple, Ginger Salsa:

2 cups pineapple, small-diced

2 red tomatoes, small-diced

⅓ cup red onion, finely chopped

2 tablespoons rice wine vinegar

2 tablespoons roasted sesame oil

2 tablespoons Bluegrass Soy Sauce

1 tablespoon fresh ginger, peeled and grated

1 tablespoon Bourbon Smoked Sesame Seeds

½ cup cilantro leaves, chopped

1. For the marinade, whisk together soy sauce, sesame oil and fresh ginger. Pour marinade over salmon and marinade for 2 hours or overnight.

2. For the glaze, whisk together all ingredients to combine. Refrigerate until needed. Serve at room temperature, whisking before serving.

3. To make the salsa, combine all the ingredients, except the cilantro, in a medium bowl. Add cilantro to salsa right before serving.

4. To cook the salmon, preheat a grill or grill pan. Remove salmon from marinade, wiping away excess marinade with a paper towel. Grill salmon, flesh side (opposite of skin side) down, 2-3 minutes. Flip and grill 2 minutes more. To serve salmon, drizzle chipotle sorghum over fillets and top with pineapple salsa. Garnish with extra cilantro, if desired.

Thai Marinated Chicken Thighs

I love it when chefs give us recipes like this because it's an example of something he'd do at home.

— Recipe by Chef Matt McCallister, FT33, Dallas, Texas

Makes 8 Chicken Thighs

For the Marinade:

3 garlic cloves, roughly chopped

1 shallot, peeled and roughly chopped

½ cup Bluegrass Soy Sauce

2 tablespoons fish sauce

2 tablespoons sambal chili paste

2 tablespoons ginger, chopped

¼ teaspoon cloves, ground

1½ cups cilantro, leaves and stems, roughly chopped, plus extra leaves for garnish

Juice of 2 limes

½ cup Bourbon Smoked Sugar

½ cup water

For Chicken Thighs:

8 chicken thighs, preferably with bone in and skin on

2 tablespoons vegetable oil

1. In a food processor or blender, add all of the marinade ingredients except for the smoked sugar and water. Process or blend until smooth. Add smoked sugar and water. Blend to combine. Marinate the chicken in a plastic bag or a shallow pan, preferably overnight or 30 minutes to an hour if you have less time.

2. Preheat oven to 425 degrees. Heat a large cast iron or oven-proof skillet on high heat. Remove chicken from the marinade and shake off excess. Add the oil to the pan. Lay chicken thighs, skin side down, in the pan. Do not move the chicken. Allow the skin to render out fat and begin to brown, about 2-3 minutes. Reduce heat to medium-high. Once the chicken releases easily, occasionally move the thighs to different parts of the pan to brown the skin evenly. Cook chicken for another 10 minutes or until the skin is very crispy and golden brown. Flip the thighs and place the skillet in the lower third of the oven.

3. Roast for about 15 minutes. Arrange on a serving platter, garnish with chopped cilantro leaves, and serve.

Ahi Tuna Tostada

Katsuji Tanabe is a Japanese-Mexican chef who cooks kosher at his restaurants. He's been begging me to make my soy sauce kosher.

— Recipe by Chef Katsuji Tanabe, MexiKosher, Los Angeles, California, NYC and Barrio, Chicago

Makes 6 servings

6 corn tortillas

Vegetable oil, for brushing

¼ cup Bluegrass Soy Sauce

Juice of 1 lime

5 shishito peppers, thinly sliced

1 habanero pepper, deseeded and thinly sliced

1 dash of Bourbon Barrel Aged Madagascar Vanilla Extract

8 ounces sushi-grade ahi tuna, cut into small cubes

1 grapefruit, suprême (peeled, sliced segments)

1 orange, suprême (peeled, sliced segments)

¼ cup red onion, thinly sliced

1 cup cilantro leaves, for garnish

½ teaspoon Bourbon Smoked Sea Salt, plus extra for garnishing

1. Preheat oven to 400 degrees. Line a baking sheet with aluminum foil. Brush the tortillas on both sides with the vegetable oil. Lay the tortillas in a single layer on the baking sheet and bake for 5 minutes. Flip the tortillas and bake for another 5 minutes. Remove the tortillas from the oven and allow them to cool.

2. In a medium-sized mixing bowl, combine the soy sauce, lime juice, shishito and habanero peppers and vanilla extract. Mix well to combine and allowed to marinate for 30 minutes.

3. In a large bowl, combine the tuna with all the citrus segments and sliced red onion. Season with smoked salt. Pour the soy sauce and lime mixture over the top and gently fold to combine. Top each tostada with a few spoonsful of the tuna mixture. Garnish with some cilantro leaves and a sprinkle of smoked sea salt. Serve immediately.

Parmesan Crusted Chicken Breasts

This one is from food and travel writer Gwen Pratesi. Actually, her husband created it. It looks basic, but it's not. Our Bourbon Smoked Paprika really elevates it. This was one of my favorite dishes while taste-testing these recipes. Gwen says, "You can brine them for at least four, and up to eight, hours before coating and baking them. This will make them incredibly tender and add another layer of flavor. For a bit of kick, we like to add some red pepper flakes to a basic brine of kosher salt, sugar, aromatics and black pepper."

— Recipe by Gwen Pratesi, food and travel writer, PratesiLiving.com

Serves 4

- 4 large boneless, skinless chicken breasts
- 20 saltine crackers
- ½ cup finely grated Parmesan cheese
- 2 teaspoons Bourbon Smoked Sea Salt
- 1 teaspoon Bourbon Smoked Pepper
- 1 teaspoon Bourbon Smoked Paprika
- 1 teaspoon red pepper flakes
- ⅛ teaspoon dried oregano
- 1 teaspoon garlic powder
- 1 egg, lightly beaten
- 2 tablespoons milk (whole milk preferred)
- 2 tablespoons unsalted butter, melted
- Bourbon Smoked Sea Salt, for finishing

1 Preheat oven to 375 degrees. Spray a baking rack with baking spray or grease lightly with oil and place into an appropriate-sized baking pan and set aside. Rinse, pat chicken breasts dry and set aside.

2 Add saltine crackers to a large plastic bag and, with a rolling pin, beat them into smaller pieces and then roll them to make fine crumbs. Add Parmesan cheese, smoked salt, smoked pepper, smoked paprika, red pepper flakes, oregano and garlic powder. Shake the bag well to combine all the ingredients. In a small, shallow bowl, whisk together the egg and milk. Dredge the chicken breasts in the egg and milk mixture and then place in the bag with the saltines and seasonings. Add two at a time to avoid over-crowding. Shake well to coat.

3 Place chicken breasts on prepared baking rack. Drizzle melted butter evenly on chicken breasts. Place in preheated oven and cook for 30-40 minutes, until internal temperature reaches 160 degrees on an instant-read thermometer. Remove them from the oven and sprinkle more smoked sea salt over them. Let them rest for 5-10 minutes before serving.

Tonkatsu

(Crispy, Breaded Pork Cutlets)

I had tonkatsu for the first time in Tokyo Station, toward the end of my second trip to Japan. It was probably the most Western thing I had to eat when I was there. The enormous pork chop looked daunting. They cut it for you, then shred pretty much an entire head of napa cabbage onto it. And you don't think you're gonna eat the whole thing, but then you do. Plus a 22-ounce beer.

Makes 4 Cutlets

4 small, boneless, ½ inch thick pork chops

Bourbon Barrel Smoked Salt, to taste

Bourbon Barrel Smoked Pepper, to taste

¼ cup all-purpose flour

2 large eggs, beaten

1 cup panko (Japanese bread crumbs)

Canola or vegetable oil, for frying

½ small head of green cabbage, sliced very thinly*

The Original Henry Bain's Famous Sauce, for serving

1. Using a meat mallet or small frying pan, pound the pork chops between two sheets of plastic wrap to a ¼ inch thickness. Using the tip of a knife, make small cuts all over each pork chop. This prevents the chops from curling up while cooking. Season each chop on both sides with smoked salt and pepper.

2. Place the flour in a shallow bowl or pan. In another shallow bowl, beat the eggs. In one more shallow bowl, add the panko. Bread the pork chops. Coat lightly in flour, then dip in egg, allow excess to drip off. Dip into panko, coating evenly on all sides. Set aside on a sheet pan. Repeat with remaining chops.

3. Fill a medium to large frying pan with oil to come up to about ½ inch. Heat over medium high heat. When oil begins to ripple (about 350 degrees), carefully lay the cutlets into the oil and fry until golden brown, about 2 minutes on each side. Transfer to a paper towel lined plate to drain. Fry in two batches if using a smaller pan (avoid overcrowding the pan). Season with a little more smoked salt, if desired.

4. Serve each cutlet sliced with a mound of shredded cabbage and a drizzle of Henry Bain's sauce.

Note: For very thinly shredded cabbage, a sharp vegetable peeler does an excellent job making nice, thin shreds.

Raw Egg over Hot Rice

This is definitely something I have when I visit Japan. I was a bit concerned the first time I had it because I was mixing a raw egg into a bowl of hot rice. But as I mixed in the egg, the hot rice cooked it and made everything so creamy. You could probably clean out your refrigerator with this dish. If you have half an avocado leftover, for example, it'll add some good texture to the rice. Always add a dash of soy sauce.

Makes 1 serving

1 fresh egg

1 tablespoon Bluegrass Soy, or more to taste

1 cup hot, cooked Japanese short grain rice

Bourbon Smoked Togarashi, for garnishing

Optional Toppings:

Bourbon Barrel Smoked Sesame Seeds

Ikura or masago (egg roe)

Nori strips

Diced avocado

Sliced scallions

1. Crack egg into a small mixing bowl and add soy sauce. Whisk well to incorporate. Place hot rice in a serving bowl and pour egg mixture over the top. Sprinkle with smoked togarashi. Serve. Add or substitute other toppings as you like.

Soy Braised Pork Belly and Eggs
(Kakuni)

This has all sorts of my favorite things: slow-cooked meat, eggs, soy sauce. The soy sauce gives it that brininess. The sweetness comes from the fat in the pork belly and the smoked sugar. The egg adds richness. Just layer upon layer of flavor.

Serves 6

For the Pork:

2¼ pounds pork belly (you may also use pork butt or shoulder if a leaner cut of meat is desired)

2 tablespoons vegetable oil

1 small leek, washed

2 scallions, washed

2 thumb-sized pieces of ginger, sliced

6 eggs

For the Final Braising Liquid:

1½ teaspoons dashi powder

5 cups water

½ cup sake or dry sherry

⅓ cup mirin

½ cup Bourbon Smoked Sugar

½ cup Bluegrass Soy Sauce

1 thumb-sized piece of ginger, sliced

1 mild, green chili pepper

Bourbon Smoked Togarashi, for garnishing

Note: This dish can be made ahead of time. Cool completely before refrigerating. The next day, a layer of hard fat will be on the top and can easily be scooped off. Reheat gently on the stove to serve.

1. Cut the pork belly into 2-inch pieces. Heat a heavy, large, low-sided pot over medium high heat and add the oil. Add the pork belly in a single layer and brown on all sides until nicely colored. Remove and transfer to a paper towel-lined plate. Repeat with any remaining pork. Wipe out excess fat from the pot.

2. Cut the green part of the leek into 2-inch pieces. Add the browned pork, green leek, scallions and sliced ginger to the pot. Add enough water to cover. Bring to a boil, then reduce heat to a simmer. Partially cover with a lid and cook for 2-3 hours, turning meat occasionally. (The longer you simmer, the more tender the meat will be.) Add more water, if needed, to keep meat covered.

3. Make the boiled eggs. Add 6 eggs to a pot. Cover with water. Heat over high heat and bring to a boil. Lower heat to a simmer and cook for 9 minutes. Drain eggs and place in an ice bath to cool off completely. Once cool, peel eggs. Set aside.

4. In another large pot, add all the ingredients for the final braising liquid. Remove the pork from the first pot and add to the braising liquid. Bring to a boil and reduce heat to a simmer. Partially cover with a lid. Simmer for 30 minutes. Remove the lid and add the hard boiled eggs. Simmer with the lid off for another 30 minutes, rotating meat and eggs in the sauce occasionally. Cook until sauce is reduced and the meat is nicely glazed. Serve with a perfectly cooked bowl of white rice.

Kentuckyaki Pork Burger Sliders

I love the pork burger at MilkWood, which is one of Edward Lee's restaurants in Louisville. There's not much that I crave, but that thing? It's two thin patties of pork and they get crusty on the outside. Then there's kimchi and pork cracklin' on top, with a pretzel bun. You just don't put it down. The recipe here is one of my favorites to make. Sweet, salty, spicy. It's just complete.

Makes 14 Sliders

For the Spicy Aioli:

½ cup Mayonnaise

2 tablespoons sriracha sauce

1 tablespoon lemon juice

¼ teaspoon Bourbon Smoked Sea Salt

For the Sliders:

½ small pineapple, peeled, cored, cut into thin wedges

⅓ cup Bourbon Smoked Sugar

2¼ pounds ground pork

¾ cup Kentuckyaki™ Sauce

¼ cup parsley, chopped

¼ cup cilantro, chopped

¼ cup scallions, finely sliced

14 mini pretzel buns or regular mini slider buns

 In a small bowl, combine all the ingredients for the aioli. Whisk well to combine. Set aside in the refrigerator. For the pineapple, roll the wedges lightly in the smoked sugar and set aside.

 Preheat a griddle pan or prepare an outdoor grill. For the burgers, combine the pork, Kentuckyaki sauce, parsley, cilantro, and scallions. Using about 3 ounces, form 14 patties. Flatten into a slightly larger size than the slider buns.

 Grill patties for about 3 minutes per side. Cover and allow to rest. Grill the pineapple slices, turning to caramelize each slice. Place slider buns on grill briefly to warm and toast slightly. Cut the pineapple wedges to fit each slider.

 Assemble the sliders. Spoon a little aioli on the bottom of a bun. Top with a pork patty and slices of grilled pineapple. Serve immediately.

Bluegrass Fried Chicken

My daughter was four or five — she was in the big-girl car seat — and we were at Doll's Market that used to be in Louisville. Whenever they were frying chicken, the smell filled up the entire store and I always had to buy some. I'd always get two drumsticks — one to eat while shopping, the other for the drive home. After loading the groceries into the car, I started eating the second one and Maddie goes, "What are you eating?" I responded, "It's a chicken leg, babe." Maddie said, "Can I have some?" I handed the whole thing back to her and she started gnawing on it. She became a daddy's girl right there in the rear-view mirror.

Makes 8-10 pieces

For the Buttermilk Marinade:

4 cups buttermilk

¼ cup Bluegrass Soy Sauce

2 teaspoons Bourbon Smoked Garlic Salt

2 teaspoons Bourbon Smoked Pepper

1 teaspoon Bourbon Smoked Paprika

1 teaspoon Bourbon Smoked Chili Powder

1 teaspoon dried thyme

For the Chicken:

1 whole fryer chicken, cut into 8-10 pieces

Canola oil, for frying

Bourbon Barrel Aged Pure Cane Sorghum, for drizzling

For the Flour Dredge:

3 cups all-purpose flour

1 tablespoon Bourbon Smoked Paprika

1 tablespoon Bourbon Smoked Chili Powder

2 teaspoons Bourbon Smoked Sea Salt

1 teaspoon Bourbon Smoked Pepper

1 teaspoon cayenne or Korean chili flakes (optional, more or less to suit your taste)

1 brown paper grocery bag

1. In a large bowl, add all the ingredients for the buttermilk marinade. Whisk well to combine. Add the chicken pieces and stir to coat. Cover and leave in the refrigerator to marinate at least 2 hours or, preferably, overnight.

2. Heat a large cast iron skillet or any heavy, high-sided skillet with enough canola oil to fill the skillet about halfway. Heat the oil to 325 degrees. A thermometer will help monitor the temperature and keep it consistent.

3. Combine the ingredients for the flour dredge in the brown paper grocery bag and shake to combine. Remove a piece of chicken from the marinade and allow excess to drip off. Drop into the flour mixture. Add 2-3 more pieces of chicken, fold over top to close, and shake bag to coat chicken completely.

4. Carefully drop chicken pieces into the hot oil. Repeat with remaining chicken pieces but do not overcrowd the skillet. Adjust the heat to maintain a steady temperature as more chicken is added to the pan. Fry, turning chicken only once. Chicken is done when golden brown on both sides. White meat should register 155 degrees and dark meat 165 degrees. Drain on a wire rack set into a rimmed baking sheet or on paper towels. Season the chicken with a little extra smoked sea salt, if desired. Serve hot or room temperature with a drizzle of sorghum and Chive and Smoked Pepper Biscuits (See recipe, page 259).

Indian Karahi Chicken

My CFO Alifiya, is from Mumbai, India. The heart of the Bollywood film industry. She brings me food all the time. I love going out for Indian food and I like it even more when she suggests what to order. She knows what's good and she knows how to cook. Her husband loves our smoked chili powder. She's currently the most important woman in my life.

— Recipe by Alifiya Chasmawala CFO of Bourbon Barrel Foods, Louisville, Kentucky

Serves 5-6

For the Chicken Marinade:

2 tablespoons plain yogurt

Juice of half a lemon

2 teaspoons Bourbon Smoked Paprika

1 teaspoon Bourbon Smoked Sea Salt

1 teaspoon ginger, grated

1 teaspoon garlic, minced

½ teaspoon turmeric powder

1 whole chicken, cut into small pieces (12 or more)

For the Curry:

¼ cup vegetable oil

2 tablespoons butter

2 cloves, whole

2 cinnamon sticks

2 cardamom pods, cracked

1 teaspoon cumin seeds

2 teaspoons dried fenugreek leaves (also called methi leaves)

2 medium-sized onions, finely diced

2 teaspoons fresh ginger, grated

1 garlic clove, grated

6-8 medium tomatoes, finely chopped

2 serrano or Anaheim chilies, slit on one side (optional)

2 teaspoons Bourbon Smoked Pepper

1 tablespoon Bourbon Smoked Sea Salt (or to taste)

2 teaspoons Bourbon Smoked Chili Powder

1 teaspoon cumin, ground

1 teaspoon coriander, ground

½ cup water

1 green bell pepper, diced

½ cup cilantro leaves

1 teaspoon garam masala

Juice of half a lemon

2 tablespoons of ginger, julienned, for garnish (optional)

1. In a large plastic storage bag, combine all the ingredients for the marinade. Add the chicken pieces and toss to coat well. Marinate in the refrigerator for at least an hour or overnight, if possible.

2. Heat the oil and butter in a large sauté pan, on high heat. Add the whole spices (cloves, cinnamon sticks, cardamom and cumin seeds). Once the spices start to sputter, add the fenugreek leaves, followed by the chopped onion. Lower heat to medium and sauté until the onions are soft, translucent and start to turn golden. Add the ginger and garlic, followed by the chopped tomatoes and one serrano or Anaheim chili. Cook for 10 minutes or until the tomatoes reduce and thicken.

3. Raise heat to high. Add the chicken pieces and sauté in the sauce for 5 minutes. Add the smoked pepper, smoked salt, smoked chili powder, ground cumin, coriander and water. Bring to a boil, partially cover the pot, and reduce heat to low. Simmer for 20 minutes, stirring occasionally. Add the chopped bell pepper and another serrano or Anaheim chili, as well as half the cilantro leaves. Uncover, adjusting heat to maintain a good simmer, and cook for another 10-15 minutes. The bell pepper should be soft and the sauce should be reduced. If sauce is still loose, continue simmering until sauce is a thicker consistency.

4. Stir in the garam masala and lemon juice. Cover, remove from heat and allow to rest for 20 minutes. Taste and adjust seasoning. Garnish with the julienned ginger and remaining cilantro leaves. Serve with basmati rice or naan bread.

Smoky Cioppino

This seafood stew is one of my favorite things to make. I know I've said this before, but seriously, the smokiness of our paprika tastes like you cooked something with a little bacon in it. You've gotta have a hearty whitefish in there, like a monkfish, that's not going to totally break down. Some shellfish, some shrimp — even some squid or octopus.

Serves 8-10

3 tablespoons olive oil

1 large fennel bulb, thinly sliced

1 large onion, diced

2 large shallots, diced

4 garlic cloves, minced

2 tablespoons Bourbon Smoked Paprika

1 teaspoon red pepper flakes

1 tablespoon Bourbon Smoked Sea Salt

¼ cup tomato paste

½ cup Kentucky bourbon

½ cup dry vermouth

½ cup Campari

1 28-ounce can diced tomatoes

4 cups chicken stock

1 cup clam juice

1 bay leaf

1 pound clams, scrubbed

1 pound mussels, scrubbed

1 pound shrimp, peeled and deveined

1 pound fish (any firm fleshed fish such as salmon, halibut, monkfish or cod) cut into 2-inch chunks

1 In a very large pot or Dutch oven, heat the oil over high heat. Add the fennel, onion, and shallots. Sauté for 10 minutes. Add the garlic, smoked paprika, red pepper flakes and smoked salt. Sauté for another 2 minutes. Stir in the tomato paste and cook for 1 minute more. Add the bourbon, vermouth and Campari to deglaze the pan. Simmer for 5 minutes or until reduced by half. Add the diced tomatoes, chicken stock, clam juice and the bay leaf. Cover and bring to a boil. Reduce heat to medium-low and simmer, covered, for 30 minutes.

2 Add the clams and mussels to the pot. Cover and cook for 5 minutes. Add the shrimp and fish and gently simmer, covered, until just cooked through, about another 5 minutes. Discard any clams or mussels that do not open. Taste and adjust seasoning as desired. Ladle into bowls and serve with warm, crusty bread.

Bluegrass Soy, Citrus Braised Lamb Shanks with Farro Pilaf

This is a good way to showcase Western-style cooking with soy sauce. In Japan they don't understand how we use it. They're captivated when we talk about it as an ingredient in barbecue sauce because barbecue sauce is so American. As the soy sauce cooks down, the flavors, like tobacco and leather, become more pronounced.

Serves 4

4 lamb shanks (about 4 pounds), trimmed

1 tablespoon whole coriander seeds, coarsely ground in a spice grinder or mortar and pestle

1 tablespoon Bourbon Smoked Sea Salt

½ tablespoon Bourbon Smoked Citrus Pepper

2 tablespoons vegetable oil

2 medium onions, diced

3 garlic cloves, minced

2 stalks of lemongrass, smashed and chopped

2 inch piece of ginger, peeled and coarsely chopped

1 chili, red or green, coarsely chopped

¼ cup white wine

¾ cup orange juice, fresh squeezed

¾ cup Bluegrass Soy Sauce

½ cup Bourbon Barrel Aged Pure Cane Sorghum

1 tablespoon Bourbon Barrel Aged Worcestershire Sauce

2 cups chicken stock

Water

1. Heat a large dutch oven or high-sided skillet on high heat. While pan is heating, season the lamb shanks with the coriander, smoked salt and smoked pepper, pressing the seasonings into the meat. Add the oil to the pan. Brown the shanks in batches, if necessary, to avoid overcrowding the pan. Brown the shanks well on all sides. Remove and set aside. Add the diced onions and garlic and sauté for 3-5 minutes. Add the lemongrass, ginger, and chili and sauté for another 2-3 minutes. Deglaze the pan with the white wine and orange juice. Cook and reduce liquid by half.

2. Place the lamb shanks back in the pot and pour in the soy sauce, sorghum, Worcestershire sauce and chicken stock. The shanks should be just covered in liquid. Top off with water, if needed. Bring to a boil and cover pot with lid. Lower heat to low and simmer for 3 hours. When done, the meat should be falling off the bone.

3. Remove the lamb shanks from the pot and cover with foil to keep warm. Strain the liquid in the pot through a mesh strainer and pour back into the pot. Bring to a boil and cook over high heat. Reduce liquid by about one-third, cooking for 25-30 minutes, or until thick, glossy and sauce-like. It should easily coat the back of a spoon. Taste and adjust seasoning with more smoked salt and smoked pepper, if needed. Serve lamb shanks warm with the sauce and Farro Pilaf (see recipe, page 240).

Bourbon Smoked Meatloaf

I made this one day for "family lunch" at work and we struggled to re-create it for the book. The employees were asking me for the recipe. This was a clean-the-refrigerator-out dish. I knew that, if it sucked, at least the bacon would make it better. It's got all those things you'd see in a Bolognese — ground pork, ground beef — but it's just a slab of meat. Man, just talking about it — I'm gonna have to make it again soon.

Serves 12-14 (makes 2 meatloaves)

1 cup day-old bread, cubed, crusts removed

1 cup heavy cream

¼ pound smoked bacon (about 5 slices), sliced into lardons

1½ pounds ground beef

1½ pounds ground pork

2 tablespoons Bourbon Barrel Aged Worcestershire Sauce

1 tablespoon Bourbon Smoked Sea Salt

½ teaspoon Bourbon Smoked Pepper

¼ cup parsley, chopped

2 teaspoons sage, chopped

1 teaspoon rosemary, chopped

1 teaspoon thyme, chopped

¼ pound (4 ounces) Cheddar cheese, grated

2 eggs, lightly beaten

1. In a small bowl, combine bread with cream and set aside to soften, about 10 minutes. Cook the bacon in a small skillet over medium-high heat until browned but not crisp, about 8 minutes. Drain on a paper towel-lined plate.

2. In a large bowl, combine the beef, pork and cooked bacon. Add the Worcestershire sauce, smoked salt, smoked pepper, herbs and cheese. Using hands, gently knead seasoning into the meat. Combine soaked bread with beaten eggs. Pour mixture over seasoned meat and knead until well combined.

3. Preheat oven to 350 degrees. Line a rimmed baking sheet with parchment or foil. Divide the mixture in half and form two loaves, placing on pan. Bake for 40 to 45 minutes or until a thermometer inserted in the center registers 160 degrees. Let meatloaves rest for 10 minutes before slicing and serving.

Sorghum Glazed Meatloaf

You know how the sugars caramelize on a honey-glazed ham? Same concept here but with sorghum.

Serves 10-12

¾ pound (12 ounces) smoked bacon, sliced into lardons

1 cup onion, finely diced

3 cloves garlic, minced

2 large eggs

½ cup buttermilk

2 tablespoons Bourbon Barrel Aged Worcestershire Sauce

1 tablespoon dry mustard

2 teaspoons Bourbon Smoked Sea Salt

¾ teaspoon dried thyme

½ teaspoon Bourbon Smoked Pepper

Dash of hot sauce (optional)

1½ pounds ground beef

1½ pounds ground pork

¾ cup dry breadcrumbs or panko

⅓ cup parsley, finely chopped

¼ cup Bourbon Barrel Aged Pure Cane Sorghum

2 tablespoons Dijon mustard

Cook bacon in a medium skillet over medium-high heat until browned but not crisp, about 8 minutes. Transfer to paper towel-lined plate to drain. Pour off all but 2 tablespoons of the fat from the pan. Lower heat, add onion, and sauté until soft, about 3 minutes. Add garlic to pan. Cook for 1 minute more. Remove from heat and set aside.

Preheat oven to 375 degrees. In a medium bowl, whisk together the eggs, buttermilk, Worcestershire sauce, dry mustard, smoked salt, thyme, smoked pepper and hot pepper sauce.

In a large bowl, combine beef, pork, breadcrumbs, cooked bacon, the onion mixture and the wet ingredients. Using your hands, toss lightly to mix. Add parsley and gently knead until combined. Line a rimmed baking sheet with parchment or foil. Form mixture into a loaf on baking sheet.

In a small bowl, whisk together sorghum and Dijon mustard. Brush or spoon a thick layer of the mixture over the meatloaf. Bake for 1 hour and 15 minutes or until a thermometer inserted into the center registers 160 degrees. Let the meatloaf rest for 10 minutes before slicing and serving.

Bacon, Pimento Cheese and Jalapeño Burger

This is another one from Robyn Lindars. If I'm gonna have some heat, it's gotta be a fresh jalapeño. I hate those off-colored green ones from a can. They're like eating canned mushrooms. You've gotta use fresh.

— Recipe by Robyn Lindars, food writer, GrillGirl.com

Makes 4 burgers

1 tablespoon olive oil

3 jalapeños, deseeded and sliced in ¼-inch slices

8 strips bacon

1-1¼ pounds ground beef

Bourbon Smoked Sea Salt, for seasoning burgers

Bourbon Smoked Pepper, for seasoning burgers

4 onion rolls (or bun of your choice)

2 cups pimento cheese (store-bought or see our recipe, page 105)

1. Preheat a grill pan or set up an outdoor grill for direct heat. In a small sauté pan, add the olive oil and heat over high heat. Add the sliced jalapeños and sauté for 2-3 minutes. Set aside. Microwave the bacon strips for 3 minutes or until crispy. Drain on paper towels and set aside. Divide the beef into four equal portions and form into patties. Put an indentation in the middle with your thumb, which will help the burger stay flat while cooking. Season both sides with a little smoked salt and smoked pepper.

2. Grill the burgers until they have reached an internal temperature of 140 degrees for a medium burger. Let the burgers rest, covered loosely, for 5-10 minutes to reabsorb the juices. While they are resting, quickly toast the buns on the grill.

3. Assemble the burgers. Layer some pimento cheese, bacon, and jalapeños on each burger. Have additional condiments such as ketchup, mayo or mustard out for people to help themselves. They probably won't be needed! Enjoy a trifecta of creamy pimento cheese, coupled with bacon and the spiciness of the jalapeños.

Barbecued Chicken Legs

There's just something about eating chicken straight off the bone that appeals to me. My grandmother was the same way. My oldest memory of barbecuing is basting chicken legs on a grill. I just remember the way the barbecue sauce caramelized on the grill right over the fire, the way the skin got nice and crispy. For our barbecue sauce, the sorghum adds sweetness to the meat. The salt, pepper and paprika add a ton of smokiness. When I did these at a wine tasting, I served them over fresh-cut rosemary. Having that rosemary blossom underneath the warm chicken legs was pretty and it tasted awesome. One of my favorite things in the book.

Serves 6

4 tablespoons Bourbon Smoked Sea Salt

1 tablespoon Bourbon Smoked Pepper

1 cup boiling water

3 cups cold water

6 chicken drumsticks, trimmed of excess fat

6 chicken thighs, trimmed of excess fat

2 cups Bourbon Barrel Barbecue Sauce, plus extra for serving

1. In a large bowl or container, add the smoked salt, smoked pepper and 1 cup boiling water. Stir until salt is dissolved. Add the cold water and stir. Drop in the chicken pieces and place into the refrigerator. Leave chicken to brine for 1-2 hours or overnight.

2. Heat a grill for indirect grilling. Light charcoals, burn until ash gray and dump them all onto one side of the grill. Alternately, turn on just one side of a gas grill. Once grill is hot, clean and oil the grate. Remove chicken from brine and place onto paper towels to dry. Place chicken, skin side down, on the cool side of the grill, away from coals. Cover with a lid. Cook for 20-25 minutes or until chicken starts to brown, turning once or twice.

3. Move chicken closer to coals (the hot side) but not directly over them. Cook and begin to flip chicken often, brushing liberally with the barbecue sauce every 5 minutes until sticky, for about 10-15 minutes more. Remove from grill and rest for 5 minutes before serving. Serve with extra barbecue sauce on the side.

Grilled Togarashi Skirt Steak

I did this recipe for the *Courier-Journal* newspaper in Louisville. Our togarashi accentuates all meat and vegetables. It's packed with umami flavor and has a little kick from cayenne. It's an all-purpose seasoning for the Japanese — both savory and sweet dishes. I've seen it on cheesecake. We do a caramel corn with it.

Makes 4-6 servings

For the Marinade:

¼ cup Bourbon Barrel Aged Pure Cane Sorghum

3 tablespoons Bluegrass Soy Sauce

1 tablespoon Korean chili paste (also known as gochujang)

1 tablespoon rice vinegar

1 teaspoon fish sauce

3 tablespoons Bourbon Smoked Togarashi, plus extra for garnishing

For the Steak:

1½-2 pounds skirt steak

4 radishes, thinly sliced, for garnish

¼ cup cilantro, chopped, for garnish

1. Combine marinade ingredients in a large bowl. Place steak in the bowl or plastic bag and turn to completely coat with the marinade. Chill and marinate for at least 2 hours or overnight.

2. Prepare grill for high, direct heat with one part of the grill for lower, indirect heat. The grill is hot enough when you can hold your hand about an inch over the hot side for only a second.

3. Remove steak from the marinade and shake off excess. Lay steak on the hot side of the grill. Grill for 1-2 minutes on each side to get a good sear, then move the steak to the cooler side of the grill and cook a few minutes more or until done to your liking. Rest steak for 5 minutes. Slice against the grain of the meat. Garnish with the radishes, cilantro and smoked togarashi before serving.

Pollo a la Brasa with Aji Verde Sauce

Chicken is never as tender as when you cook it whole.

Serves 4-6

For the Marinade:

1 (4-pound) chicken

2 tablespoons vegetable oil

2 tablespoons white vinegar

2 tablespoons cumin

1 tablespoon Bluegrass Soy Sauce

1 tablespoon Bourbon Smoked Paprika

1 tablespoon Bourbon Smoked Sea Salt, plus extra for seasoning

1 teaspoon Bourbon Smoked Pepper

2 teaspoons hot sauce

For the Aji Verde Sauce:

1-2 jalapeños, ribs and seeds removed, coarsely chopped

1 garlic clove, chopped

Juice of 1 lime

1 cup cilantro, packed and coarsely chopped

½ cup mayonnaise

¼ cup queso fresco or feta cheese, crumbled

1 tablespoon hot sauce (more or less to taste)

½ teaspoon Bourbon Smoked Sea Salt

¼ teaspoon Bourbon Smoked Pepper

1. Rinse chicken and dry well with paper towels. In a large bowl or large plastic bag, add the ingredients for the marinade. Whisk well to combine. Place the chicken in the marinade and rub into the meat, using your hands. Allow the chicken to marinate, breast side down, overnight in the refrigerator.

2. The following day, remove chicken from the refrigerator 30 minutes before cooking. Preheat the oven to 425 degrees. Place the chicken in a roasting pan or on a rimmed baking sheet lined with parchment paper or foil. Tie the legs together, if desired. Season the outside of the chicken with a little more smoked salt. Roast the chicken for 15 minutes. Reduce the temperature to 375 degrees and roast for about an hour or until a thermometer inserted into the thickest part of the thigh registers 165 degrees.

3. Remove from the oven and tent with foil. Allow the chicken to rest for 10-15 minutes before carving. While chicken is resting, make the sauce.

4. Combine all the ingredients for the sauce in a blender. Blend until puréed. Add a couple of teaspoons of water if too thick. Taste and adjust seasoning, if necessary. Serve chicken with aji verde sauce. Extra sauce keeps in the refrigerator for 3 days.

Smoked Paprika Shrimp and Grits

It's a total Low Country thing, a crowd-pleaser that restaurants put on their menus. The first time I had it was at Jack Fry's, a historic restaurant in Louisville where I worked from age 22 to 24. I was probably the worst server in the history of Jack Fry's, but it did give me an appreciation for food. We always ordered the shrimp and grits after shifts.

Serves 4

For the Grits:

4 cups water

1 teaspoon Bourbon Smoked Sea Salt

1 cup finely ground grits or cornmeal (also called "instant grits" or "polenta")

2 tablespoons butter

1 cup sharp Cheddar cheese, grated

1 teaspoon Bourbon Smoked Pepper

For the Shrimp:

1 tablespoon butter

1 tablespoon olive oil

4 scallions, sliced, whites and greens separated

2 garlic cloves, minced

1 pound shrimp, peeled and deveined

2 teaspoons Bourbon Smoked Paprika

1 teaspoon Bourbon Smoked Sea Salt

½ teaspoon Bourbon Smoked Citrus Pepper

Juice of ½ lemon

¼ cup parsley, chopped, plus more for garnish

1. In a large pot, bring water and salt to a boil. Pour grits in slowly, whisking vigorously, to combine. Once simmering, lower heat to a gentle bubble and cook grits for 10-12 minutes, stirring occasionally. Remove from heat and stir in butter, Cheddar cheese and smoked pepper. Cover pot with a lid to keep warm.

2. Heat a large skillet over high heat. Add butter and olive oil to pan. Once melted, add the scallion whites and sauté for 1 minute. Add the garlic and shrimp and cook until shrimp turn pink and opaque, about 2 minutes. Season with the smoked paprika, smoked salt and smoked citrus pepper. Toss and cook for another minute. Remove from heat. Add the lemon juice, scallion greens and parsley. Stir to combine.

3. Spoon grits into a serving bowl. Pour shrimp on top and garnish with parsley. Serve immediately.

Vietnamese Grilled Chicken Thigh Salad

I love cooking with chicken thighs as opposed to chicken breasts. The darker meat has so much more flavor and holds up well to braising. I almost want to describe the flavor of this dish as floral. It just tastes healthy. The mint combined with the salted peanuts is one of my favorite combinations.

Serves 4

For the Marinade:

¼ cup Bluegrass Soy Sauce

Juice of 3 limes

2 tablespoons ginger, grated

1 tablespoon toasted sesame oil

2 garlic cloves, crushed

1¼ pounds boneless, skinless chicken thighs

For the Dressing:

¼ cup Bluegrass Soy Sauce

2 tablespoons rice wine vinegar

2 teaspoons fish sauce (optional)

2 small jalapeños, seeded and chopped

½ teaspoon Bourbon Smoked Salt

¼ teaspoon Bourbon Smoked Pepper

¼ cup neutral oil, such as canola

For the Salad:

1 large cucumber, thinly sliced

2 large carrots, julienned or grated

3-4 radishes, thinly sliced

¼ cup cilantro, chopped

¼ cup mint, chopped

½ teaspoon Bourbon Smoked Sea Salt

¼ teaspoon Bourbon Smoked Pepper

¼ cup roasted, salted peanuts, chopped

1. In a shallow pan, combine all the ingredients for the marinade and whisk well to combine. Add the chicken thighs and turn well to coat. Set aside in the refrigerator to marinate for at least an hour.

2. Combine all the ingredients for the dressing, except the oil. Pour the oil in a slow stream and whisk. Set aside.

3. Light a grill for medium-high heat. Remove the chicken from the marinade. Place the chicken on the grill and grill each side for 5-6 minutes, flipping a few times to prevent burning. Transfer to a cutting board and allow to rest.

4. In a large bowl, combine all the ingredients for the salad, except the peanuts. Add the dressing a bit at a time and toss. Add more dressing, as needed. Place salad on a serving platter. Slice chicken and add to salad. Garnish with peanuts and serve.

BATCH 217-15

BOTTLE NUMBER 186

SIDES

222

Grilled Corn, Mexican Style

I have this great photo from when my daughter Maddie was five years old. She would smear the cheese, butter and paprika all over her corn on the cob and go to town. She took a big ol' bite, smiled at me and looked like the Joker with a big clown mouth.

Makes 4-5 servings

¼ cup mayonnaise

¼ cup Mexican crema or sour cream

½ cup Cotija or feta cheese, finely crumbled

½ teaspoon Bourbon Smoked Chili Powder, plus extra for garnish

1 garlic clove, finely minced

¼ cup cilantro, chopped, plus extra for garnishing

½ teaspoon Bourbon Smoked Sea Salt

¼ teaspoon Bourbon Smoked Pepper

4-5 ears corn, shucked

1 lime, cut into wedges

1. Preheat a grill or grill pan for high-heat grilling. While the grill is heating, combine all the ingredients in a medium bowl, except the corn and lime. Stir well.

2. Grill corn, rotating frequently, until cooked and charred on all sides, about 8 minutes total. Using a large spoon or brush, coat cheese mixture evenly on all sides of the grilled corn. Dust with more smoked chili powder and garnish with chopped cilantro. Serve immediately with lime wedges.

Baked Sweet Potatoes with Kalbi Butter

"This recipe makes a good portion of kalbi butter, which can be used for many other purposes: cooking shrimp, slathering on cornbread, putting it on top of grilled steak. You can roll extra butter into logs in parchment paper and store in the freezer until needed."

— Recipe by Chef Edward Lee, 610 Magnolia and MilkWood Restaurants, Louisville, Kentucky

Makes 4 servings, plus extra butter

For the Sweet Potatoes:

4 sweet potatoes, washed and scrubbed

¼ cup corn oil

Bourbon Smoked Sea Salt

2 scallions, chopped, for garnish

For the Kalbi Butter:

⅓ cup Bluegrass Soy Sauce

3 tablespoons Bourbon Smoked Sugar

1 tablespoon toasted sesame oil

3 garlic cloves, roughly chopped

2 tablespoons ginger, grated

2 scallions, roughly chopped

1 teaspoon Korean chili flakes

1 pound unsalted butter, softened

1. Brush potatoes with corn oil. Roll in smoked salt and let sit at room temperature for an hour. Meanwhile, preheat oven to 375 degrees. Bake on a rimmed baking sheet for 1-1½ hours or until soft when pierced with a knife.

2. Make kalbi butter while potatoes are roasting. In a small saucepan, combine the soy sauce, smoked sugar and sesame oil. Bring to a boil and simmer for 5 minutes. Let cool until just slightly warm.

3. In a food processor, add the garlic, ginger, scallion and chili flakes. Pulse until fully blended. Add the softened butter and pulse to combine. Drizzle in the warm soy sauce and process to incorporate. Divide the butter between two sheets of parchment or foil and form into 1½ inch-wide logs. Twist ends of parchment or foil to seal. Chill logs until firm before using.

4. When potatoes are cooked, remove from the oven and split the middle of the potato. Add a generous portion of the kalbi butter. Garnish with the chopped scallions and serve immediately.

Spicy Cold Chinese Noodles

I asked everybody in the office if they wanted to contribute a recipe and this is something one of my old employees, Dalton and his step-dad, Eric, make at home. It's one of their comfort-food dishes.

— Recipe by Dalton Gahafer and Eric Buryn, Bourbon Barrel Foods Friends, Louisville, Kentucky

Serves 6-8

For the Noodles:

12 ounces dried spaghetti or Chinese egg noodles

1 tablespoon vegetable oil

1 English cucumber, julienned

2 carrots, peeled and julienned

2 teaspoons Bourbon Smoked Sesame Seeds

2-3 scallions, green parts only, thinly sliced

For the Sauce:

1 tablespoon vegetable oil

2 teaspoons garlic, minced

2 teaspoons ginger, grated

3 tablespoons tahini

3 tablespoons rice vinegar

3 tablespoons Bluegrass Soy Sauce

3 tablespoons hot water

2 tablespoons smooth peanut butter

2 tablespoons toasted sesame oil

2 tablespoons Bourbon Smoked Sugar

2 teaspoons sambal chili paste (or hot sauce)

½ teaspoon ground Sichuan pepper (optional)

1. Bring a large pot of water to a boil and cook spaghetti or noodles until al dente. This is usually the minimum amount of time according to package instructions. Drain and rinse with cold water. Drain thoroughly and toss with 1 tablespoon of vegetable oil. Set aside in a large mixing bowl.

2. Heat 1 tablespoon of vegetable oil in a small frying pan over medium heat. Quickly sauté the garlic and ginger for 30 seconds or until just fragrant. Remove from the heat and add to a medium sized bowl. Add the remaining ingredients for the sauce and whisk until smooth. Thin with a little additional hot water, if needed.

3. Add the cucumbers and carrots to the noodles. Pour the sauce over the noodles and toss well. Transfer to a serving bowl or platter and garnish with sesame seeds and scallions. Noodles may be made ahead and kept in the refrigerator or served immediately at room temperature. Leftovers will keep in the refrigerator for 2-3 days.

Pommery Potato Salad

This is something I had to make every single day at the restaurant where I worked in Gainesville. It's warm potato salad, which I love. You get it to that temperature where you see the mayonnaise start to separate a little bit.

Serves 5-6 as a side

2 pounds Yukon gold potatoes, washed and cut into 1½ inch chunks

1 tablespoon Bourbon Smoked Sea Salt

½ cup Pommery mustard or other whole grain mustard

⅓ cup mayonnaise

½ cup shallot or red onion, finely diced

¼ cup parsley, chopped

3 tablespoons apple cider vinegar

1 tablespoon Bourbon Barrel Aged Worcestershire Sauce

1 tablespoon prepared horseradish (optional)

1-2 teaspoons Bourbon Smoked Sea Salt

1 teaspoon Bourbon Smoked Pepper

1. Place cut potatoes and salt into a large pot and cover with cold water by 2 inches. Bring to a boil over high heat. Reduce heat and simmer until potatoes are just tender, about 6-8 minutes. Do not overcook. Drain potatoes in a colander and leave to steam dry for 5 minutes.

2. In a large bowl, combine the remaining ingredients and whisk well to combine. Add the potatoes and gently toss to combine. Serve warm or at room temperature.

Sorghum and Soy Braised Collard Greens

We were trying not to be a Southern cookbook, but you can elevate collard greens so easily with our sorghum and soy.

Serves 4 as a side dish

1½ pounds collard greens, washed

1 teaspoon olive oil

¼ pound bacon, cut into 1-inch pieces

1 medium onion, diced

5 cloves garlic, thinly sliced

½ -1 teaspoon crushed red pepper flakes (optional)

½ cup beer (any kind will do)

2 cups low sodium chicken broth

2 tablespoons Bourbon Barrel Aged Pure Cane Sorghum

2 tablespoons apple cider vinegar

1 tablespoon Bluegrass Soy Sauce

1 tablespoon Bourbon Barrel Worcestershire Sauce

2 teaspoons Bourbon Smoked Sea Salt

½ teaspoon Bourbon Smoked Pepper

1. Prepare collard greens by cutting away the tough stems from the leaves. Stack the leaves, roll tightly and cut into ½ inch ribbons. Heat a large pot over medium high heat. Add the olive oil and bacon pieces. Cook until the fat renders out and the bacon is crisp. Remove the bacon with a slotted spoon and drain on a paper towel-lined plate.

2. Add the onion to the bacon fat in the pot. Lower heat to medium and sauté the onion, about 5-6 minutes. Add the garlic and red pepper flakes and sauté for 1 minute more. Add the collard greens, stirring until wilted. Turn heat to high and add the beer. Cook for 1 minute, scraping bottom of pan to deglaze. Add the remaining ingredients along with the reserved bacon and stir well to combine. Bring to a boil. Cover with a lid, reduce heat to low and simmer for 30 minutes or until the greens are soft and tender with just a slight bite. Taste for seasoning and adjust as necessary. Serve hot.

Fried Rice with Broccoli and Mustard Greens

His specialty is vegetables. You'll see why when you taste the mustard greens.
— Recipe by Chef Steven Satterfield of Miller Union in Atlanta, Georgia

Serves 4 as an entrée, 8 as a side dish

4 scallions, thinly sliced, white and light green parts (dark green part reserved for garnish)

5 garlic cloves, minced

2 tablespoons ginger, peeled and minced

1 small hot pepper, seeded and minced

3 tablespoons Bluegrass Soy Sauce (more or less to suit your taste)

1 tablespoon sriracha sauce

Juice of half a lime

4 tablespoons peanut or canola oil, for cooking. Also, the quantity should be divided.

5 large eggs, whisked

2 cups broccoli florets (from 1 small head)

½ cup celery, thinly sliced

½ cup carrots, thinly sliced or julienned

1 bunch (½ pound) mustard greens, washed, trimmed, roughly chopped

5 cups cooked rice, chilled (leftover rice is best)

2 tablespoons roasted sesame oil

Bourbon Smoked Sea Salt (to taste)

3 tablespoons Bourbon Smoked Sesame Seeds, for garnish

1 In a small bowl, combine the white and light green parts of the scallions, garlic, ginger and hot pepper. In another small bowl, combine the soy sauce, sriracha and lime juice. In a large, wide skillet or a wok, heat 1 tablespoon oil over high heat. When the oil begins to shimmer, pour in the whisked eggs and quickly swirl them against the hot surface with the back of a spoon or wooden spatula to make a thin layer. Remove the egg from the pan as soon as it solidifies. Set aside.

2 Add another tablespoon of oil to the pan. When hot, add the broccoli, celery and carrots. Quickly toss to coat. Add about one-third of the scallion mixture and toss well. Spoon over one-third of the soy sauce mixture and toss well. Pour vegetables into a rimmed baking sheet in one layer. Do not pile the vegetables in a mound or they will continue to cook.

3 With the skillet or wok still on high heat, add another tablespoon of oil. Add the mustard greens and one-third of the scallion mixture and one-third of the soy sauce mixture to the pan. Toss to coat well and cook until greens have just wilted. Spread out over the broccoli mixture on a sheet pan.

"I said, 'Who is this Matt Jamie? He's blond and so white. There's no way this stuff tastes good.' But then I tried the soy sauce, which has an incredibly deep and rich umami flavor. Matt has embraced the ancient art."

— Chef Steven Satterfield

Steven & Matt

4 Add another tablespoon of oil to the pan and add the cold rice and the remaining scallion mixture. Toss well, breaking up any clumped rice. Pour the remaining Bluegrass Soy Sauce mixture over rice, stirring frequently to avoid sticking. When rice is hot, add all the vegetables and egg. Toss or stir to combine. Taste and adjust seasoning with extra Bluegrass Soy Sauce or Bourbon Smoked Sea Salt. Pour 2 tablespoons of sesame oil over rice and stir. Remove from heat. Garnish with green, sliced scallions and Bourbon Smoked Sesame Seeds. Serve immediately.

Edamame and Shiitake Salad

This is always popular during tastings in our kitchen studio. Get the shiitake mushrooms nice and crisp. They'll soak up the soy sauce, which accentuates the umami flavors even more.

Serves 8-10 as a side dish

2 tablespoons vegetable oil

8 ounces shiitake mushrooms, stems removed, sliced

1 tablespoon Bourbon Smoked Sea Salt

1 pound shelled edamame, frozen

1 bunch green onions, thinly sliced

4 large radishes, julienned

2 tablespoons Bluegrass Soy Sauce

1 tablespoon rice vinegar

½ tablespoon Bourbon Smoked Togarashi

2 teaspoons toasted sesame oil

1. Heat a large skillet over high heat. Add the vegetable oil and sauté mushrooms for 8-10 minutes or until browned and crispy. Remove from pan, placing on a paper towel-lined plate and allow to cool.

2. Fill a medium saucepan with water and bring to a boil. Add smoked salt and edamame. Blanch for 2-3 minutes. Drain in a colander and rinse with cold water to stop the cooking.

3. Combine mushrooms, green onions edamame and radishes in a large bowl and toss with soy sauce, rice vinegar, smoked togarashi and toasted sesame oil. Serve immediately.

Matt's Smoky Roasted Root Vegetables

Perfect in the fall when you have those gorgeous carrots that are all different colors. I made up this recipe at the last minute. I had some of our chili powder and sorghum and just tossed the carrots in there. Sometimes if they're a little larger, like a potato, I'll hard-boil them to prevent all the moisture from escaping in the oven. You want them all to be similar in size. Find the smallest one and cut the bigger ones like that.

Makes 4 servings

1 pound parsnips, peeled

1 pound carrots, peeled

2 teaspoons Bourbon Smoked Chili Powder

1 teaspoon Bourbon Smoked Sea Salt

½ teaspoon Bourbon Smoked Pepper

2 teaspoons olive oil

2 tablespoons Bourbon Barrel Aged Pure Cane Sorghum, plus extra for garnish

2 tablespoons parsley, chopped, for garnish

1. Preheat oven to 400 degrees. Line a baking sheet with parchment paper. Cut parsnips and carrots in half lengthwise. Cut any thicker vegetables in half again (all the vegetables should roughly be about the same size for even cooking). Place vegetables in a large bowl and add the bourbon smoked chili powder, smoked salt, smoked pepper, olive oil and sorghum. Toss well to combine.

2. Spread vegetables out on a baking sheet in a single layer. Roast for 20 minutes. Flip vegetables with a spatula. Roast for another 15 minutes or until tender and caramelized. Serve on a platter and garnish with a drizzle of sorghum and chopped parsley. Serve immediately.

Smoky Bourbon and Blue Cheese au Gratin Potatoes

She threw the whole cupboard in there. To me, the best part of this dish are the crispy bits stuck to the corners.

— Recipe by Chef Madeleine Dee, Fond Restaurant, Louisville, Kentucky

Serves 10

10 medium sized Yukon gold potatoes, peeled and washed

2½ teaspoons Bourbon Smoked Sea Salt, divided

2½ cups heavy cream

½ teaspoon Bourbon Smoked Pepper

1 teaspoon Bourbon Smoked Paprika

1 tablespoon Bluegrass Soy Sauce

1 teaspoon Bourbon Barrel Worcestershire Sauce

1 tablespoon garlic powder

Zest of 1 lemon

4 ounces blue cheese, crumbled

4 ounces cream cheese, cut into small pieces

2 tablespoons chopped chives, for garnish

 Preheat oven to 375 degrees. Slice the potatoes thinly with a mandolin, discarding the ends. In a large bowl, toss potatoes with 2 teaspoons of smoked salt. Set aside.

 In a medium saucepan, add the heavy cream, ½ teaspoon smoked salt, smoked pepper, smoked paprika, soy sauce, Worcestershire sauce, garlic powder and lemon zest. Bring to a boil and remove from the heat. Stir in the blue cheese and cream cheese until smooth. Butter or spray a 9 x 13-inch baking dish and spread half the potatoes in an even layer. Pour half the cream mixture on top. Add the remaining potatoes in an even layer and pour over the remaining cream mixture. Make sure all the potatoes are submerged.

 Cover the pan tightly with foil and cut a few slits on top to vent. Bake for 1 hour, remove the foil and bake for another 30-40 minutes or until the top is golden brown and the potatoes are tender. Remove from oven and cool for 10 minutes. Garnish with chopped chives and serve.

Farro Pilaf with Mushrooms and Swiss Chard

Farro is one of those ancient grains that's popular these days. Essentially you're just boiling wheat until it pops open. The farro will absorb whatever you're putting on it. Sometimes I'll just go into our warehouse, grab a cup of our wheat and cook that.

Serves 4-6

12 ounces cremini and/or shiitake mushrooms, stems removed, sliced

2 tablespoons butter

½ teaspoon Bourbon Smoked Sea Salt

½ teaspoon red pepper flakes

2 tablespoons olive oil

1½ cups pearled farro (regular farro is fine but will take longer to cook)

1 medium onion, diced

½ cup white wine

4½ cups chicken or vegetable stock

½ bunch Swiss chard, stems removed, green leaves finely sliced

¼ cup grated Parmesan, plus more for garnish

1 teaspoon Bourbon Smoked Sea Salt, divided

½ teaspoon Bourbon Smoked Pepper

1. Heat a large skillet on high heat. Add butter and melt. Add the mushrooms and sauté, in two batches if necessary, until mushrooms are browned and crispy around the edges. Season with ½ teaspoon smoked salt and red pepper flakes. Set aside.

2. Heat a large saucepan or dutch oven over high heat. Add the olive oil and onions. Sauté for 3-5 minutes or until soft and translucent. Add the farro, stirring until toasted, about 1 minute. Add the wine and cook, until reduced by half. Pour in the stock and bring to a boil. Reduce heat to medium and simmer, stirring occasionally, until farro is tender and creamy, about 20-25 minutes. Right before farro is done, add the swiss chard and stir until wilted. Add the cooked mushrooms. Remove from heat and add the Parmesan cheese, remaining smoked salt and smoked pepper. Stir well to combine. Serve hot.

Grilled Chili-Lime Cauliflower Steaks

For the last few years, the trendy vegetable was Brussels sprouts. Now it's cauliflower. Cut 'em thick to get those cauliflower "steaks" everybody likes.

Serves 4-5

2 large heads of cauliflower

¼ cup extra virgin olive oil

Zest and juice of 2 limes

2 teaspoons Bourbon Barrel Aged Pure Cane Sorghum

1 tablespoon Bourbon Smoked Chili Powder

1 tablespoon Bourbon Smoked Garlic Salt

3 tablespoons cilantro, chopped

Lime wedges, for garnish

1. Heat a charcoal or gas grill on high heat. Remove the outer leaves from each cauliflower. Cut two or three "steaks" about 1½ inches thick from the middle of each cauliflower. There will be extra florets from the sides, which may also be grilled, along with the steaks. Slice about the same thickness as the steaks for even cooking.

2. Whisk the olive oil, lime juice, zest and sorghum together in a small bowl. In another small bowl, mix together the smoked chili powder and smoked garlic salt. Brush each cauliflower steak and the florets with the olive oil mixture. Season with the chili powder mixture. Lay the steaks, seasoned side down, onto the grill. Brush and season the other side of each steak and the florets on the grill. Grill, turning every 4-5 minutes and basting occasionally with the olive oil mixture. Continue grilling until browned and slightly charred on both sides. Cauliflower should be cooked but still a little al dente.

3. Remove from grill and arrange on a platter. Brush with any remaining olive oil mixture and garnish with chopped cilantro and the lime wedges.

Black Rice with Shiitake Mushrooms, Bacon and Kale

Black rice is kinda fancy. It's often called "forbidden rice" because it supposedly is an aphrodisiac. Plus, this dish has two feel-good items: bacon and shiitake mushrooms. This should be on a Valentine's Day menu.

Serves 9-10 people

2 cups Forbidden Black Rice (substitute 6 cups cooked brown or white rice if black rice is not available and skip step 1)

Pinch of salt plus 2 tablespoons, divided

3½ cups water

1 bunch kale (lacinato or curly), washed and stems stripped away

5 slices bacon, sliced into ¼ inch pieces

1 medium onion, small dice

2 tablespoons fresh ginger, chopped

3 cups (6 ounces) Shiitake mushrooms, stems removed, sliced

1 teaspoon Bourbon Smoked Sea Salt

1 teaspoon Bourbon Smoked Pepper

2 tablespoons vegetable oil

¼ cup Bluegrass Soy Sauce

¼ cup Kentuckyaki™ Sauce

1 tablespoon toasted sesame oil

3 scallions, green parts only, sliced

2 tablespoons Bourbon Smoked Sesame Seeds

1. Combine rice, a pinch of salt and water in a large saucepan. Bring to a boil over high heat. Cover and reduce heat to low. Cook for 30-35 minutes or until all the water has absorbed and rice is cooked. Remove from heat. Let stand for 5 minutes, covered, then fluff with a fork. Allow to cool. Rice can be made up to two days ahead of time. Cool completely before refrigerating in an airtight container.

2. Bring a medium sized pot of water to a boil. Add 2 tablespoons of salt. Once boiling, add the kale and blanch the leaves for 1 minute. Drain into a colander and rinse with cold water until cool. Squeeze kale to remove excess water, roll into a ball and chop into fine shreds. Set aside.

3. In a large skillet or wok, add bacon and cook over medium high heat. Cook until bacon is crispy and brown. Remove onto a paper towel-lined plate with a slotted spoon, leaving fat in pan. Add onion and ginger. Sauté until onions are soft and translucent, about 5 minutes. Add the shiitake mushrooms and sauté for 10 more minutes or until cooked and crisping around the edges. Season with smoked salt and smoked pepper. Pour oil into the pan and add the cold rice, breaking up the rice with your hands or a large spoon. Stir fry for 6-8 minutes. Add the kale, bacon, soy sauce and Kentuckyaki sauce, stirring well to combine. Remove from heat and stir in the sesame oil. Transfer to a serving bowl and garnish with sliced scallions and smoked sesame seeds.

Spring Peas and Edamame with Soy, Lemon Butter

One of my favorite things about the spring is pea shoots, whether you're having a salad or garnishing with them.

Serves 4 as a side dish

12 ounces frozen peas

1 pound frozen edamame, shelled

2 tablespoons olive oil

5 scallions, green and white parts separated, sliced

3 tablespoons Bluegrass Soy Sauce

4 tablespoons butter, cut into pieces

1 teaspoon Bourbon Smoked Sea Salt

½ teaspoon Bourbon Smoked Pepper

Zest of 1 lemon

Juice of half a lemon

⅓ cup fresh mint leaves, roughly torn or chopped

3 cups pea shoots, reserve some for garnish

Bourbon Smoked Togarashi, for garnish

1. Bring a medium pot of water to a boil. Add the frozen peas and edamame. Boil for 1 minute. Drain in a colander and rinse with cold water. Heat a large skillet on high heat. Add the olive oil and scallion whites. Sauté for 1 minute. Add the peas and edamame and toss. Sauté for 5 minutes and add the soy sauce, butter, smoked salt and smoked pepper. Toss to combine.

2. Remove from heat. Add the lemon zest, juice, mint leaves, pea shoots and reserved scallion greens. Transfer to a serving bowl and garnish with extra pea shoots and smoked togarashi. Serve immediately.

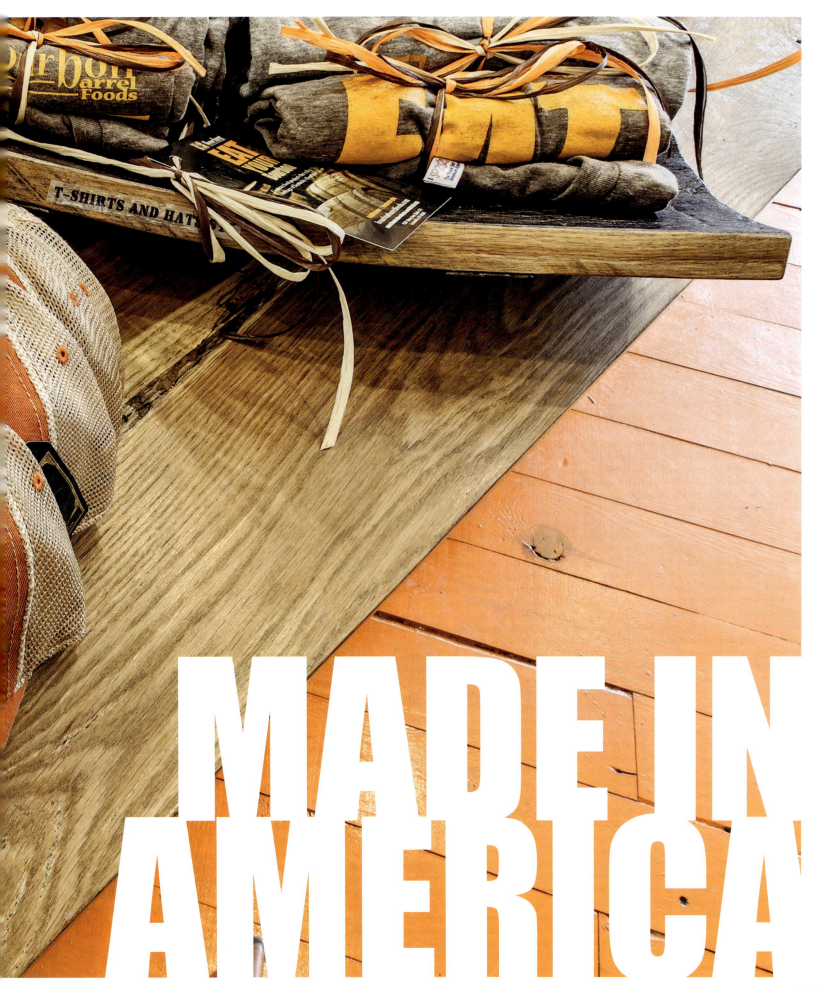

BAKED GOODS & SWEETS

Blackberry Cobbler with Johnnycake

Baking is chemistry. Cooking is more of a creative process. So I've said before that it's easy to mess up baked desserts. Unless you're making cobbler. This is one of my favorite things to make. I had a friend in Florida who would always say, "Matt, when are you gonna make me your cobbler again?" Essentially, you're just taking the best fruit you can find — toss it in some sugar, maybe add a little bourbon — and put it in a bowl, then put biscuit dough on top of the fruit and bake it. A Johnnycake is like a drop biscuit. You can tell it's done when the filling starts to come out the edges.

Makes 6-7 servings

For the Fruit Filling:

- 3 tablespoons butter
- 6 cups (5 pints) blackberries, divided
- ½ -¾ cup Bourbon Smoked Sugar
- 1 tablespoon cornstarch
- 2 tablespoons water

For the Dough:

- 1½ (190 grams) cups all-purpose flour
- ½ cup (70 grams) cornmeal, finely ground
- 3 tablespoons Bourbon Vanilla Sugar
- 1 tablespoon baking powder
- ½ teaspoon baking soda
- ½ teaspoon Bourbon Smoked Sea Salt, plus extra for sprinkling
- 4 tablespoons (½ stick) cold, unsalted butter, cut into pieces
- 1¼ cups heavy cream, cold

For the Bourbon Whipped Cream:

- 1 cup heavy cream, cold
- 1 tablespoon Bourbon Vanilla Sugar
- 1 tablespoon Kentucky bourbon
- 1 teaspoon Bourbon-Madagascar Vanilla Extract

1. Preheat oven to 400 degrees. Melt butter in a large saucepan over medium heat. Add two-thirds of the blackberries and enough sugar to achieve the desired sweetness. Stir to dissolve sugar. Bring to a boil. Simmer gently to soften fruit and to cook down some of the juices, about 10 minutes. Dissolve the cornstarch and water together to make a slurry. Add the remaining blackberries and more sugar, if necessary, and stir. While the mixture is bubbling, pour in the cornstarch slurry and stir to combine. Remove from heat once mixture has thickened. Set aside.

2. In a food processor, combine the flour, cornmeal, vanilla sugar, baking powder, baking soda and smoked salt. Pulse to combine. Add the pieces of cold butter and pulse 6-7 times. Pour in the heavy cream and pulse just until a dough ball forms.

3. Divide the fruit mixture between six or seven standard sized ramekins, filling about halfway full. Mound the dough on top of the fruit. It will seem like a lot of dough. Sprinkle each cobbler with a pinch of smoked salt and place on a parchment or foil lined baking sheet. Place baking sheet on the center rack of the oven and bake for 14-15 minutes or until the tops are nicely browned. Cool for 10 minutes.

4. To make whipped cream, add all the ingredients into a bowl. Whisk, using a hand mixer or stand mixer, until soft peaks form. Serve cobblers warm, with a dollop of whipped cream.

Soft Pretzels with Bourbon Smoked Sea Salt

There's a part in here that is not gonna be optional: You need to boil the dough. Boiling the dough will give it that crust on the outside.

Makes 8 large pretzels

1½ cups warm water

1 tablespoon Bourbon Smoked Sugar

2 teaspoons kosher salt

1 package (7 grams) active dry yeast

4½ cups (560 grams) all-purpose flour

4 tablespoons (2 ounces) unsalted butter, melted

Vegetable oil or cooking spray, for bowl and pan

10 cups water, for boiling

⅔ cup (165 grams) baking soda

1 large egg yolk, beaten with 1 tablespoon water

Bourbon Smoked Sea Salt, for topping

1. Combine the warm water, sugar and kosher salt in the bowl of a stand mixer and sprinkle the yeast on top. Stir and allow to sit for 5 minutes or until the mixture begins to foam. Add the flour and butter. Using the dough hook attachment, mix on low speed until well combined. Increase to medium speed and knead until the dough is smooth and pulls away from the side of the bowl, approximately 4 to 5 minutes. Remove the dough from the bowl and oil the bowl well with vegetable oil. Return the dough to the bowl, cover with plastic wrap and leave in a warm place for approximately 1 hour or until the dough has doubled in size.

2. Preheat the oven to 450°F. Line two half-sheet pans with parchment paper or silicone mats and generously brush or spray with vegetable oil. Set aside. Bring water and the baking soda to a rolling boil in an 8-quart saucepan or a large roasting pan. In the meantime, turn the dough out onto a work surface and divide into eight equal pieces. Roll out each piece of dough into a 24-inch rope. Make a U shape with the rope. Holding the ends of the rope, cross them over each other and then press ends into the bottom of the U in order to form the shape of a pretzel. Carefully transfer pretzel onto the lined sheet pan.

3. Place the pretzels into the boiling water, one by one, for 30 seconds, using a large spoon to gently push the pretzels down into the water. Remove them from the water using a large, flat spatula or spider. Place onto the half-sheet pan, brush the top of each pretzel with the egg wash and generously sprinkle with the smoked salt. Bake until dark golden brown in color, approximately 13 to 15 minutes. Transfer to a cooling rack for at least 5 minutes before serving.

(Step-by-step guide on page 255)

Line two half-sheet pans with parchment paper or silicone mats and generously brush or spray with vegetable oil.

The dough is ready when it has doubled in size.

Turn the dough out onto a work surface and divide into eight equal pieces.

Roll out each piece of dough into a 24-inch rope.

Make a U shape with the rope.

Holding the ends of the rope, cross them over each other.

Press the ends into the bottom of the U in order to form the shape of a pretzel.

8. Place the pretzels into the boiling water, one by one, for 30 seconds, using a large spoon to gently push the pretzels down into the water.

9. Carefully remove them from the water using a large, flat spatula or spider and place on lined sheet pan.

10. Brush the top of each pretzel with the egg wash.

11. Generously sprinkle with the smoked salt and bake.

Bourbon Crème Brûlée

Patrick Roney came to Louisville to work at the famous Oakroom in the even more famous Seelbach Hotel. Now he's the chef at Harvest in Louisville. He's one of the most talented chefs in town. This dish is pretty simple, but sometimes simple — and executed perfectly — is the best.

— Recipe by Chef Patrick Roney, Harvest, Louisville, Kentucky

Makes 8 servings

1 quart (32 ounces) heavy cream

½ cup (155 grams) Bourbon Vanilla Sugar, plus extra for topping

3-4 tablespoons Kentucky bourbon

2 teaspoons Bourbon-Madagascar Vanilla Extract

7 egg yolks

1. Preheat oven to 300 degrees. In a large saucepan on medium heat, combine heavy cream, vanilla sugar and bourbon. Cook, stirring occasionally, just until the mixture begins to bubble. Remove from heat and add vanilla extract. In a medium bowl, whisk yolks. Ladle ½ cup of the warm cream mixture in a slow, steady stream into the egg yolks while whisking. Pour the egg mixture into the cream mixture, whisking to combine.

2. Set eight 5-6 ounce ramekins into a roasting pan. Fill the ramekins with the custard mixture. Carefully pour hot water into the roasting pan to come about halfway up the ramekins. Bake for 25-30 minutes or until the custards have only a slight ripple when tapped. Remove the custards from the water bath and allow to cool to room temperature. Refrigerate for at least an hour but preferably overnight. Covered custards will keep in the refrigerator for 3 days.

3. Sprinkle 1 tablespoon of vanilla sugar evenly over the top of each ramekin of custard. Using a blowtorch, melt and caramelize the sugar. Serve immediately.

"Being the chef of a restaurant that sources everything locally, having Bourbon Barrel Foods a mile from my restaurant is such a win for me. Matt's always coming up with something a little bit different."

— Patrick Roney

Chive and Smoked Pepper Biscuits

I would make these for picnics back when I was in love.

Makes 9 biscuits

6 tablespoons unsalted butter, frozen or refrigerated

2 cups (250 grams) all-purpose flour

1 tablespoon baking powder

¼ teaspoon baking soda

½ teaspoon Bourbon Smoked Salt, plus extra for garnishing

1½ teaspoons Bourbon Smoked Pepper

⅓ cup chives, chopped

1 cup buttermilk, cold

3 tablespoons unsalted butter, melted and cooled

1. Preheat oven to 425 degrees. Line a baking sheet with parchment paper. Set aside. Using a box grater, grate butter into a small bowl and place in the freezer. In a large bowl, whisk together flour, baking powder, baking soda, smoked salt and smoked pepper. Add the chives and grated butter and stir to combine.

2. Make a well in the center of the flour mixture. Pour in the buttermilk. Stir with a large spoon just until a dough forms. Transfer dough to a lightly-floured surface. Gently pat dough into a rectangle. Fold rectangle into thirds. Pat down into a rectangle again and repeat folding into thirds. Pat the dough into a square about 1-inch thick. With a sharp knife, cut (pushing knife straight down and not with a sawing motion) dough into 9 equal squares. Place on baking sheet about 1 inch apart. Place baking sheet into the refrigerator or freezer for 10 minutes to chill.

3. Brush chilled biscuits with melted butter and sprinkle lightly with smoked salt. Bake for 10-12 minutes or until golden brown. Serve immediately.

Note: Leftover biscuits can be reheated in a 375 degree oven for 5 minutes.

Apple Cake with Bourbon Whipped Cream

Early on, we'd make this for tasting events because it was easy for somebody other than me to make it. Serve it warm, so the whipped cream melts a little.

Makes 1 (9 x 13-inch) sheet cake

For the Cake:

2 cups (250 grams) all-purpose flour

1 tablespoon baking powder

2 teaspoons Bourbon Smoked Sea Salt

2 sticks (16 tablespoons) unsalted butter, softened (plus extra for the pan)

2 cups (450 grams) granulated sugar

2 large eggs, lightly beaten

2 teaspoons Bourbon-Madagascar Vanilla Extract

½ cup (115 grams) Bourbon Smoked Sugar

juice of ½ a lemon

2 teaspoons cinnamon

5-6 tart apples, such as Granny Smith, Honeycrisp, or Macintosh

For the Bourbon Whipped Cream:

2 cups heavy whipping cream, cold

2 tablespoons confectioner's sugar

2-3 tablespoons Kentucky Bourbon

2 teaspoons Bourbon-Madagascar Vanilla Extract

1. Preheat oven to 375 degrees. Butter a 9 x 13-inch baking pan. In a small bowl, whisk together the flour, baking powder and smoked salt. In a large bowl or stand mixer, cream together the butter and 2 cups of granulated sugar until pale and fluffy. Add the eggs and vanilla extract and mix. Add the flour mixture and beat until combined. Batter will be thick. Spread mixture evenly into the prepared pan. Set aside.

2. In a small bowl, mix the smoked sugar and cinnamon. Peel, core and slice the apples into a large bowl and toss with the lemon juice. Add the cinnamon smoked sugar and toss well to combine. Arrange and shingle the sugared apples on top of the batter to completely cover the cake, pressing in lightly. Bake for 40-45 minutes or until a toothpick inserted into the cake comes out clean

3. While the cake is baking, make the whipped cream. In a large bowl, combine all the ingredients for the whipped cream. Using a hand mixer or large whisk, whip cream until soft peaks form. Cover bowl with plastic wrap and set aside in refrigerator.

4. Cool cake on a wire rack for 10-15 minutes. Serve with the bourbon whipped cream.

Sorghum Sugar Cookies

These cookies became so popular that we now have a company making them for us. The only person who doesn't like them soft and chewy is my dad. Whenever we screw up a batch and they're crunchy, we give them to him. The black pepper in there makes them taste a little like a gingersnap. These cookies are also now part of our charity, Cookies With Cause. One-hundred percent of the proceeds go to the West End School in Louisville, Kentucky. and other charities that our cookie bakers choose.

Makes 40-45 cookies

¾ cup (1½ sticks) unsalted butter, softened

1 cup (200 grams) granulated sugar

1 egg

¼ cup Bourbon Barrel Aged Pure Cane Sorghum

2 cups (250 grams) all-purpose flour

2 teaspoons baking soda

1 teaspoon ground cinnamon

½ teaspoon Bourbon Smoked Pepper

½ teaspoon Bourbon Smoked Sea Salt

½ teaspoon ground ginger

½ teaspoon ground cloves

Bourbon Smoked Sugar, for dipping

1. In a medium bowl or stand mixer, cream together butter and sugar. Add egg and sorghum and mix. In a separate bowl, add dry ingredients and whisk to combine. Add the dry mix to the butter mixture. Mix until smooth. Cover bowl with plastic wrap and chill dough for 1 hour or overnight.

2. Preheat oven to 350 degrees. Line baking sheets with parchment paper. Pour some smoked sugar into a small bowl or plate. Roll one tablespoon of dough into a ball and roll in smoked sugar. Place two inches apart on a baking sheet. Bake 9-11 minutes or until light golden brown. Cool on baking sheet for 10 minutes, then cool completely on a wire rack. Store cookies in an airtight container.

Sorghum Cookie Ice Cream Sandwiches with Smoked Cacao Nibs

Spicy cookie, sweet ice cream. It's just a good contrast. This recipe uses vanilla ice cream, but in the summertime, strawberry is my favorite.

Makes 8 ice cream sandwiches

16 sorghum sugar cookies (see recipe, on previous page)

1 pint vanilla ice cream, (or your favorite flavor) softened

Bourbon Smoked Cacao Nibs, for coating

1. Scoop approximately ¼ cup ice cream onto one cookie. Top with another cookie and gently press down to flatten slightly. Smooth sides of ice cream with an offset spatula or butter knife.

2. Roll the sides of the ice cream sandwiches in smoked cacao nibs. Place on a small sheet pan or on a plate. Repeat with remaining cookies and ice cream. Freeze for 1 hour to firm up.

Flourless Peanut Butter Cookies

Peanut butter cookies are my favorite cookies. At Desserts by Helen, I get the Dreamsicle™ cake. They have a big one and a small one. I've mastered eating the small one while driving.

— Recipe by Chef Craig Friedman of Desserts by Helen, Louisville, Kentucky

Makes 72 cookies

2 cups (16 ounces) smooth or chunky peanut butter (use "dessert style" peanut butter, such as Jif® or Skippy®)

2 cups (400 grams) Bourbon Vanilla Sugar

2 large eggs

2 teaspoons Bourbon-Madagascar Vanilla Extract

1 teaspoon Bourbon Smoked Sea Salt, plus extra for topping

Bourbon Smoked Sugar, for topping

1. Preheat oven to 325 degrees. Line 3 baking sheets with parchment paper. Using a mixer, beat peanut butter and vanilla sugar until well combined. Add eggs, vanilla extract and smoked salt and mix until completely incorporated.

2. Using a tablespoon scoop, make well-packed scoops and place on baking sheets about ½-inch apart. These cookies do not spread much. Flatten each scoop with either a spatula or the tines of a fork. Sprinkle smoked sugar and a small pinch of smoked salt on top of each cookie. Bake for 13-14 minutes. Cool on baking sheets for 10-15 minutes before transferring to a wire rack. Cool completely before storing in an airtight container.

Lime, Pistachio, Cardamom Pound Cake

I have a very early memory of making pound cake with my mom. It was out of a box and I mostly remember liking to lick the bowl. This recipe is a fancy version of that.

Makes 2 loaves

For the Pound Cake:

1 cup (2 sticks) unsalted butter, room temperature

2 cups (400 grams) Bourbon Vanilla Sugar

5 large eggs

3 cups (375 grams) all-purpose flour

1½ teaspoons cardamom

1½ teaspoons Bourbon Smoked Sea Salt

½ teaspoon baking powder

½ teaspoon baking soda

¾ cup buttermilk

⅓ cup lime juice, freshly squeezed

Zest of 2 limes

1 cup roasted pistachios, coarsely chopped

For the Glaze:

2 cups (220 grams) powdered sugar

3-4 tablespoons lime juice

¼ cup roasted pistachios, coarsely chopped

Zest of 1 lime

1. Preheat oven to 350 degrees, with a rack in the lowest position. Grease and flour two 4½ x 8-inch loaf pans.

2. Using a mixer, cream together butter and vanilla sugar until fluffy. Add eggs, one at a time, beating well after each addition. In a separate bowl, whisk together flour, cardamom, smoked salt, baking powder and baking soda. In another small bowl, combine buttermilk, lime juice and zest. Alternate adding flour and buttermilk into the butter, ending with the flour. Beat just until smooth. Gently fold in chopped pistachios.

3. Bake for 50 minutes to 1 hour or until a toothpick inserted into the cake comes out clean. Tent with foil if the cake begins to over brown. Cool cakes on a wire rack for 10 minutes. Run a knife around the edges and turn out onto a wire rack set into a rimmed baking sheet and allow to cool completely.

4. Make the lime glaze. In a medium bowl, combine the powdered sugar and 3 tablespoons of lime juice. Whisk until a thick but pourable glaze forms. If mixture is too thick, whisk in additional lime juice. Pour and spread glaze on cooled cakes, allowing excess to run down the sides. Scatter chopped pistachios and lime zest on top of glaze. Slice and serve.

Spiced Pecan Carrot Cake

I hate raisins, so I always leave them out.

Makes one (9 x 13-inch) sheet cake

For the Cake:

1 cup (195 grams) vegetable oil

2 cups (400 grams) Bourbon Smoked Sugar

1 teaspoon Bourbon Smoked Sea Salt

4 large eggs

1 teaspoon Bourbon-Madagascar Vanilla Extract

2 teaspoons cinnamon

½ teaspoon ginger, ground

¼ teaspoon cloves, ground

2 cups (250 grams) all-purpose flour

2 teaspoons baking soda

3 cups (325 grams) carrots, grated (from about 1 pound carrots)

1 cup (100 grams) Bourbon Barrel Spiced Pecans, finely chopped, plus extra for garnish

½ cup (70 grams) raisins, gold or dark

For the Cream Cheese Frosting:

½ cup (8 tablespoons) unsalted butter, softened

8 ounces cream cheese, softened

¼ teaspoon Bourbon Smoked Sea Salt

2 teaspoons Bourbon-Madagascar Vanilla Extract

2½ cups (285 grams) confectioner's sugar, plus more if needed

1. Preheat oven to 350 degrees. Lightly butter or spray a 9 x 13-inch pan.

2. In a large bowl or stand mixer, beat together the oil, smoked sugar, smoked salt, eggs, vanilla extract and spices. Whisk the flour with the baking soda and stir into the wet mixture. Add the carrots, nuts, and raisins and mix just until incorporated. Pour into prepared pan. Bake for 35-45 minutes or until a toothpick inserted into the center comes out mostly clean. Cool cake completely on a wire rack.

3. Make the frosting. In a large bowl or stand mixer, beat the butter and cream cheese until smooth. Add the smoked salt and vanilla extract and mix. Beat in the confectioner's sugar, a little at a time, on low speed. If frosting is too thin, add a little more sugar. If too thick, add a teaspoon of milk.

4. Either remove the cake from the pan to frost or frost cake directly in the pan. Decorate top with extra pecans and any other embellishments, as desired.

Chocolate Pavlova with Summer Berries

This is a great one for Forth of July when summer berries are at their best.

Serves 8-10 for dessert

For the Meringue:

6 large egg whites

1½ cups (300 grams) granulated sugar

3 tablespoons cocoa powder, sieved

1 teaspoon white vinegar

⅓ cup (50 grams) dark chocolate, chopped

2 tablespoons Bourbon Smoked Cacao Nibs

For the Whipped Cream:

2 cups heavy cream, cold

2 teaspoons Bourbon-Madagascar Vanilla Extract

1 tablespoon Bourbon Smoked Sugar

For Garnishing:

2 pints summer berries (blackberries, raspberries, etc.)

1-2 teaspoons Bourbon Smoked Cacao Nibs

1 bar of dark chocolate, chilled, for shaving

Tip: A nice accompaniment is our Bourbon Barrel Blackberry Sauce (see our recipe, page 336).

1. Preheat oven to 350 degrees and line a baking sheet with parchment paper. Using a ruler and pencil, lightly draw a 9-inch circle onto the parchment paper. Set aside. In the bowl of a stand mixer, add the egg whites and whip until foamy and peaks just start to hold. Start adding the sugar, a tablespoon at a time, and whip until stiff, shiny peaks form. Sprinkle in the cocoa powder, vinegar, chopped chocolate and smoked cacao nibs and gently fold in with a rubber spatula until incorporated.

2. Mound meringue onto the parchment paper in a large circle, using the circle you drew as a guide. Smooth the tops and the sides with the rubber spatula. Place into the oven and turn the temperature down to 300 degrees. Bake for about 1 hour or until meringue looks dry on top but the center feels soft when poked. Do not be alarmed if there are large cracks in it. Turn off the oven, leave the door slightly open and allow the meringue to cool completely in the oven.

3. Right before assembly, whip the cream with the vanilla extract and the smoked sugar until soft peaks form. Set aside in the refrigerator until needed. Using a large spatula, remove the cooled meringue from the baking sheet and place onto serving tray. Mound the whipped cream on top of the meringue and top with all of the berries. Scatter the smoked cacao nibs on top. With a sharp knife, vegetable peeler or coarse grater, shave the chocolate bar. Garnish top of pavlova with chocolate shavings. Serve immediately.

Focaccia with Red Grapes and Rosemary

We used to have to make focaccia every day at the restaurant where I worked in Gainesville. It was our sandwich bread and can double as pizza dough.

Makes 1 (9 x 13-inch) focaccia

1 package (7 grams) active dry yeast

1 tablespoon Bourbon Barrel Aged Pure Cane Sorghum

1¼ cups lukewarm water

4 cups (500 grams) bread flour

½ teaspoon Bourbon Smoked Sea Salt, plus extra for sprinkling

3 tablespoons extra virgin olive oil, divided, plus extra for drizzling

Baking spray or soft butter, to grease the pan

1 tablespoon cornmeal or semolina

1 cup small, red grapes, washed

1½ tablespoons rosemary, roughly chopped

1 teaspoon Bourbon Smoked Sugar

1. In a small bowl, add the yeast and sorghum to the lukewarm water. Stir well to combine. Set aside. In a large mixing bowl, add the bread flour, smoked salt and 1 tablespoon of olive oil. Pour the yeast mixture into the flour and stir with a spoon or fork. Once a dough starts to form, flour a clean surface and the dough. Knead the dough for 10 minutes or until smooth and elastic. This step may also be done in a stand mixer with a dough hook. Place dough in an oiled bowl and cover with plastic wrap. Leave in a warm place to rise for 40 minutes.

2. Spray or butter a 9 x 13-inch baking pan. Scatter cornmeal or semolina over the bottom of the dish. Remove the risen dough from the bowl and gently stretch into a rectangle roughly the size of the pan. Lay dough into the pan and drizzle 2 tablespoons of olive oil over the top. Using just your fingertips, push into the dough to create dimples all over the top. Scatter grapes and rosemary over the surface, pushing some grapes into the dough. Cover with plastic wrap and leave to rise again for 45 minutes.

3. Preheat oven to 400 degrees. Remove plastic wrap and sprinkle dough with a little more smoked salt and the smoked sugar. Bake for 25 minutes or until top is golden brown. Remove from the oven, drizzle with a little more olive oil and allow to cool for 10 minutes before serving.

Chocolate Chunk Cookies With Smoked Salt

Salty. Sweet. Smoky

Makes 2 dozen cookies

½ cup (1 stick) unsalted butter, softened

¼ cup (50 grams) Bourbon Vanilla Sugar

¾ cup plus 2 tablespoons (165 grams) packed light brown sugar

1 egg

1 teaspoon Bourbon-Madagascar Vanilla Extract

¼ teaspoon Bourbon Smoked Sea Salt, plus extra for sprinkling

¾ teaspoons baking soda

1¾ cups (220 grams) all-purpose flour

½ pound (8 ounces) semi-sweet or bittersweet chocolate, cut into ½ inch chunks

1. Preheat oven to 350 degrees. In the bowl of a stand mixer, cream the butter and sugars together until light and fluffy. Add egg and vanilla extract. Beat until incorporated, scraping down sides as needed. Add smoked salt and baking soda. Add flour and stir at low speed until just mixed. Fold in chocolate with a wooden spoon or rubber spatula.

2. Scoop 1½ tablespoons of dough for each cookie. Space cookies 2 inches apart on parchment-lined baking sheets. Sprinkle with a little extra smoked salt on top of each cookie. Bake for 11-12 minutes or until golden on the top but still soft in the center. Cool on baking sheet for 5 minutes before transferring to a wire rack.

Blackberry Chip Ice Cream with Smoked Cacao Nibs

Cacao is a super food, like kale and avocados. Have you heard people say that chocolate is an aphrodisiac? It's mostly because of what's in the cacao. They're somewhat bitter, so you need something to eat with them.

Makes approximately 1 quart

- 1½ cups whole milk
- 1½ cups (320 grams) Bourbon Vanilla Sugar
- 1½ cups heavy cream
- 4 egg yolks
- 2 teaspoons Bourbon-Madagascar Vanilla Extract
- 18 ounces blackberries, blended in a blender and strained to remove seeds (about 2 cups blackberry purée)
- 1 tablespoon freshly squeezed lemon juice
- 4 ounces semi-sweet or bittersweet chocolate, coarsely chopped
- 2 tablespoons Bourbon Smoked Cacao Nibs

1. In a medium saucepan, combine the milk and vanilla sugar. Gently warm over medium heat, stirring occasionally, just until it begins to bubble. Remove pan from heat. Pour the heavy cream into a large bowl and set a fine mesh strainer over the bowl.

2. In a medium bowl, whisk together the egg yolks and vanilla. Add a small ladle of the warm milk into the eggs, whisking constantly. Add a little more milk and whisk. Pour the remaining milk into the eggs and whisk to combine. Pour the mixture back into the saucepan and heat over medium heat, stirring constantly, until it thickens and easily coats the back of a wooden spoon. Pour mixture through the strainer into the heavy cream. Add the blackberry purée and lemon juice. Stir well.

3. Leave to cool or place bowl into an ice bath to quickly chill. Once cool, cover and chill in the refrigerator at least a couple of hours or overnight.

4. Using your ice cream maker, churn the custard according to the manufacturer's directions, adding the chopped chocolate and smoked cacao nibs during the last few minutes of churning. Ice cream will be soft after churning. Transfer ice cream to a lidded container and freeze for several hours before serving.

Sorghum Buttermilk Irish Soda Bread

I love it whenever we can incorporate sorghum into something people wouldn't imagine it in, like bread. As opposed to, you know, just dipping biscuits in it.

Makes 1 loaf

2 cups (250 grams) bread flour

1¼ cups (155 grams) whole wheat flour (optional- all bread flour may be used)

1 teaspoon Bourbon Smoked Sea Salt

1 teaspoon baking soda

1⅓ cups buttermilk

1 large egg, beaten

1 tablespoon Bourbon Barrel Aged Pure Cane Sorghum

1. Preheat oven to 375 degrees. Line a baking sheet with parchment paper. In a large bowl, combine flours, smoked salt and baking soda. Whisk to combine. In a small bowl, combine the buttermilk, egg and sorghum. Stir. Make a well in the center of the dry ingredients and pour in the wet mixture. With a wooden spoon, bring the ingredients together to form a dough.

2. Turn dough onto a floured surface and lightly dust with flour. Knead dough gently a couple of times to bring dough together, if needed. Form dough into a round loaf. Transfer loaf onto the prepared sheet pan. Using a sharp knife, cut an X into the top of the loaf, about ½ inch deep.

3. Bake for 35 minutes. The bread should be golden brown and the bottom should sound hollow when tapped. Remove to a wire rack and allow to cool for 10 minutes before slicing. Enjoy warm with butter and our smoked strawberry jam. (see our recipe page 329)

Sweet and Salty Chocolate Bark

My kids and I made this bark for Christmas last year. Somebody gets the fun job of crunching up pretzels and peanuts and the finished product looks pretty.

Serves 8-10

8 ounces chocolate (dark, semi-sweet, or milk chocolate), roughly chopped

⅓ cup peanuts, roasted and roughly chopped

½ cup pretzels, roughly chopped

2 teaspoons Mint Julep Sugar

2 teaspoons Bourbon Smoked Cacao Nibs

½ teaspoon Bourbon Smoked Sea Salt

1. Set a medium size saucepan filled with 2 inches of water on high heat. Put the chopped chocolate in a heat proof mixing bowl and set on top of the saucepan. Once the water is boiling, turn heat to low. Allow the chocolate to melt, stirring occasionally. Lay a large sheet of parchment paper on a sheet pan. Once the chocolate is completely melted, pour chocolate onto the parchment paper and spread out in a thin layer with a spoon or rubber spatula.

2. Scatter the peanuts and pretzels evenly over the chocolate. Sprinkle the mint sugar, smoked cacao nibs, and smoked salt on top. Chill the chocolate bark in the refrigerator for at least 2 hours to set. To serve, break apart in chunks. Store in an airtight container in the refrigerator for up to a week.

Smoked Sesame Wafers

A lot of the products that we do, like the cacao nibs or the sesame seeds, are more chef-driven. The oil inside the sesame seeds holds that smoke flavor really well. I snack on these wafers. They're sweet, not savory.

Makes 36 cookies

1½ tablespoons unsalted butter, room temperature

1 cup (213 grams) light brown sugar

1 large egg

2 tablespoons all-purpose flour

¼ teaspoon Bourbon Smoked Sea Salt

1 teaspoon Bourbon-Madagascar Vanilla Extract

½ cup Bourbon Smoked Sesame Seeds

Baking spray

Ice water

1. Preheat oven to 350 degrees. In a medium bowl with an electric hand mixer, cream together the butter and light brown sugar. Add the egg, all-purpose flour, smoked salt and vanilla extract, beating to combine. Add the smoked sesame seeds and stir to combine.

2. Line baking sheets with parchment paper and lightly coat with baking spray. Drop a scant teaspoon of batter about 3 inches apart on the baking sheets. Slightly flatten each cookie with an offset spatula or knife dipped in ice water. Bake for about 6 minutes (on middle rack) until lightly golden brown. Allow to cool completely on baking sheets. Remove with an offset or thin spatula. Store in an airtight container.

Salted Chocolate Mint Brownie Cookies

Our Mint Julep Sugar isn't too overpowering.

Makes about 1 dozen cookies

1 scant cup (120 grams) all-purpose flour

1 teaspoon baking powder

¼ teaspoon Bourbon Smoked Sea Salt, plus extra for sprinkling

14 ounces (395 grams) 60-70% dark chocolate, chopped

3 tablespoons (50 grams) unsalted butter, chopped

4 large eggs

1¼ cups (270 grams) Mint Julep Sugar

1 teaspoon Bourbon-Madagascar Vanilla Extract

1. Whisk together dry ingredients. Set aside. In a heatproof bowl, combine the chocolate and butter. Place over a pot of gently simmering water or microwave in 30 second intervals, stirring in between, until completely melted.

2. In the bowl of an electric mixer, combine the eggs and the mint sugar and whisk on medium speed for 5-6 minutes until it's pale and tripled in size. Scrape the chocolate into the bowl, add the vanilla and whisk on a low speed to combine. Add the dry ingredients and whisk slowly to combine. Scrape down the sides of the bowl with a spatula and stir by hand to fully incorporate.

3. Refrigerate batter for one hour to firm up. Preheat oven to 355 degrees. Line two baking sheets with parchment. Using a large (⅓ cup) ice cream scoop, scoop cookies about 3 inches apart on baking sheets. Flatten each cookie slightly with the palm of your hand. Sprinkle with smoked salt. Bake for 12-13 minutes until puffed and dry looking around the edges but still slightly soft in the middle. Cool completely on cookie sheet before serving.

BATCH
217-15

BOTTLE NUMBER
186

DRINKS

Bourbon Barrel Boulevardier

It's a negroni minus the gin. I can't drink gin responsibly, so I'm always subbing in bourbon or vodka. Finding out that there was an actual name for what I was drinking was awesome. I love the flavors of Campari and vermouth — that anise flavor, though I hate black licorice. This cocktail transcends all seasons. Refreshing in the summer, warming in the winter. And it's easy to make. You don't have to put on your herringbone vest and get out your mixology tools. You can eyeball it. If you want more bourbon, put more bourbon in it.

Makes 1 serving

1½ ounces Kentucky bourbon

1 ounce Campari

1 ounce sweet vermouth

1 dash bitters

Ice

Orange slice, for garnish

Maraschino cherry, for garnish

1. In a cocktail shaker, add all the ingredients, except the orange and cherry. Stir well to combine. Strain into a chilled cocktail glass. Garnish with an orange slice and Maraschino cherry.

Classic Mint Julep

If you have been transplanted to Louisville or are a hipster, you tend to talk down the mint julep. A good julep is like lemonade — you don't want it to be too sweet. Just a little tang that's refreshing.

Makes 1 serving

3 ounces Kentucky bourbon

1 ounce Mint Julep Simple Syrup (see recipe, page 333)

3 fresh mint leaves

Crushed ice

Mint sprig, for garnish

1. Add bourbon, Mint Julep Simple Syrup and three mint leaves to a chilled mint julep cup or tall bar glass. Gently bruise the mint leaves with the back of a spoon and stir. Fill the cup with plenty of crushed ice and garnish with a fresh mint sprig.

Tequila Barrel

Who doesn't have a tequila story? Let me tell you about how I used to hang out with Sammy Hagar. Just kidding. For this cocktail, I love seeing how Katsuji paired tequila with some of our bourbon-smoked products.

— Recipe by Chef Katsuji Tanabe of Mexikosher, Los Angeles, CA

Makes 1 serving

1 ounce vanilla simple syrup, plus extra for glass rim (see recipe, page 333)

Bourbon Smoked Sugar, for glass rim

1 ounce tequila

1 ounce lime juice

1 egg white

4 dashes bitters

Pinch of Bourbon Smoked Sea Salt

Ice

Maraschino cherry, for garnish

1. Pour a little vanilla simple syrup into a saucer. Dip the rim of a cocktail glass into the syrup, then the smoked sugar. Fill with ice.

2. In a cocktail shaker, combine the tequila, 1 ounce vanilla simple syrup, lime juice, egg white, bitters and smoked salt. Add some ice and shake well, until frothy. Strain cocktail into glass. Garnish with a Maraschino cherry.

Vanilla Bourbon Fashioned

Everybody in Louisville knows the Old Fashioned was founded at the Pendennis Club. Adding vanilla is a nice riff on it. This recipe is from Tim Laird, co-host of *Secrets of Bluegrass Chefs*, which films in our kitchen studio.

— Recipe by Tim Laird, cookbook author and Chief Entertaining Officer of Brown-Forman, Louisville, Kentucky

Makes 1 serving

2 inch strip of orange peel

¼ -½ ounce Vanilla Simple Syrup (see recipe, page 333)

2 ounces Kentucky bourbon

2 dashes bitters

Ice, preferably large cubes

1. In an old-fashioned or rocks glass, add the orange peel and gently muddle to release the oils. Add the vanilla simple syrup, bourbon and bitters, stirring to combine. Add a few ice cubes and enjoy.

Bridle Leather Cocktail

This is from Kathy Teree, a customer of ours and a librarian. I met her at a Southern Foodways Alliance convention in Jackson, Mississippi. This drink has a great name. The sorghum gives it that leathery, earthy flavor.

— Recipe by Kathy Teree of Kentfield, CA, Bourbon Barrel Foods consumer

Makes 1 serving

1 ounce aged rum

1 ounce Kentucky bourbon

½ ounce raspberry liqueur

½ ounce Bourbon Barrel Aged Pure Cane Sorghum

¾ ounce fresh lemon juice

Ice

Dash or two of bitters

1. In a cocktail shaker, combine all the ingredients, except the bitters. Add ice and shake.

2. Strain into a cocktail glass filled with crushed ice or serve straight up in a chilled glass. Top with a dash or two of bitters and gently stir.

Cucumber and Mint G & Ts

A lot of effort goes into this, but it's one of the best summer drinks I've ever had.

Makes 4 cocktails

1 (about 13 ounces) large cucumber, washed

2 Persian cucumbers, washed

For Each Cocktail:

1 ounce cucumber juice

½ ounce Mint Julep Simple Syrup (see recipe, page 333)

1½ ounces gin (Hendrick's, preferably)

Ice

Tonic water

Mint sprigs, for garnish

1. Grate the large cucumber into a sieve set into a bowl. Press down with the back of a spoon to extract as much of the cucumber juice as possible. You should have ½ cup. Set aside.

2. Using a vegetable peeler, mandoline or knife, peel or cut 12 long, thin strips of Persian cucumber. Wind three strips of cucumber around the inside of four cocktail glasses.

3. For each cocktail glass, pour in the cucumber juice, Mint Julep Simple Syrup and gin. Stir. Fill glass with ice and top with tonic water. Garnish with a sprig of mint.

Strawberry and Smoked Pepper Shrub

This is from my operations manager, Josh Rust. He's been working for me for seven or eight years. He brews every barrel of soy sauce and has taken over a lot of our cocktail program, like the products we've developed for Woodford Reserve and Old Forester. You know how every office has that one person who'll say something really funny when you say something dead serious? That's Josh. I'll be having an important meeting, and I'll look at him and say, "Alright, insert funny comment here." Anyway, Josh's shrubs are phenomenal. It's almost like you're making a really, really thin jam.

— Recipe by Josh Rust, Bourbon Barrel Foods, Louisville, Kentucky

Makes 1¼ cups shrub syrup

For the Shrub:

1 cup apple cider vinegar

½ cup Bourbon Smoked Sugar

2 tablespoons Bourbon Smoked Pepper

8 ounces (about 2 cups) fresh strawberries, hulled and sliced

To Make Drinks | Cocktails:

Sparkling water

Vodka

Ice

Strawberries, for garnish

1. In a small saucepan, combine the apple cider vinegar, smoked sugar and smoked pepper. Heat over medium-high heat and stir to dissolve sugar. Add the strawberries to a clean quart container or jar with a lid. Pour the vinegar mixture over the strawberries, cap the lid and shake to combine.

2. Allow mixture to sit in the refrigerator for 2 days, shaking well once a day. Strain the shrub through a fine mesh sieve into a clean jar or container.

3. To make a non-alcoholic drink, fill a tall glass with ice. Add 1-2 tablespoons shrub syrup (or to taste) and fill with sparkling water to make a refreshing drink. Add 2 ounces vodka (before topping off with sparkling water) to turn this into a cocktail. Garnish with a fresh strawberry and a sprinkling of smoked pepper. Extra syrup will keep in the refrigerator for 2 weeks.

302

Bourbon, Orange, Ginger Cooler

Those large sugar crystals suck in a lot of that smoke flavor. When we made a simple syrup out of our sugar, we didn't know if the Kentucky flavor would survive the melting process. Totally does.

Makes 1 serving

For the Smoked Ginger Syrup:

½ cup sliced, fresh ginger

¾ cup Bourbon Smoked Sugar

1½ cups water

½ teaspoon Bourbon-Madagascar Vanilla Extract

For the Cocktail:

2 ounces Kentucky bourbon

1 ounce triple sec

3 tablespoons smoked ginger syrup

3 ounces fresh orange juice

Ice

Orange peel and fresh ginger slice, for garnish

1. Make the ginger syrup. In a small saucepan, combine all the ingredients except the vanilla extract. Heat over high heat and bring to a boil. Reduce heat and simmer for 10-15 minutes, reducing to about 1 cup liquid. Remove from heat and add the vanilla extract. Leave to cool completely. Strain through a fine mesh sieve. Syrup keeps in the refrigerator for up to 2 weeks.

2. To make the cocktail, combine the bourbon, triple sec and orange juice. Stir. Pour into an ice-filled glass. Garnish with an orange peel and a slice of ginger.

Bourbon and Sorghum Peach Smash

Sorghum in a cocktail, especially mixed with fruit, gives it earthiness, sweetness and nice depth.

Makes 1 serving

5 mint leaves, plus mint sprigs for garnish

1 large lemon wedge

1 teaspoon Bourbon Barrel Pure Cane Sorghum

2 ounces Kentucky bourbon

1 teaspoon peach jam

Ice

Mint sprig and fresh peach slice, for garnish

1. In a cocktail shaker, muddle the mint leaves and lemon wedge. Add the sorghum, bourbon and jam, and stir.

2. Add ice to a shaker and shake well. Strain into a cocktail glass filled with crushed ice. Garnish with a mint sprig and a peach slice.

Watermelon Mint Cooler

This is another great batch cocktail. If you're having a cookout, it's nice to make those big pitchers so you're not playing bartender all day.

Makes 10 (6 ounce) cocktails

4 cups seedless watermelon, chopped

⅓ cup Mint Julep Simple Syrup (see recipe, page 333)

½ cup lime juice, freshly squeezed

2 cups vodka

Mint sprigs, for garnish

Lime slices, for garnish

1. In a blender, add the watermelon and blend until completely puréed. Pour into a large pitcher. Add the Mint Julep Simple Syrup, lime juice and vodka. Stir well to combine.

2. Fill cocktail glasses with ice and pour in watermelon cooler. Garnish each glass with a sprig of mint and a lime slice.

Smoked Blackberry Caipirinha

When I first started making drinks, the first thing I made was a Caipirinha — probably on some North Florida beach like Destin.

Makes 1 serving

6-8 blackberries

1 teaspoon Bourbon Smoked Sugar

3 lime wedges, divided

2 ounces cachaça or white rum

Ice

1. In a cocktail shaker, muddle the blackberries, smoked sugar and 2 lime wedges. Add the cachaça or white rum and some ice. Shake well.

2. Strain into a rocks glass filled with fresh ice and garnish with the remaining lime wedge.

Bourbon Champagne Cocktail

This is what we pass out during filming of *Secrets of Bluegrass Chefs*, which tapes in our kitchen studio. We also like serving it in a Mason jar. Usually you'd top it off with brandy, but we always like to add bourbon.

Makes 1 serving

2 tablespoons Vanilla Simple Syrup (see recipe, page 333)

2 dashes bitters

2 ounces Kentucky bourbon

Champagne or Prosecco

Maraschino cherry, for garnish

1. In a chilled champagne flute, add the vanilla simple syrup and bitters. Pour in the bourbon and stir. Slowly pour in the champagne or Prosecco and garnish with a cherry.

Strawberry Mint Champagne Cocktail

You're essentially making a Champagne smoothie.

Makes 4 cocktails

1 cup fresh strawberries, hulled, plus extra for garnish

¼ cup Mint Julep Simple Syrup (see recipe, page 333)

Champagne or Prosecco

Mint sprigs, for garnish

1. Place strawberries and simple syrup in a blender. Blend until completely puréed. Fill Champagne flutes about one-third full of purée. Slowly top with Champagne or Prosecco. Lightly stir and garnish with a strawberry and mint sprig.

Bourbon Smoked Bloody Mary

No, I don't know why we haven't come up with our own Bloody Mary mix, given that we make so many things that make a good Bloody Mary. Most Worcestershire sauces have anchovies in them. Ours doesn't, which speaks to a broader crowd. This one is from Joy Perrine, a famous Louisville bartender who has written several books, including *The Kentucky Bourbon Cocktail Book*.

— Recipe by Joy Perrine, bourbon expert and mixologist

Makes 1 serving

5 ounces tomato juice

2 ounces vodka

1 tablespoon fresh lemon juice

2 teaspoons Bourbon Barrel Worcestershire Sauce

2 teaspoons grated horseradish

1 teaspoon hot sauce (more or less to suit your taste)

¼ teaspoon Bourbon Smoked Sea Salt

⅛ teaspoon Bourbon Smoked Pepper

Pinch Bourbon Barrel Smoked Paprika

Assorted pickles, olives, celery sticks and lemon slice for garnish

1. Combine all the ingredients, except the garnishes, in a shaker with ice. Shake well. Strain into a tall pint glass with fresh ice. Garnish with pickles, olives, celery and a lemon slice.

Hot Bourbon Lemonade

I came up with this one on my own. It's kind of like a Hot Toddy that I make for myself when I'm sick.

Makes 2 servings

4 cups water

2 tablespoons Bourbon Vanilla Sugar (or to taste)

Juice of 2 lemons

Kentucky bourbon, to taste

Fresh mint sprigs

Lemon slices, for garnish

1. In a small saucepan, bring water to a boil. Add vanilla sugar and stir to dissolve. Remove from heat. Add lemon juice and bourbon. Stir.

2. Fill mugs or cups with several sprigs of mint. Pour in Hot Bourbon Lemonade. Add more vanilla sugar, if desired. Garnish with lemon slices and serve.

312

Spiced and Buttered Hot Cider and Bourbon

You've gotta know what you're doing to make a hot cocktail. This one's complicated but worthwhile. Definitely a crowd-pleaser. Good for people who like to go Christmas caroling.

Makes 4 servings

4 cups apple cider

1 cup water

6 tablespoons Bourbon Smoked Sugar

6 whole cloves

2 cinnamon sticks

5 tablespoons unsalted butter, chilled

1½ cups Kentucky bourbon

¼ cup freshly squeezed lemon juice

Ground nutmeg, for garnish

1. Combine first five ingredients in a large saucepan. Bring to a boil and remove from heat. Cover pan with a lid and allow to steep for 15 minutes. Add 4 tablespoons of butter to the pan and bring back to a boil. Remove from heat and whisk in bourbon and lemon juice.

2. Strain cider into a large pitcher. Cut remaining tablespoon of butter into 4 pieces. Divide cider between 4 mugs or cups and add a piece of butter to each mug. Garnish with a sprinkle of nutmeg and serve.

Bourbon Barrel Michelada

We'll send email-blasts of recipes and for this one we sold the ingredients as a bundle. I couldn't believe how much people loved it. Seriously, I was so surprised.

Makes 1 serving

Lime wedges, for garnish and rimming the glass

Bourbon Smoked Sea Salt, for rimming the glass

Juice of lime

⅓ cup tomato juice

1 teaspoon Bluegrass Soy Sauce

2 teaspoons Bourbon Barrel Worcestershire Sauce

1 teaspoon Chef Ed Lee's Sambol Hot Sauce (or to taste)

Ice

12 ounces Mexican beer

Bourbon Smoked Pepper, for garnish

1. Rub the rim of a pint glass with a wedge of lime, then dip into smoked salt. Pour in the lime juice, tomato juice, soy sauce, Worcestershire sauce and hot sauce. Stir to combine. Add ice, then slowly top off with beer. Garnish with a wedge of lime and a sprinkling of smoked pepper.

AMERICA'S ONLY MICRO BREWED

PANTRY STAPLES

BATCH 217-15   BOTTLE NUMBER 186

Bourbon Smoked Buttermilk Dressing

Who doesn't like buttermilk dressing? It's kind of like ranch dressing, but ours tastes better because it has Bourbon Smoked Pepper. Use it on raw vegetables, salads, chicken wings — anything. Some people put it on their pizza.

Makes 1½ cups

1 cup mayonnaise

½ cup buttermilk

2 teaspoons Dijon mustard

1 tablespoon lemon juice

½ teaspoon Bourbon Smoked Sea Salt

¼ teaspoon Bourbon Smoked Pepper

1. In a medium bowl, whisk ingredients together. Chill and serve. Dressing keeps for 5-6 days in the refrigerator.

Bourbon Smoked Paprika Oil

This is a great finishing oil — Kentucky with a piquant bite of paprika. You can dress pastas with it. I'd drizzle it on grilled steak.

— Recipe by Chef Annie Pettry of Decca Restaurant, Louisville, Kentucky

Makes 1 cup

2 tablespoons extra virgin olive oil, plus 1 cup, divided

2 garlic cloves

4 tablespoons Bourbon Smoked Paprika

1. In a small frying pan, add two tablespoons of olive oil and heat over medium heat. Add the garlic cloves and toast for a couple of minutes until fragrant and lightly browned. Remove from heat. Add the remaining olive oil and smoked paprika and whisk to combine. Leave to infuse for at least an hour. Strain through a double layer of cheesecloth or coffee filter-lined mesh strainer. Store in an airtight container in the refrigerator for up to 2 weeks.

Bourbon Barrel Foods Seasoned Flour and Egg Wash

If I tell my son we're gonna have fried chicken tenders for dinner, he makes the seasoned flour and egg wash. He knows exactly what to do. It's kind of his thing.

For the Seasoned Flour (makes 2¼ cups)

2 cups all-purpose flour

1 tablespoon Bourbon Smoked Garlic Salt

1 tablespoon Bourbon Smoked Paprika

1½ teaspoons Bourbon Smoked Pepper

1½ teaspoons mustard powder

1 In a medium bowl, whisk together all the ingredients.

For the Egg Wash (makes 1 cup):

¼ cup milk or water

2 eggs

1 tablespoon Bourbon Barrel Worcestershire Sauce

1 In a medium bowl, whisk together all the ingredients.

Sorghum Vinaigrette with Lime and Cumin

Put this on grilled chicken, vegetables, any kind of salad greens.

— Recipe by Chef Jenn Louis of Lincoln restaurant, Portland, OR

Makes about 2 cups

1 tablespoon coriander seed

1 tablespoon cumin seed

½ cup Bourbon Barrel Aged Pure Cane Sorghum

½ cup + 2 tablespoons lime juice

¼ cup red wine vinegar

½ cup + 2 tablespoons olive oil

Zest of ½ orange

Zest of ½ lime

1 teaspoon Bourbon Smoked Sea Salt

½ teaspoon Bourbon Smoked Pepper

1. Place coriander and cumin seeds in a small frying pan and toast over medium heat until fragrant and lightly toasted. Once cool, finely grind in a spice grinder or mortar and pestle.

2. In a medium sized bowl, combine ground spices with remaining ingredients and whisk until smooth. Vinaigrette keeps in a jar in the refrigerator for 1 week.

Bourbon Tomato Jam

Smear this jam on a BLT.
— Recipe by Joyce Pinson, food writer, FriendsDriftInn.com

Makes 5-6 pint jars

5 pounds tomatoes, coarsely chopped with skin left on

3 cups Bourbon Smoked Sugar

½ cup light brown sugar

½ cup fresh lemon or lime juice

1 tablespoon Bourbon Smoked Sea Salt

2 teaspoons fresh ginger, grated

1 teaspoon thyme, fresh, chopped

1 teaspoon cinnamon

1-2 teaspoons red pepper flakes (optional)

½ teaspoon cayenne pepper

⅓ cup Kentucky bourbon

2 tablespoons apple cider vinegar

1. In a large saucepan, combine everything except the bourbon and cider vinegar. Bring to a rolling boil. Reduce heat to a gentle simmer. Cook for approximately 1 hour and 30 minutes, stirring occasionally or until the consistency is nice and thick, resembling a very rich jam. As the mixture thickens, you will need to stir more frequently.

2. Sterilize jars, lids and rings. Leave them in a water bath canner with the heat turned to a low simmer while the jam cooks.

3. At about the hour and fifteen minute mark, check to see if the mixture has started to thicken. When it looks close to being finished, add the bourbon. Cook until you've reached the desired consistency. Add the cider vinegar and cook for 2 minutes more.

4. Fill sterile jars to ¼ inch from the rims, wiping edges clean with a damp cloth, if needed. Add lids and rings, closing them "finger tight". Process jars in the hot water bath canner for 20 minutes. Cool on a towel lined counter until room temperature before storing in a dark, cool place.

Oven Roasted Tomatoes

At my first chef gig, we would have to oven-roast tomatoes every day. We would use them to finish almost everything we made or as a garnish or the basis for a sauce. Sometimes we'd peel them and just use the skins.

Makes 10 servings

3 pounds plum tomatoes, stems removed and cut in half, length-wise

3-4 tablespoons extra-virgin olive oil

3 garlic cloves, minced

1 tablespoon Bourbon Smoked Paprika

1 tablespoon fresh thyme, chopped

½ teaspoon Bourbon Smoked Sea Salt

½ teaspoon Bourbon Smoked Pepper

½ teaspoon Bourbon Smoked Sugar

1. Preheat the oven to 225 degrees. Place a rack set in the middle of the oven. In a large bowl, toss cut tomatoes with the olive oil. Add the remaining ingredients and toss well to combine. Lay the tomato halves on a parchment lined baking sheet, cut side up.

2. Slow roast the tomatoes for 2½–3 hours. When finished, they should look a little shriveled but still a bit juicy in the middle. Store in an airtight container in the refrigerator for up to 1 week.

Serving suggestions: in omelettes, with roasted chicken or fish, tossed with pasta, in panini sandwiches, added to grain salads or cous cous, or served antipasti style with olives and mozzarella cheese.

Worcestershire Caramelized Onions

Put 'em in a jar and they'll keep for a while. Pull them out when you're grilling, roasting, making a salad dressing. They're great to have on-hand.

Makes about 2½ cups

2 pounds yellow or Vidalia onions, cut into ½ inch wedges

2 tablespoons olive oil

1 tablespoon Bourbon Smoked Sea Salt

2 teaspoons Bourbon Smoked Sugar

⅓ cup Bourbon Barrel Worcestershire Sauce

1 teaspoon Bourbon Smoked Pepper

3 tablespoons fresh parsley, chopped (optional)

1 Heat a large, wide, thick-bottomed pan or skillet on medium-high heat. Add the oil. Add the onions and cook for 10 minutes, stirring occasionally. Add the smoked salt and smoked sugar, lower heat to medium low and cook, stirring often, for 30-50 minutes. Once the onions start to really caramelize, you may need to lower the heat even more and stir more often. If the onions are sticking to the bottom of the pan, add 2-3 tablespoons of water and scrape the bottom of the pan.

2 When onions are very soft and a rich, dark brown, pour in the Worcestershire sauce and add the smoked pepper. Cook for 2 minutes more. Remove from heat and add parsley, if desired.

Serving suggestions: on burgers, with steak, in sandwiches, on pizzas, tossed with pasta and fresh tomatoes or served alone, as a side dish.

Smoked Strawberry Jam

Step one: Make our soda bread. Step two: Make this strawberry jam. Step three: Put jam on soda bread. Step four: EAT YOUR BOURBON.

Makes about 2½ pints

2½ pounds strawberries, washed and hulled

2 tablespoons fresh lemon juice

1 teaspoon lemon zest

3 tablespoons classic pectin

3½ cups Bourbon Smoked Sugar

2 tablespoons Bourbon-Madagascar Vanilla Extract

1. Combine the strawberries, lemon juice and zest in a large pot. Using a potato masher, crush the strawberries. Stir in the pectin. Cook over high heat and bring to a rolling boil, stirring constantly. Add the sugar and stir to dissolve. Stir and boil for 1 full minute. Remove from heat and skim off any foam. Add the vanilla extract.

2. Ladle jam into clean jars and seal with a lid. Leave to cool completely before storing in the refrigerator. Jam keeps in the refrigerator for up to 1 month.

Note: For longer storage, freeze or can and process in a water bath as directed for strawberry jam in canning cookbooks and manuals.

Chocolate Ganache

It can sound complicated, but it's really easy. You're basically melting chocolate.

Makes about 1½ cups

1 cup heavy cream

8 ounces semi-sweet chocolate, finely chopped

1 pinch Bourbon Smoked Sea Salt

1. Place chocolate in a medium bowl. Heat cream in a small saucepan over medium-high heat until it almost comes to a boil. Pour cream into the chocolate and allow the mixture to sit for 2 minutes. Add the smoked salt and stir until smooth, combined and glossy.

2. Use immediately to glaze or as a dip for desserts and pastries. Once cooled, ganache will be nearly solid. To re-melt, microwave ganache in 30 second intervals, stirring in between. Heat and stir until desired consistency. Ganache will keep for 1 week in the refrigerator.

Smoked Salt Caramel Sauce

Make it ahead of time, pull it out of the refrigerator, warm it up. I love it on cupcakes.

Makes 1¾ cups

½ cup (1 stick) unsalted butter, cut into pieces

1¼ cups Bourbon Smoked Sugar

½ cup heavy cream

1½ teaspoons Bourbon Smoked Salt

1. In a medium, heavy bottomed saucepan, combine the butter and smoked sugar. Heat over medium-high heat until butter is melted. Pour in cream and whisk until sugar dissolves and sauce is smooth, about three minutes. Lower heat, if needed, to maintain a gentle bubble.

2. Add smoked salt and whisk to combine. Pour into a jar. Allow to cool for 15 minutes before enjoying. To reheat, microwave sauce in 30 second intervals, stirring in between. Heat and stir until desired consistency.

Mint Julep Simple Syrup

For a richer simple syrup, use two parts sugar to one part water

Makes 1 cup

1 cup Mint Julep Sugar

1 cup water

Combine sugar and water in a small saucepan. Bring to a boil over high heat. Remove from heat and stir to dissolve sugar. Allow to cool. Store syrup in a jar or airtight container. Syrup keeps for 2 weeks in the refrigerator.

Vanilla Simple Syrup

Makes 1 cup

1 cup Bourbon Vanilla Sugar

1 cup water

Combine vanilla sugar and water in a small saucepan. Bring to a boil over high heat. Remove from heat and stir to dissolve sugar. Allow to cool. Store syrup in a jar or airtight container. Syrup keeps for 2 weeks in the refrigerator.

Blackberry Sauce

Blackberries are my favorite fruit during the summer and they're Kentucky's indigenous fruit. People should use more local fruit. When making this sauce, it's important to strain out the big seeds.

Makes 1 cup

2 cups blackberries, washed

¼ cup Bourbon Smoked Sugar

¼ cup water

¼ teaspoon Bourbon-Madagascar Vanilla Extract

1 teaspoon lemon juice

1 teaspoon lemon zest

1. In a small saucepan, combine blackberries, smoked sugar and water. Bring to a boil over high heat. Crush berries with a potato masher. Reduce heat to medium and simmer for 10-15 minutes until berries are completely broken down and the juice has thickened to a sauce-like consistency.

2. Remove from heat and add the vanilla extract and lemon juice. Pass sauce through a fine mesh sieve, pressing against solids with a rubber spatula. Add lemon zest to sauce and stir. Cool completely before refrigerating in an airtight container. Sauce keeps for 1 week in the refrigerator.

Elizabeth's Chocolate Sauce

This is from Elizabeth Daunhauer, who's one of those special Bourbon Barrel Foods employees who suffered through being my assistant. Now she's grown into a full-fledged sales person. Elizabeth is always bringing in recipes she makes at home, and she is really proud of this chocolate sauce. When you're using chocolate sauce, it's always a good idea to put one of our bourbon cherries on top.

— Recipe by Elizabeth Daunhauer, Bourbon Barrel Foods, Louisville, Kentucky

Makes 2 cups

1 stick (8 tablespoons) unsalted butter

⅓ cup cocoa powder

½ teaspoon espresso powder (optional)

1 cup heavy cream

1 tablespoon Bourbon-Madagascar Vanilla Extract

¼ teaspoon Bourbon Smoked Sea Salt

1. In a small saucepan over medium-low heat, melt the butter. When melted, whisk in the cocoa and espresso powder. Mix well. Slowly pour in the heavy cream and whisk to combine. Bring to a boil and gently simmer for 5 minutes. Off heat, add the vanilla extract and smoked salt and stir. Cool slightly before serving. Leftover sauce keeps in the refrigerator for 1 week.

NOTE: To reheat, microwave at 30 second intervals, stirring in between, until desired consistency.

This is the most important page and possibly the most difficult to complete. While I wrote this page and edited and re-edited it, memories of starting this company overwhelmed me. It's emotional, to say the least. Everyone mentioned here played an important role in the past, present and future success of Bourbon Barrel Foods. I have an amazing group of people surrounding me, who make me look smarter than I really am.

Thank you to:

My kids, Max and Madeline. You two don't know me doing anything other than Bourbon Barrel Foods. If you had known me before this — well, I used to be the type of person who had a job for maybe two years before getting fired.

My mom, for giving me a couple hours, then a day, then a couple days, then a couple weeks, then months, then years without getting paid.

My dad, for still putting up with me.

Annie, my best friend, for believing in what we were trying to do and for making the sale happen.

Karen, for being with me the longest. You've seen this company grow the most. You always believed and always delivered. BEST LOGO EVER!

Ty Adams, for making that IUS class worthwhile. Things happen for a reason.

Susan, for being a total ball-buster and working tirelessly on this book.

Leanne Doll. Every company should have a Leanne.

My employees, past and present. I have learned and grown with all of you. You make it all happen!

Chris Witzke, you've been amazing all theses years. So glad to work with you.

Josh Moss, my tribe is bigger now with you in it. Amazing work on your part. Rockstar.

Tom Wurzbach, for being there with me when I came up with the idea. Thanks for the reminder, Tom.

Edward Lee, for eating disgusting gas station food with me on our 15-hour car ride to Virginia and back. Without that trip, I might never have expanded my business the way I have. I owe you a lot, Ed. Thank you.

My mentor, Bert Gill, at Mildred's Big City Food in Gainesville, Florida. You helped me turn a hobby into a passion.

My investors (Don, Ron, Steve, Mike, Caldwell, Schuyler, Kent, Ted, Bruce).

Greater Louisville Inc., the Nia Center and the University of Louisville's entrepreneurship program for all the free help.

The University of Kentucky Agricultural Economics and Agricultural Marketing departments, for introducing me to Chris Kummer and Bernard Peterson, who grow the most amazing soybeans in Kentucky.

Ron Fox with SCORE, for your patience and guidance.

Mark Bittman, for taking the time to talk to a nobody with an idea.

John T. Edge, for putting us on the map with one of the best articles that's ever been written about Bourbon Barrel Foods.

Francine Maroukian, for making it rain.

Old National Bank, for my first loan.

Whitney, regardless, you are a part of this. Thanks.

Heine Brothers' Coffee, for being my makeshift office in the beginning. I think my mail was getting delivered there.

Oldham County because it's where I grew up. Crescent Hill because it's where I live now. Butchertown because it's my company's home.

The Craft House, for staying open late while we wrote this cookbook.

Andy Blieden, for taking a risk on me, even though you'll say it wasn't a risk.

Toshio Shinko, for being the best soy sauce maker in the world and greeting me with an open mind.

Danny Ray Townsend, for your sorghum.

Lodge, for outfitting our kitchen.

Brown-Forman, for making my company more introspective.

General Electric, for partnering with us.

Secrets of Louisville Chefs.

West End School, for helping us make a difference.

Kentucky Proud, for helping all the small producers in the state.

Hi

John Hassmann at A Taste of Kentucky, for taking in my product in November. Nobody adds new product in November.

Caroline Keller, for making us better.

A BIG thank you to our customers. Your support is so important and so very much appreciated. I hope we continue to amaze you all!

All the chefs who have made our products household names.

The bourbon industry. Without your success I don't think I'd have a company.

Louisville, Kentucky. I love this city.

Community Involvment

West End School, Louisville, KY
Since 2013, we have provided dinner for the students and faculty the third Wednesday of each month. Bourbon Barrel Foods donates the cost of food and employee time to shop, prepare and serve dinner. West End School is a free, private college preparatory elementary and middle school for at risk young men. Admission is open to boys entering pre-kindergarten through second-grade, or sixth grade, who are on a free or reduced-lunch program, are capable of doing academic work at grade level or above, and who would benefit from a safe environment and high expectations. West End School does not charge students for room, board or tuition. Local community support plays a critical role in the school's success. Meals are provided by many dedicated, generous volunteers who prepare and serve two meals a day, five days a week.

Cookies with Cause, Louisville, KY
In the Fall of 2015 a group of young girls (friends and family of Bourbon Barrel Foods employees) held a cookie exchange in our Kitchen Studio on the first day of Holiday Break. Each young girl chose her favorite charity and invited as many friends as possible. It was a huge success, raising over $2,000. The girls decided to carry on their mission by participating in fund-raising events throughout the year, i.e. Alex's Lemonade Stand (childhood cancer research). We now work with local bakers to assist with baking the group's signature sorghum cookie, donating one-hundred percent of the profits. Bourbon Barrel Foods has generously supported the group and plans on supplying one-hundred percent of supplies needed for the Cookies with Cause sorghum cookie venture.

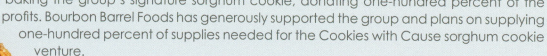

BATCH	BOTTLE NUMBER
217-15	186

PRODUCT INFORMATION

Product Index | Resource Page

Bluegrass Soy Sauce is microbrewed in small batches using only whole Kentucky-grown Non-GMO soybeans, soft red winter wheat and the purest limestone-filtered Kentucky spring water. We ferment and age the soybean mash in re-purposed bourbon barrels. It's Kentucky and brothy with hints of oak and a mild sweetness reminiscent of fine Kentucky bourbon.

Bourbon Barrel Foods Worcestershire Sauce ia a southern twist on the British classic. The tartness of real tamarind and the sweetness of Kentucky sorghum blended with our own spice blend. It's vegetarian and Non-GMO.

Boubon-Madagascar Vanilla Extract is aged in bourbon barrels that were once filled with some of the Bluegrass State's finest bourbon. Rich, sweet and aromatic with a bit of southern heritage and charm.

Pure Cane Sorghum is Kentucky's Maple Syrup™. It's earthy and sweet with hints of exotic spice. Our sorghum is estate grown and hand-harvested. Use in place of other syrups or as an antioxidant-rich, all-natural alternative.

Kentucky Style Teriyaki that is sweetened with pure cane sorghum. Flavored with bourbon, fresh ginger and garlic. Use it as a marinade for any meat or add it to stir fry. Vegetarian. Natural. Non-GMO.

Kentucky Style Hot & Spicy Teriyaki is sweetened with Kentucky pure cane sorghum flavored with bourbon and made with fresh ginger and garlic. This sauce has a great kick. Use it as a marinade for any meat or add it to stir fry. Vegetarian. Natural. Non-GMO. The 2017 Good Food Awards Winner.

Bourbon Barrel Barbeque Sauce has a sweet Kentucky and tangy twist. Made with bourbon smoked spices, Kentucky sweet cane sorghum and Kentucky bourbon. Great on beef, pork, chicken and seafood.

 Our cracked peppercorns are slow smoked in aged bourbon barrels. This gives them a wispy hint of smoke and a subtle oaky flavor that is reminiscent of fine Kentucky bourbon.

 A bourbon smoked, easy-to-use, extremely flavorful version of a classic garlic spice blend. Excellent on all meats and vegetables.

 All natural, solar evaporated, domestically harvested sea salt smoked with oak that has been soaking up bourbon for 7 years.

 Bourbon smoked blend of mild chilies and spices. This unique blend adds a robust flavor to any dish.

 Many paprikas are smoked, but none of them are bourbon smoked. Try this combination of sweet, piquant paprika and the mellow, oaky flavors of fine Kentucky bourbon.

 Bourbon smoked cracked peppercorns are slow smoked in aged bourbon barrels. This gives them a wispy hint of smoke and a hint of citrus that is excellent on all meats and vegetables.

 Bourbon smoked sesame seeds have a unique flavor with a nutty taste and a delicate, almost invisible crunch. Use them in salads, on breads, desserts, sushi, dressings, spice blends and rice.

 Shichimi togarashi is a traditional Japanese pepper blend that typically contains 7 ingredients. We bent the rules a bit. This blend is an excellent seasoning for soups, noodles, rice, potatoes, vegetables, all meats and our favorite...cheesecake!

 Cacao Nibs are cacao beans that have been roasted, separated from their husks, and broken into smaller pieces. They have a chocolatey taste, but they're not quite as sweet as chocolate, which can make them more versatile. You can snack on raw cacao right out of the bag, add it to trail mixes or smoothies, or use it whole or powdered in your cooking and baking.

 Our all natural Demerara sugar is packed and aged with Bourbon-Madagascar vanilla beans to enhance the molasses flavors of the sugar with the richness of vanilla.

 Named for the official drink of the Derby, Mint Julep Sugar has all the rich caramel flavors of raw sugar as well as the refreshing flavors of mint.

 Raw sugar cane smoked with repurposed bourbon barrel staves. Sweet caramel flavors and the richness of smoked oak.

 These pecans are sweet and savory with a hint of spice. Perfect for cheese trays, salads and of course as an accompaniment to your favorite bourbon cocktail! Our pecans are seasoned with our Bourbon Smoked Sea Salt, Bourbon Smoked Pepper, Bourbon Smoked Paprika and a blend we call Woodford Reserve® Bourbon Smoked Chefs Blend.

Please go to **Bourbonbarrelfoods.com** for more information

Matt with Josh Rust

Index

21c Museum Hotel, Nashville 157
211 Clover Lane 174, 175
610 Magnolia 75, 225
Agedashi Tofu 112
Ahi Tuna Tostada 186
Aioli, spicy 196
Alamo, Tennessee 14, 150
Amazon 136
Apple Cake with Bourbon Whipped Cream 262
APPS & SNACKS 74
Argentina 20
Asparagus and Country Ham Frittata 70
Atlanta, Georgia 231
Baby Kale Salad with Soy-Sesame Dressing
Bacon 59, 163, 206, 208, 210, 230, 243
Bacon, Pimento Cheese and Jalapeño Burger 210
BAKED GOODS AND SWEETS 250
Baked Sweet Potatoes with Kalbi Butter 225
Barbecue Sauce, White 84
Barbecued Chicken Legs 212
Bardstown, Kentucky 10, 11
Beans
   black 128
   kidney 128
   pinto 128
Beef
   filets 174
   flanken 171
   ground 128, 137, 206, 208, 210
   picnic ribs 171
   short ribs 171
   skirt steak 213
Beer 102, 128, 230, 316
Benedictine and Shaved Vegetable Canapés 98
Big Band dancing 39
Biscuits 59, 67
   Chive and Smoked Pepper 259
Bittman, Mark 11
Bizarre Foods America 17
Black Rice with Shiitake Mushrooms, Bacon and Kale 243
Blackberry Chip Ice Cream with Smoked Cacao Nibs 280
Blackberry Cobbler with Johnnycakes 252
Blackberry Sauce 336
Bluegrass Fried Chicken 197
Bluegrass Soy, Citrus raised Lamb Shanks with Farro Pilaf 203
Bluegrass Soy Roasted Tofu and Red Quinoa Salad 144
Bluegrass Soy Steamed Mussels 80
Bluegrass State 24
Bollywood 200
Bourbon 59, 75, 163, 174, 202, 252, 258, 262, 292, 294, 296, 297, 303, 304, 307, 311, 314, 326, 337, 343, 344
Bourbon Barrel Barbecued Chicken Legs 212
Bourbon Barrel Beer Cheese 102
Bourbon Barrel Foods Egg Wash 323
Bourbon Barrel Foods Seasoned Flour 323

Bourbon Barrel Smoked Pimento Cheese 105
Bourbon barrels 343, 344
Bourbon Brown Butter 75
Bourbon Crème Brûlée 258
Bourbon Smoked Buttermilk Dressing 321
Bourbon Smoked Chili 128
Bourbon Smoked Meatloaf 206
Bourbon Smoked Paprika Oil 322
Bourbon Smoked Spiced Pecans 96
Bourbon Tomato Jam 326
Bourbon Whipped Cream 252
Bread 98, 206
   buns 196, 210
   Irish Soda 281
   Monkey 59
   rolls 210
   Spiced 55
BREAKFAST and BRUNCH 42
Brock, Sean 17, 166, 168
Brown-Forman 296
Buryn, Eric 228
Butchertown 11, 34, 37, 208
Buttermilk 65, 103, 125, 197, 208, 259, 269, 281, 321
Cacao 280
Cachaça 306
Cake
Apple 262
Pound 269
Spiced Pecan Carrot 272
Calico Jack's 7
Campari 202, 292
Canapés, Benedictine and vegetable 98
Capers 177
Champagne 307, 308
Charcoal Grilled Baby Back Ribs with Kentuckyaki Glaze 166
Charleston, South Carolina 17, 166
Chasmawala, Alifiya 200
Cheese
   blue 238
   Cheddar 70, 102, 105, 206, 217
   Cotija 223
   cream 65, 98, 238, 272
   feta 132, 133, 216, 223
   goat 116
   Gouda 70
   Parmesan 177, 187, 240
   pimento 105, 106
   queso fresco 216
Chex® cereals 99
Chicken 197, 200, 216
   and Egg Miso Ramen 136
   and Smoked Pepper Dumplings 125
   breasts 187
   cutlets 177
   fingers 169

legs and thighs, barbecued 212
   thighs 183, 212, 220
wings 84
Chicago 163, 179
Chili 128
Chips, bagel 99
Chive and Smoked Pepper Biscuits 259
Chocolate 49, 71, 273, 277, 280, 283, 288
  bark 283
  Ganache 67, 31
Chocolate Chunk Cookies with Smoked Salt 277
Chocolate Pavlova with Summer Berries 273
Cider, apple 314
Cinnamon Rolls 65
Cioppino, Smoky 202
Citrus Pepper Chicken with Artichokes, Capers and Angel Hair Pasta 177
Clams 202
Cod 202
Coconut 53
Community involvement 341
Condé Nast Traveler 11
Cookies
  Chocolate Chunk 277
  Peanut Butter 268
  Salted Chocolate Mint Brownie 288
  Sorghum Sugar 264
Corn 223
Corn Dogs 104
Corn, Grilled 223
Cornmeal 104, 217, 252, 276
Courier-Journal 213
Crème Brûlée, Bourbon 258
Crock-Pot 137
Crostini, Hot Pimento Cheese 106
Culinary Institute of America 7
Curry 200
Dallas, Texas 183
Dashi powder 193
Daunhauer, Elizabeth 337
Decca 89, 322
Dee, Madeline 238
Derby Pie 179
Desserts by Helen 268
Destin, Florida 306
Deviled Eggs (Two Ways) 119
DINNER & MAIN DISHES 162
Doll's Market 197
Dougan, Glenn 84
Doughnut Holes and Toppings 67
Dressings and Vinaigrettes
  Bourbon Smoked Buttermilk 321
  Buttermilk 107
  Dressing 220
  Sorghum Vinaigrette with Lime and Cumin 324
  Soy-Ginger 132
  Soy-Sesame 142
  Soy Vinaigrette 75
  Vinaigrette 133
DRINKS 290
  Bourbon and Sorghum Peach Smash 304
  Bourbon Barrel Boulevardier 292
  Bourbon Barrel Michelada 316
  Bourbon Champagne Cocktail
  Bourbon, Orange, Ginger Cooler 303
  Bourbon Smoked Bloody Mary 310
  Bridle Leather Cocktail 297
  Cider, Spiced and Buttered 314
  Classic Mint Julep 294
  Cucumber and Mint G&Ts 299
  Hot Bourbon Lemonade 311
  Smoked Blackberry Caipirinha 306
  Spiced and Buttered Hot Cider and Bourbon 314
  Strawberry and Smoked Pepper Shrub 301
  Strawberry Mint Champagne Cocktail 308
  Tequila Barrel 295
  Vanilla Bourbon Fashioned 296
  Watermelon Cooler 305
Dumplings 125
Edamame 234, 246
Eggs
  deviled 119
  roe 191
scrambled 63
soy brined tea 89
Esquire 37
Farro 203, 240
Farro Pilaf with Mushrooms and Swiss Chard 240
Fatback 163
Fire Roasted Gazpacho 129
Firestone, Janet 137
Fish and Seafood
  See individual
Flourless Peanut Butter Cookies 268
Focaccia with Red Grapes and Rosemary 276
Fond Restaurant 238
Food Crafters 17
Fort Bragg, California 10
Frankfort, Kentucky 16
French Toast 41
with Blackberry and Cherry Sauce 58
Friedman, Craig 268
friendsdriftinn.com 326
Frittata, Asparagus and Country Ham 70
Frosting, Cream Cheese 272
Fruit(s)
  apples 262
  avocados 129, 191, 280
  bananas 49, 71
  blackberries 46, 58, 252, 273, 280, 306, 336
  blueberry(ies) 132
    pancakes 46
  cherries 58
  grapes 276
    Smoked Pickled Grapes 88
  grapefruit 186
  mangos 49
  oranges 186

peaches 49, 133
pears 171
pineapple 182, 196
raspberries 49, 273
strawberries 49, 301, 308, 329
tangerines 142
watermelon 133, 303
FT33 183
Fukume'-ni 93
Gahafer, Dalton 228
Gahafer-Buryn, Karen 5
Gainesville, Florida 7
Galbi-style 171
Ganache, Chocolate 67
Garden and Gun 102
Gin 299
Glaze 166, 269
  Chipotle Sorghum 182
  Honey, Chili, Lime 84
Goat Cheese and Sorghum Onion Jam Tartlets 116
Granola, Sorghum and Pomegranate Molasses 53
Grill Girl 129, 210
Grilled Bourbon Smoked Cauliflower 242
Grilled Corn, Mexican Style 223
Grilled Oysters with Bourbon, Brown Butter and Soy
  Vinaigrette 75
Grilled Togarashi Skirt Steak 213
Grilled Watermelon and Peach Arugula
Salad with Feta 133
Grits 217
Halibut 202
Ham, country 70
Harvest restaurant 258
Heine Brothers' Coffee 10
Heintzman, Chef Allen 174
Hot Brown 39
Hot Pimento Cheese Crostini 106
How It's Made 17
Husk restaurant 17, 166
Husk Bar 166
Ice cream
  Blackberry Chip 280
  Sandwiches, Sorghum Cookie
  vanilla 265
Ikura 191
Indian Karahi Chicken 200
Jack Fry's 7, 217
Jam
  onion 116
  peach 304
  Smoked Strawberry 329
Jamie, Carol 158
Jamie, Madeline 63, 67, 197, 223
Jamie, Max 47, 49, 169
Japan 10, 11, 14, 19, 20, 21, 99, 112, 156, 190, 191, 203
Joy of Cooking 17
Kakuni 193
Kalbi Butter 225
Kanji 21
Ken's Favorite Bolognese Sauce 163

Kentfield, California 297
Kentuckyaki L.A. Style Galbi 171
Kentuckyaki Pork Burger Sliders 196
Kikkoman 20
Kitchen tools 21
Knife, French and German 21
Koji 10, 20, 153
Kokokuji Temple 20
Kombu 136
Kroger 171
Kummer, Chris 10
Laird, Tim 296
Lamas, Anthony 81, 91, 182
Lamb 203
Lauer, Matt 17
Lee, Edward 35, 36, 75, 84, 86, 196, 225
Lemonade, Hot Bourbon 311
Lime, Pistachio, Cardamom Pound Cake 269
Lincoln restaurant 324
Lindars, Robyn 129, 210
Louis, Jenn 324
Louisville 7, 10, 11, 14, 20, 34, 37, 39, 75, 77, 78, 80, 84, 90,
  91, 98, 102, 174, 179, 182, 196, 197, 200, 213, 217, 225,
  228, 238, 258, 264, 268, 294, 296
Low Country 217
Madeline's Pancakes 46
Madeline's Quick Scrambled Eggs 63
Maker's Mark 10
Marinades 182, 183, 197, 200, 213, 216, 220
Marion County 10
Masago 191
Mash 7, 10, 11, 14, 19, 157
Mason jar 307
Matt's Smoky Roasted Root Vegetables 235
Max's Chicken Fingers with Sorghum-Mustard
  Dipping Sauce
Max's Smoothies
McCallister, Matt 183
McCrady's 166
Meat
  See individual
Meatloaf, Sorghum Glazed 208
Melrose Inn 179
MexiKosher restaurant 295
Mildred's Big City Food 7
MilkWood 84, 196, 225
MilkWood Wings with White Barbecue Sauce 84
Miller Union 231
Mini Shrimp Corn Dogs 104
Mint Julep Simple Syrup 333
Miso 10, 36, 112, 119, 136, 139
Molasses, pomegranate 53
Monkfish 202
Montgomery County 16
Moromi 11, 19, 156
Moss, Josh 5
Mumbai 200
Mushrooms 93, 136, 142, 234, 240, 243
Mussels 80, 202
Naan 55

Napa Valley 14
Nation, John 5
Netherlands, the 20
New York Times 11, 16, 37
Nguyen, Susan 5, 180
Nori 191
Nuts
  almond flakes 132
    peanuts 53, 283
    pecans 59, 96, 133, 272
    pistachios 269
Ohio River 179
Old Forester 301
Oldham County 179
Omelette, Spanish 62
Onions, 55, 62, 116, 128, 136, 163, 200, 203, 234, 240, 243, 303 328
Original Henry Bain's Famous Sauce, The 190
Oysters
  Grilled 75
  Pan-fried 107
Pancakes 46
  Blackberry Lemon Poppy Seed 46
  Blueberry 46
Pancetta 163
Pan-Fried Oysters 107
Panko 169, 190, 208
PANTRY STAPLES 320
Parmesan Crusted Chicken Breasts 187
Pasta/Noodles
  angel hair 136, 177
    Chinese egg noodles 228
    spaghetti 136, 228
Peanut butter 268
Peppers
  Anaheim 200
  habanero 186
  jalapeño 216, 210, 220
  poblano 129
  serrano 200
  shishito 122, 186
Perrine, Joy 310
Pettry, Annie 89, 322
Pilaf, Farro with Mushrooms and Swiss Chard 240
Pimento Cheese 210
  Smoked 105
Pinson, Joyce 326
Pita 55
Polenta 217
Pollo a la Brasa with Aji Verde Sauce 216
Pomegranate molasses 53
Pommery Potato Salad 229
Pork
  belly 193
  Belly Pot Stickers 113
  butt 193
  chops 190
  cutlets 190
  ground 113, 128, 136, 163, 196, 206, 208
  ribs 166
  sausage 163
Pot Stickers, Pork Belly 113

Potato(es) 62
  Salad, Pommery 229
    Smoky Bourbon and Blue Cheese Au Gratin 238
    sweet 225
Pratesi, Gwen 187
Pretzels 253
Prosecco 307, 308
Puff pastry 116
Quinoa 144
Raisins 53, 272
Ramen 136
  bars 99
Raspberry liqueur 297
Raw Egg over Hot Rice 191
Ribs 166, 167
Rice 191, 243
  Fried 231
Roasted Broccoli and Wheatberry Salad with Sesame, Miso Dressing 139
Roney, Patrick 258
Rub
  Dry, for chicken wings 84
Rum 297, 306
Rust, Josh 301
Salads
  Baby Kale 142
  Edamame and Shiitake 234
  Red Quinoa 144
  Roasted Broccoli and Wheatberry 139
  Spinach and Blueberry 132
  Vietnamese Grilled Chicken Thigh 220
Salmon, 182, 202
Salsa, Pineapple, Ginger 182
Salted Chocolate Mint Brownie Cookies 288
Satterfield, Steven 232
Sauces
  Aji Verde 216
  Blackberry 336
  Blackberry and Cherry Sauce 58
  Bolognese 163
  Caramel, Smoked Salt 67, 32
  Dipping 113, 169
  Elizabeth's Chocolate Sauce 337
  Fruit 58
  Sorghum-Mustard 169
  White Barbecue 84
Sausage, pork 163
Seafood and Fish
  See individual
Secretary of State, Kentucky 16
Secrets of Bluegrass Chefs 308
Seviche restaurant 81, 91, 182
Shakshuka with Eggs and Spiced Bread 55
Shinko, Toshio 19, 20
Shrimp 104, 202, 217
SIDES 222
Simpsons, The 89
Smoked Paprika Shrimp and Grits 217
Smoked Pickled Grapes 88
Smoked Pimento Cheese 105
PRODUCT INFORMATION 342
Smoked Salt Caramel Sauce 332

Smoked Sesame Wafers 286
Smoked Strawberry Jam 329
Smoky Bourbon and Blue Cheese Au Gratin Potatoes 238
Smoky Cioppino 202
Smoothies 49
   Chocolate, Raspberry, Oat 49
   Mango, Peach, Ginger 49
   Strawberry, Banana, Orange 49
   Superfood Cocoa and Banana 71
Soft Pretzels with Bourbon Smoked Sea Salt 253
Sorghum 34, 36, 37, 46, 49, 53, 59, 71, 116, 137, 166, 169, 182, 197, 203, 208, 213, 230, 235, 242, 264, 265, 276, 281, 297, 304, 324
   and onion jam 116
   and Pomegranate Molasses Granola 53
   and Soy Braised Collard Greens 230
   Buttermilk Irish Soda Bread 281
   Cookie Ice Cream Sandwiches with Smoked Cacao Nibs 265
   glaze 182
   Sugar Cookies 264
   Vinaigrette with Lime and Cumin 324
Southern Pride BBQ Pits & Smokers 14, 150
SOUPS AND SALADS 124
Soups and Stews
   Beef and Barley Soup in a Crock-Pot 137
   Cioppino, Smoky 202
   Gazpacho, Fire Roasted 129
Soy Braised Collard Greens 230
Soy Braised Pork Belly and Eggs 193
Soy Braised Shiitake Mushrooms 93
Soy Brined Tea Eggs 89
Soy Sauce Avenue 20
Spanish Omelette (Tortilla Española) 62
Spiced Pecan Carrot Cake 272
Spicy Cold Chinese Noodles 228
Spinach and Blueberry Salad with Soy-Ginger Dressing 132
Spring Peas and Edamame with Soy, Lemon Butter 246
Steak au Poivre "Louisville Style" 174
Super Bowl 104
Superfood Cocoa and Banana Smoothie 71
Sweden 20
Sweet and Salty Chocolate Bark 283
Syrup
   Mint Julep Simple 333
   Vanilla Simple 295, 296, 333
Taco Bell 16
Tanabe, Chef Katsuji 186
Tartlets, Goat Cheese and Sorghum Onion Jam 116
Tequila 295
Teree, Kathy 297
Thai Marinated Chicken Thigs 183
The New York Times 11
Today 17
Tofu 112, 144
Togarashi Grilled Shishito Peppers 122
Togarashi, skirt steak grilled 213
Togarashi Snack Mix 99
Tomato(es) 55, 70, 128, 129, 137, 163, 182, 200, 202, 326, 327, 328 129
   Bourbon Jam 326
   juice 310
   Oven Roasted 327
Tonkatsu 190
Tortilla Española 62
Tortillas 186
Tostada, Ahi Tuna 186
Townsend, Danny Ray 16, 36
Triple Sec 303
Tuna ahi 91
tostada 186
   Ceviche 91
Umami 213, 36
University of Florida 7
University of Kentucky, Department of Agricultural Economics 10
University of Louisville 10
Vanilla Simple Syrup 333
Veal, ground 163
Vegetable(s)
   artichokes 177
   asparagus 70
   beets 98
   bell pepper 139, 200
   broccoli 139, 231
   cabbage 190
   carrots 125, 137, 163, 220, 228, 231, 235, 272
   cauliflower 240
   celery 231
   cucumbers 98, 129, 132, 220, 228, 299
   fennel 202
   greens
      collard 230
      kale 142 243
   mixed 132
   mustard 231
   leek 193
   parsnips 235
   radishes 91, 98, 142, 213, 220, 234
   Roasted Root 235
   pea(s) 125, 144, 246
   spinach 132
   Swiss chard 240
Vermouth 202, 292
Vodka 301, 305, 310
Vietnamese Grilled Chicken Thigh Salad 220
Wakayama, Japan 10, 20
Wallace, Levon 157
Weber grill/chimney 146, 166, 167
West End School 264, 340, 341
Wheatberries 139
Whipped Cream, Bourbon 262
Whole Foods 14
Wild Alaskan Salmon with Chipotle Sorghum Glaze and Pineapple, Ginger Salsa 182
Winchester, Kentucky 36
Wine 203
Witzke, Chris 5
Woodford Reserve 11, 301
Worcestershire Caramelized Onions 328
Wurzbach, Tom 7
Yogurt 49, 200
YouTube 19
Zimmern, Andrew 17, 82

EAT YOUR Bourbon